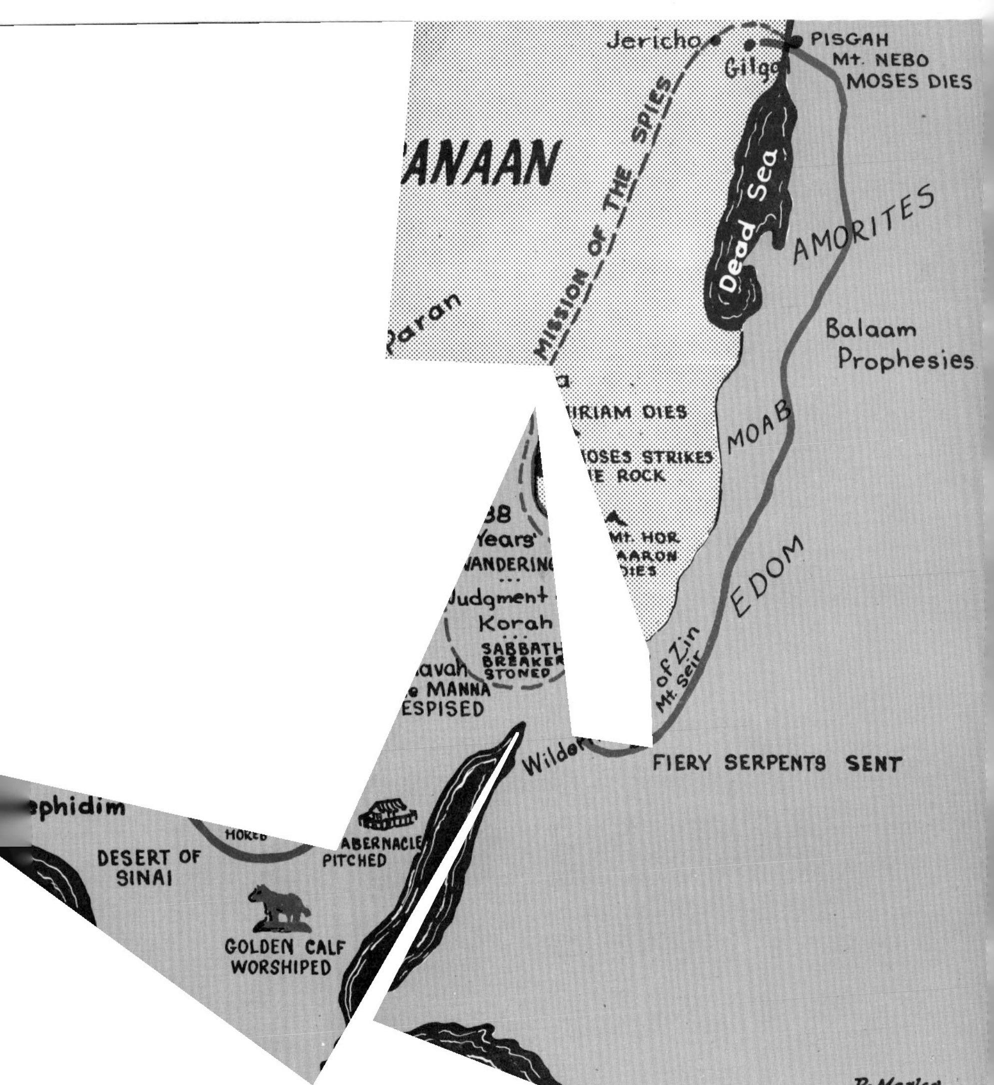
Jericho
PISGAH
Mt. NEBO
MOSES DIES
MISSION OF THE SPIES
Dead Sea
AMORITES
Balaam
Prophesies
MOAB
Mt. HOR
EDOM
Korah
SABBATH
BREAKER
STONED
Mt. Seir
FIERY SERPENTS SENT
DESERT OF
SINAI
GOLDEN CALF
WORSHIPED
PITCHED
R. Marler

# THE WILDERNESS JOURNEY

# THE WILDERNESS JOURNEY

*Christian Principles Illustrated by Israel's Desert Wanderings*

Charles H. Stevens

MOODY PRESS · CHICAGO

To
*Grace Weaver Stevens,*
fellow companion in a blessed ministry,
mother of my two lovely daughters and my two stalwart sons,
sweetheart wife for more than forty years,
God's greatest earthly gift

Library of Congress Catalog Card Number 71-143474

*Printed in the United States of America*

# CONTENTS

# FOREWORD

I HAVE READ CAREFULLY the manuscript of *The Wilderness Journey*. A sense of inadequacy is upon me as I evaluate this remarkable book. Giving evidence of scholarly study, close scrutiny, wise interpretation on the part of the author—a study reaching over a period of forty years—it is most illuminating, informative, and inspiring.

As with a microscope, we see worlds in a drop of water; as with telescope, we view landscapes millions of miles away; as with spectrograph, we learn the constituent elements of remotest astral bodies: so within the covers of this book we discover worlds of redemptive revelations, view continents of Bible truth and history, and firmaments of wisdom contracted to the compass of a page.

Truly this volume is all scriptural organs in one diapason. An ocean of God's truth lifts high tides within its covers.

I have never read a book which has given me more pleasure and profit. Space does not permit mention of all the types and events and truths the author mentions with such illumination. Showing the worth of typology as the handmaiden of theology, the author, picturing the historical account from Egypt to Canaan, illustrates the whole Christian journey from bondage to liberty. In so doing, he shows how the whole drama of redemption finds historical demonstration in the journey of Israel from Egypt to Canaan.

In the whole of this book we find the truth that Christ is the theme of the Bible. All the Bible's types, analogies, pictures, and truths are so related to Christ Jesus that He alone explains them, and the explanation is filled with such perfection of harmony in all details that the relationships between them and our Lord Jesus is strikingly self-evident. The diversified and systematic sacrifices of the Jews—significant shadows of the redemptive entity still ahead, the adumbrations of a substance yet to come—were elemental, preparatory, rudimental, and introductory, and they pointed to Christ, the propellant Center to which the faith of mankind, before and since, gravitates.

The ceremonies of Judaism mean Christ, just as the light that burns in prophecy means Christ. The author shows that Christ alone is the secret of the Bible's strength, beauty, and unity. To take Christ out of the Bible is like taking heat out of fire, melody out of music, numbers out of mathematics, and fact out of history. All this the author sets forth as he declares that, while the Old Testament promises Christ, the New Testament presents Christ. The Old Testament prophecies Christ, but the New Testament produces Christ. The Old Testament localizes Christ, while the New Testament universalizes Christ.

The author has made all who read and study this book beneficiaries of his diligent study and explanations and interpretations of Bible realities. All teachers, preachers, Bible lovers, Bible students—all who desire to know more of the Bible's rich contents—will cheat themselves and burglarize their own lives if they fail or refuse to read and study this remarkably illuminating book.

Robert G. Lee

# PREFACE

My purpose in writing this book is to give an over-all, comprehensive view of God's redemptive plan as outlined and dramatized in the account of Israel's journey from Egypt to Canaan. A study of this journey, as commended by the apostle Paul (1 Co 10:1-11), opens a whole vista of divine truth. Actually, this body of scriptural truth is a course in biblical typology given in historical sequence. The events recorded in the books of Exodus, Numbers, Deuteronomy, and Joshua "happened unto them [the children of Israel] for ensamples [types]: and they are written for our admonition upon whom the ends of the world [age] are come" (v. 11).

The material contained in this volume has been drawn from many sources over a long period of study and research. While the writer claims no great originality, he has attempted to distill the truth to a form that will be more easily apprehended and comprehended.

While full recognition cannot be given to all contributing sources, the writer would like to recognize in particular some of the major sources that have proved helpful in this study. Among these are such works as John Ritchie's helpful book *From Egypt to Canaan;* Charles H. MacKintosh's *Notes on Pentateuch; The Saviour in the Shadows,* by Robert L. Moyer; *The Alphabet of Christian Experience,* by John J. Van Gorder; and *Studies in the Book of Exodus,* by George Henderson.

The writer gratefully recognizes the invaluable help rendered by certain individuals. At the top of the list is Dr.

Gerald L. Stover, professor of Christian education and of journalism at Piedmont Bible College. Grateful recognition is also extended to Mrs. Troy Watts, Mrs. Robert H. Cox, and Mrs. Robert J. Evans for their help in typing the manuscripts, and to Mrs. Joseph Marler for the artistic work in drawing the map. It is with a deep sense of gratitude to the Lord that this volume is offered to the public.

The writer's own life has been greatly enriched in the preparation of this material, which has been in process over a period of many years, and he trusts that heavenly warmth shall be experienced by those who peruse the pages of this book.

# 1

# FROM EGYPT TO CANAAN

THE OLD TESTAMENT can well be called the kindergarten of the Bible. Intricate doctrines, abstract truths, and metaphysical concepts involved in the story of redemption as set forth in the New Testament are broken down in the Old and laid out in pieces. Someone has said that the study of types is a study of Christ in parts. The Pentateuch in particular is filled with pictures, figures, and symbols. Typology is a science within itself. A type, in its scriptural usage, is a person, thing, event, or institution in the Old Testament that foreshadows and anticipates a fuller revelation of the truth that appears later in the New Testament. Most often the truth dramatized in typology is obscure and obtuse until the substance it prefigures is revealed in divine history.

Like every great doctrine, typology has been much abused and often tortured with meanings and inferences that were never intended. Having said this, we hasten to point out that a sincere study of types will put in the hands of the believer a light which makes the whole Bible come alive. We venture to add that no one can properly understand the Bible apart from some recognition of the meaning of types.

For example, how can we understand the meaning and deep significance of the death of Christ apart from some knowledge of the levitical offerings? As a matter of fact, the greatest commentary on the death of Christ is to be found in the study of these five levitical offerings. The reverse is also true. One cannot grasp the full impact and spiritual meaning of the levitical offerings apart from their reference to the sacrificial and high priestly work of the Lord Jesus Christ. These five offerings give us a fivefold picture of Calvary.

A type without its antitype is obscure; the antitype without its type is difficult to understand. "In the Old Testament, the New Testament is contained; in the New Testament, the Old Testament is explained." Christ is the key to both the Old and the New. "In the Old, we have the portrait; in the New we have the Person."

The great doctrines of grace that find amplification in the New Testament in logical and chronological sequence appear in the Old Testament in types and shadows. That which appears in the New Testament in abstract doctrinal form finds a counterpart in the Old Testament in dramatic illustration. The Old Testament revelation is often given in kindergarten imagery. The importance of typology, so largely used in this first portion of the Scriptures, is quickly appreciated when we remember that learning processes can begin through the eye gate. An old Chinese proverb tells us: "One picture is worth more than ten thousand words." This is especially true in the early stages of the learning process. Later we must come to the abstract and spiritual truths called theology.

Typology is but the handmaiden of theology. Having first ascertained the great Bible doctrines, typology serves us well as a sort of "visual aid." In the field of visual aids we are accustomed to two forms—the still and the moving. A moving picture, for example, permits a study in action, while the filmstrip permits a study that is stationary. The types and shadows may well be compared to a filmstrip depicting in the Old Testament those persons, institutions, things, and events that foreshadow New Testament truth. A single picture may reveal many hidden facts but be little understood until seen in relation to a moving series depicted in the New Testament. A study of typology is of little value until one has viewed the truth in action as manifested in the person, work, and glory of the Lord Jesus Christ. In Old Testament typology, New Testament truth is viewed in detail. Old Testament typology might be called the microfilm of New Testament truth stored away in the Old Testament scriptures.

In our study of the great historical account, *The Wilderness Journey,* we find ourselves in a fruitful area for the study of types. This "travelogue" is graphically illustrative of the whole Christian journey. In this study we have a road map of the saint's travel experience and destination—from redemption through discipline to victory. This experience in Israel's journey from Egypt to Canaan could well be both the inspiration and the prototype of John Bunyan's *Pilgrim's Progress.*

The use of this study, tracing the journey of the children of Israel from the land of servitude and death to a land that flowed with milk and honey, has much scriptural justification. What the resurrection is to the New Testament, the journey from Egypt to Canaan is to the Old Testament. As the annual observance of the Passover commemorates the focal point of Israel's history, the Lord's Supper becomes a commemorative observance in the New Testament. "For even Christ our passover is sacrificed for us" (1 Co 5:7). Almost the entire book of Exodus and a great part of the books of Numbers and Deuteronomy are taken up with this aspect of Israel's life. Psalm 106 recounts the activities of the people of God in the wilderness. More miracles are associated with the account of the forty years in the wilderness than with all the rest of the Old Testament combined. In these wanderings God is immanent among His people. His arm is made bare, both in redemption and in judgment. The whole drama of redemption finds historical demonstration in this journey from Egypt to Canaan.

The New Testament likewise attaches great importance to Israel's experience as seen in 1 Corinthians:

> Moreover, brethren, I would not that ye should be ignorant, how that all our fathers were under the cloud, and all passed through the sea; and were all baptized unto Moses in the cloud and in the sea; and did all eat the same spiritual meat; and did all drink the same spiritual drink: for they drank of that spiritual Rock that followed them: and that Rock was Christ. But with many of them God was not well pleased: for they were overthrown in the wilderness. Now these things were our examples, to the intent we should not lust after evil things, as they also lusted. Neither be ye idolators, as were some of them; as it is written, The people sat down to eat and drink, and rose up to play. Neither let us commit fornication, as some of them committed, and fell in one day three and twenty thousand. Neither let us tempt Christ, as some of them also tempted, and were destroyed of serpents. Neither murmur ye, as some of them also murmured, and were destroyed of the destroyer. Now all these things happened unto them for ensamples: and they are written for our admonition, upon whom the ends of the world are come (10:1-11).

In this passage alone we have ample justification for the employment of this historical incident to teach Christian truth. Recounting this wilderness journey, the apostle Paul warns his Christian readers against committing the same mistakes that were made by Israel. He cites Israel's failures as examples (Greek, *tupos*). Verse 11 could be translated, "Now all these things happened unto them for types." The same word is used in verse 6. In fact, *tupos* occurs at least sixteen times in the New Testament, and is translated as follows: print, figure, fashion, form, ensample, example, manner, and pattern. The Greek *antitupon,* from which is derived our English word *antitype,* is found in two places in the New Testament, and it is rendered "figure" in both instances (Heb 9:24; 1 Pe 3:21). According to 1 Corinthians 10:1-11, then, the wilderness experiences that happened to Israel were types and were written for our admonition.

The writer to the Hebrews emphasizes the typical meaning of the wilderness experience in Hebrews 3—4. The same refrain of warning is found here as in 1 Corinthians 10.

Further justification of the use of types is found in their recurring use by our Lord. He so designates the brazen serpent and Jonah's three days and three nights in the fish's belly. He employs the days of Noah, as well as the days of Lot, as typifying the last days of this present dispensation. Too, He refers to Himself as the true Manna, the heavenly Bread: "Then Jesus said unto them, Verily, verily, I say unto you, Moses gave you not that bread from heaven; but my Father giveth you the true bread from heaven. For the bread of God is he which cometh down from heaven, and giveth life unto the world. Then said they unto him, Lord, evermore give us this bread. And Jesus said unto them, I am the bread of life: he that cometh to me shall never hunger; and he that believeth on me shall never thirst" (Jn 6:32-35).

John the Baptist used types when he said: "Behold the Lamb of God, which taketh away the sin of the world" (Jn 1:29). Paul resorted to the use of typical teaching when he wrote: "Purge out therefore the old leaven, that ye may be a new lump, as ye are unleavened. For even Christ our passover is sacrificed for us" (1 Co 5:7). Simon Peter resorted to the use of types when he wrote: "But ye are a chosen generation, a royal priesthood, an holy nation, a peculiar people; that ye should show forth the praises of him who hath called you out of darkness into his marvellous light" (1 Pe 2:9). He also wrote: "Ye also, as lively stones, are built up a spiritual house, an holy priesthood, to offer up spiritual sacrifices, acceptable to God by Jesus Christ" (v.5).

The entire book of Revelation is filled with typical meaning and constitutes the greatest of all enigmas for those who either neglect or dislike typology. The book becomes an unveiling when we interpret it in its typical meaning in the light of what is revealed in the Old Testament, especially in the book of Daniel. Old Testament types constitute the alphabet of New Testament language. What printers' type is to the words on this page, Old Testament typology is to New Testament teachings.

In the study of types we offer one word of warning: Never build a doctrine on a type or a parable, but where there is a clearly revealed New Testament doctrine, types and parables may be brought up as footlights to illuminate and to clarify the truth found therein.

One need not be abashed or intimidated in the use of types because of the harsh ridicule of many professed scholars. With such critics, teaching by type is considered as oversimplification of truth and leads to extravagance. Those who reject the full inspiration of Scripture cannot be expected to receive typical teachings, since they carry such a strong weight of authenticity. To adhere to a belief in typology is to expose oneself to the charge of low-grade scholarship. Be assured that one is in good company when he employs types in scriptural exegesis—the type of exegesis which recognizes sound principles of interpretation. Types may well constitute the watermarks of authenticity, and we should heed their lessons!

"Too much cannot be made of the fact that there is a constant analogy between the historic experience of God's people and the current experience of His saints" (J. C. Massee, *Conflict and Conquest in Holiness*).

In her book, *The Study of the Types,* Ada R. Habershon

names seven reasons for the study of types. Following is the substance of her chapter.

First, God Himself employed this method in communicating the mysteries of His message. We learn from the epistle to the Hebrews that in the construction of the tabernacle every detail was planned by Him, "according to the pattern showed to [Moses] in the mount" (Heb 8:5). For example, in speaking of the veil which divides the holy place from the holiest of all, the writer says, "The Holy Ghost thus signifying, that the way into the holiest of all was not yet made manifest, while as the first tabernacle was yet standing" (He 9:8). In other words there was a typical meaning to the veil that was not revealed until Christ came and fulfilled the type.

This aspect of divine truth necessitates the ministry of the Holy Spirit in guiding the believer into all truth. Jesus said "The Comforter . . . shall teach you all things . . . He shall receive of mine, and shall show it unto you" (Jn 14:26; 16:14). The writer makes this truth very clear as he interprets the rending of the veil that took place while Chirst hung on the cross; this miracle prefigured the new way into the holiest of all. "Having therefore, brethren, boldness to enter into the holiest by the blood of Jesus, by a new and living way, which he hath consecrated for us, through the veil, that is to say, his flesh" (He 10:19-20).

Another evidence of the importance and accuracy of types as used by the Father is found in what John records for us: "But when they came to Jesus, and saw that he was dead already, they break not his legs . . . For these things were done, that the scripture should be fulfilled, A bone of him shall not be broken" (Jn 19:33, 36). Fourteen hundred years earlier, Jehovah had ordered that not a bone of the paschal lamb should be broken. Now we know why—Imperial Rome had ordered it otherwise, but God's Word and God's type prevailed.

Second, our Lord thought much of these types. This is illustrated in His words to the two disciples who were on the way to Emmaus. "Beginning at Moses and all the prophets, he expounded unto them in all the scriptures the things concerning himself" (Lk 24:27). Those who neglect the study of types rarely become Christians with burning hearts. It is when we see Christ in Moses' writings that we more fully enter into the blessedness of His secret lowliness and beauty.

In the book of Revelation we behold Christ as the antitype of the bleeding, dying lambs offered upon the smoking altars at Israel's tabernacle gate. Twenty-nine times in this book the Lamb is mentioned.

Christ applies the manna as a type of Himself in John 6-7. He refers to the water from the smitten rock as a type of the Holy Spirit flowing from Himself.

Third, all types directly or indirectly converge and find their fulfillment in Christ. As in all things according to the will of the Father, Christ has the preeminence in types and shadows. We hear Christ say, "Had ye believed Moses, ye would have believed me: for he wrote of me" (Jn 5:46).

In addition to types, there are numerous lessons and examples to be found in God's Word which do not relate directly to Christ.

Fourth, the important use of types is emphasized by the abundant employment of them by the New Testament writers. This is indicated by the frequently recurring term, "that the Scriptures may be fulfilled" (Jn 13:18). Types and shadows of the Old Testament are fulfilled in the New. We give but one clear example: The gospel itself, the irreducible minimum of what one must believe in order to be saved, the salvation formula, is based upon Old Testament types. In 1

Corinthians 15:3-4 we read, "For I delivered unto you first of all that which I also received, how that Christ died for our sins according to the scriptures; and that he was buried, and that he rose again the third day according to the scriptures." While the death of Christ is clearly set forth in the offerings, the resurrection of Christ finds little doctrinal basis in the Old Testament as compared to the prophecies of this resurrection in types. For instance, the waving of the sheaf of firstfruits "on the morrow after the sabbath" (Lev 23:11) is made a type of Christ in 1 Corinthians 15:23; "Christ the first fruits; afterward they that are Christ's at his coming." The firstfruits in Leviticus found no explanation until it was exemplified in the resurrection of Christ.

Fifth, one of the most conclusive answers given to those who depreciate the study of types is found in the irrefutable fact that much of the New Testament cannot be understood without some measure of knowledge of Old Testament typology. For example, the epistle to the Hebrews is rooted and grounded in the Old Testament, and it is more or less obscure to those who refuse to properly observe the prototypes upon which its message rests.

Sixth, it is the typology of the Old Testament that constitutes the true commentary of the New. It is the bond that gives unity to the whole. The unexplained ceremonies of the Old Testament find their counterparts in the New. To observe this science makes the Bible one book.

Seventh, it is typology that gives the sure antidote to so-called higher criticism. The Scriptures carry the convincing evidence of their own authenticity.

# 2

# A NATION IN BONDAGE

LET US CONSIDER the historical background of Israel's wilderness journey. Since the close of Genesis, marked by the death of Joseph, Egypt's benefactor, more than a half a century has transpired. A new dynasty or family has taken over the throne, headed by a Pharaoh who does not know Joseph. Israel's outlook and expectations have been altered. As foreigners in Egypt they are now in the hands of enemies, not friends.

The Israelites were both hated and feared. They were hated because they were non-conformists. Due to their basic nature and their religious beliefs, they refused to be assimilated into the mainstream of Egyptian national life. They were people who kept to themselves, and they were feared because through a prolific birthrate, they were fast becoming a minority of alarming size. The monotheism of Israel was offensive to the Egyptians and their polytheism. As a labor contingent they were needed, but only as slaves.

The enigma of Israel's separateness and devotion to Jehovah was irritating. What the world cannot assimilate or suppress, it hates and desires to annihilate. The growing population of Israel constituted a threat to the ruling powers, and it could well hold the balance of power in case of a national crisis. The treatment of Israel at the hands of Pharaoh is set before us in the opening chapters of the book of Exodus.

## Israel's Position Personified

The covenant nation was not found in Egypt by accident More than two hundred years earlier, the Abrahamic covenant had been ratified. In Genesis 15 we read these words: "And thou shalt go to thy fathers in peace; thou shalt be buried in a good old age. But in the fourth generation they shall come hither again: for the iniquity of the Amorites is not yet full" (vv. 15-16). Israel's position in Egypt fell within the plans of divine providence. It was to be a part of their preparation for the service that God had ordained. In order to prepare a people for a world destiny it seemed necessary that they attend the "University of Hard Knocks" for four hundred years and then have a postgraduate course for forty years in the wilderness before moving back into the land of Canaan. It is the unfailing rule of God to put under rigorous discipline those whom He would greatly use.

## The Backdrop of Suffering

The first chapter of Exodus gives us a general view of Israel in Egypt. There the people were slaves of Pharaoh, and bitter was their bondage, hard was their lot, and hopeless was their outlook as they worked unceasingly at the brick kilns.

First, we see their need of redemption. Since they were unable to redeem themselves, they had to reach the end of their own way, and exhaust their own resources. We are told that they served with rigor (v. 13). Sin is servitude, and it brings slavery. "Sold unto sin" describes the sinner apart from Christ. These Israelites were shut in on every side. Egypt symbolized the world system under the control of Satan operating upon the principles of force, greed, selfishness, cruelty, ambition, and pleasure.

This need had to be felt and recognized, and the source of help had to be sought. "The children of Israel sighed by reason of the bondage, and they cried, and their cry came up unto God by reason of the bondage. (Ex 2:23). Despair and hopelessness often lead to the Saviour, who can both comfort and deliver. This is a hard lesson for men to learn.

## Divine Deliverance Is Timely

In the twelfth chapter of Exodus, we read: "And it came to pass at the end of the four hundred and thirty years, even the selfsame day it came to pass, that all the hosts of the Lord went out from the land of Egypt" (v. 41). God was on time; He is never behind schedule. Jehovah was patient and long-suffering with Pharaoh. Pharaoh hardened his own heart and in turn God hardened Pharaoh's heart. Only judgment could avail; deliverance must always come through judgment. The visitation of nine plagues upon Egypt was not enough to break her spirit and to convince Pharaoh of the power of Jehovah. The tenth plague was heaven's ultimatum —the death of the firstborn.

The firstborn represented the strength and pride of the flesh; a double portion of the inheritance went to him. Nine plagues failed to extricate Israel and to deliver her from Pharaoh's enslavement. The judgment of death alone could avail to bring salvation from God and satisfaction to His people. God saved His people in the nick of time. Moses and Aaron had been long prepared, and finally the evil had come to a head. The hour had struck, and the beginning of time for a nation had arrived. The end of travail was to bring forth a new nation under God. Exodus 12:1-2 tells us: "And the Lord spake unto Moses and Aaron in the land of Egypt, saying, This month shall be unto you the beginning of months: it shall be the first month of the year to you." So it is with the antitype, "But when the fulness of the time was come, God sent forth his Son, made of a woman, made under the law, to redeem them that were under the law, that we might receive the adoption of sons" (Gal 4:4-5).

Israel, God's earthly people, were taught by what is known today as "the kindergarten method." Through institutions, feasts, sacrifices, and observance of days, the priestly ministries served to keep the basic divine truth before the nation. The importance of the Passover is easily understood and recognized as soon as we recall the fact that God used both the judgment of the firstborn and His power to deliver His blood-redeemed people from death and bondage. Furthermore, He established the inherent truths of the Passover as a memorial for the coming generations. For fifteen hundred years, beginning with Israel's entrance into the land, the Passover was kept annually by the seed of Abraham. The importance of this study is also emphasized by the fact that we are told "Christ our passover is sacrificed for us" (1 Co 5:7). We know we are on safe ground when we find in this important event the central truth of our Christian faith.

The eleventh chapter of Exodus tells of the solemn announcement concerning the character and nature of the tenth plague—the one which involved the death of the firstborn. The divine decree was universal in its application. The sentence of death was passed upon the firstborn of man and beast (v. 5). But nothing is said about the death of the clean animals. This seems quite significant since, if these animals were under the same decree, a lamb could only die for himself. It is evident that these were not included in this decree of death. Even so, Christ could not have died for us had He been a mere man under the same decree of death. "The soul that sinneth, it shall die" (Eze 18:4). Christ was the only truly clean man this earth has seen since the fall of Adam. There was no sentence of death upon Him; therefore He alone could die for others.

God said that the execution of this sentence of death

would bring a great cry in Egypt: "And all the firstborn in the land of Egypt shall die, from the firstborn of Pharaoh that sitteth upon his throne, even unto the firstborn of the maidservant that is behind the mill; and all the firstborn of beasts" (Ex 11:5-6). God was about to make a difference between the Egyptians and the Israelites—the difference between death and life.

It is the cross that constitutes the dividing line between the believer and the world. It is not so much a matter of the saints giving up the world as it is the saints taking their assigned places as Christians. When one has taken his divinely assigned place, the world will give him up. "And the LORD said unto Moses, Yet will I bring one plague more upon Pharaoh, and upon Egypt; afterwards he will let you go hence: when he shall let you go, he shall surely thrust you out hence altogether" (v. 1). The preaching and living of the truth of the cross is the real secret of separation. Every implication of Calvary is a scandal and an offense to the lost man.

## Redemption's Development

The book of Genesis is the book of beginnings — the beginning of creation, the beginning of sin, redemption, the family, the nations, and in particular, the nation of Israel. The book closes with "a coffin in Egypt."

The book of Exodus is the book of redemption. The word "Exodus" itself means "going out" or "the way out." Exodus has been well divided under three heads: ruin, redemption, and relationship—ruin in Egypt, redemption by blood and power out of Egypt, and a relationship with Jehovah in the wilderness on the basis of the blood redemption.

There are three spheres of experience depicted for us in this journey.

## Israel In Egypt

Egypt is an example of the world; it is typical, in some respects, of this cosmos into which we were born by nature. Egypt represents this world order with all of its attractions under the domination and control of one greater than Pharaoh. If Egypt is an example of the world, then Pharaoh may well portray Satan, the god of this world. Egypt represents this cosmos with all of its mighty power, its prestige, its wealth, its glory, and its appeal.

In the day of Israel's bondage, Egypt was the mistress of the world and the granary that supplied the nations. Her ancient ruins, such as Karnak, Thebes, and Alexandria, give silent but effective testimony to her former grandeur. The Holy Spirit employs Egypt as an illustration of this world in Revelation 11:8: "And their dead bodies shall lie in the street of the great city, which spiritually is called Sodom and Egypt, where also our Lord was crucified."

The symbols of Egypt today are the pyramids, the tombs of the ancient Pharaohs. These are the silent sentinels of the centuries, testimonies to a faded glory. If one should go into any museum and look for something distinctively Egyptian, he would most easily find an Egyptian mummy. Egypt is a land of death; this world, which Egypt typifies, is also characterized by death. In spite of all the glamour that greets the eye—the boasted power, the culture, and the accomplishments of this world system—death is the dominant enemy, and the fear of death continually hangs like a pall over the world's gaiety. Longfellow wrote, "Our hearts, like muffled drums, are beating funeral marches to the grave."

The Egypt of Moses' day was a land of bondage—a land of servitude and affliction. There was heard in the land the crack of the taskmasters' whips, and the sound of the overlords' rough voices. For Israel, Egypt was a land of endless toil and hopeless despair. At the same time, none would deny that there were temporary pleasures in Egypt with its flesh-pots and its seasoned foods. But like the darkened world of the twentieth century, Egypt was a land of night and death.

Egypt was also a land of conflict—conflict between the people of God and the servants of Pharaoh. Jehovah brought judgment against the gods of Egypt, exposing their impotence and their shame. God's demand was for the Pharaoh to let His people go so they might hold a feast in His honor in the wilderness. Pharaoh's refusal and his persistent hardness of heart brought upon the land the ten infesting plagues. The last of these plagues was the death of the firstborn of man and beast. Israel had been exempt from the former plagues but not from this one. There was a blanket decree of death. "That every mouth may be stopped, and all the world may become guilty before god . . . There is no difference: for all have sinned, and come short of the glory of God" (Ro 3:19, 22-23). But for God's covenant people, there was a gracious way of redemption. It was a foolish way to the natural man, "but unto us which are saved it is the power of God" (1 Co 1:18). The way of redemption, in Egypt and elsewhere, is the way of blood. "Without shedding of blood is no remission" (Heb 9:22). If Israel was to be delivered from bondage, help must come from without; God must undertake for His people. This He did and continues to do.

## Israel in the Wilderness

The very night Israel was redeemed from death by blood the people were ordered out of Egypt. While the power of Pharaoh had been broken, the danger of servitude had not passed. Israel was redeemed, not merely from death, but unto the Lord, so that He might take a people unto Himself as "a peculiar treasure" (Ex 19:5). The wilderness is the place of testing, of discipline, and of preparation. There the people were to learn two great lessons.

First, they were to learn what the flesh is and then they were to learn what God is. Both of these truths are brought out in Deuteronomy 8:2: "And thou shalt remember all the way in which the LORD thy God led thee these forty years in the wilderness, to humble thee, and to prove thee, to know what was in thine heart, whether thou wouldest keep his commandments, or no." Like Israel of old, the child of God, having been redeemed by Christ, the Passover Sacrifice, is still in Egypt or the world. Israel was in Egypt as to fact, in the wilderness as to experience, and in Canaan as to position. The enemy in Egypt was the world; in the wilderness it was the flesh; and in Canaan it was the devil. The world, the flesh, and the devil—this unholy trinity is still with us.

For Israel, the wilderness was "the school of God." God was preparing a career people—world diplomats, a priestly nation—to represent Him among the nations of the earth. This divine purpose, though delayed, will ultimately find fulfillment. Israel was to be the nucleus and the channel of world redemption and divine beneficence. All such hope was contingent upon the coming of the promised Messiah and upon Israel's acknowledgment of Him. We know full well how miserably Israel failed.

The believer likewise has his wilderness; he is a heavenly ambassador—a divinely appointed diplomat while a stranger and a pilgrim in this world. We are being prepared not only for heavenly citizenship but also for winning others to the Lord's side by the testimony of both life and word. As believers we, with Paul, are to learn what the flesh is: "For I know that in me (that is, in my flesh,) dwelleth no good thing" (Ro 7:18). And we must have no confidence in the flesh. Our other great lesson is to know what God is as revealed in Christ through His Word and our experience.

### Israel in Canaan

Israel's passage through Jordan depicts another aspect of death. Moses, who represented the law, passed off the scene. A new Joshua (or Jesus) had to lead the way into the land that was flowing with milk and honey. Canaan was a land of warfare and victory, and there the bondslaves of Egypt were destined to become the bondslaves of Jehovah and the soldiers in the land of Canaan. Canaan is not representative of heaven, as many of our hymns mistakenly teach; it represents the land of spiritual adulthood. The book of Joshua tells of the conflicts of Canaan and is often compared to the book of Ephesians in the New Testament. Both of these symbolize the place of warfare and victory. Ephesians is the Christian's kingdom. As George Henderson said, "What is described historically in the book of Joshua is set forth doctrinally in the Epistle to the Ephesians and practically in the third and fourth chapters of Hebrews" (*Studies in the Book of Exodus*).

The journey from Egypt to Canaan serves well as a living drama of the Christian's experience reduced to its simplest equation.

# 3

# JUDGMENT UPON EGYPT

IT IS A MISTAKE to assume that the purpose of the ten plagues was to soften Pharaoh and Egypt to the point where they would let Israel go. As a matter of fact the very opposite was true. "And the LORD said unto Moses, When thou goest to return into Egypt, see that thou do all those wonders before Pharaoh, which I have put in thine hand: but I will harden his heart, that he shall not let the people go" (Ex 4:21). Note that this passage states, "I will harden his heart, that he shall *not* let the people go."

The question naturally arises concerning the real purpose of the ten plagues. Several factors seem to be involved as we search for an answer.

First, we must keep in mind the fact that the people of Israel had been slaves in Egypt for some four hundred years. The nation had seen no miracles, nor had it witnessed an exhibition of divine power. In fact, the people knew Jehovah only as "the God of Abraham, Isaac, and Jacob." Even Moses asked, "Behold, when I come unto the children of Israel, and shall say unto them, The God of your fathers hath sent me unto you; and they shall say to me, What is his name? what shall I say unto them? And God said unto Moses, I AM THAT I AM: and he said, Thus shalt thou say unto the children of Israel, I AM hath sent me unto you" (Ex 3: 13-14). The Exodus generation was far removed from the patriarchs.

The ten plagues gave evidence of the mighty power of Jehovah. This, indeed, is the first lesson that any generation must learn—that power and majesty belong to Almighty God. As we reflect upon the miracles of our Lord, we arrive at practically the same conclusion. Miracles, outward demonstrations of divine power, always occur at a time when mankind has forgotten God and His omnipotence. There was the beneficent aspect of our Lord's miracle-working ministry. However, the gospel of John in particular emphasizes that such miracles were performed as signs so that men might believe. It is interesting to note in Scripture that the miracles occur, not when God's people are living on a spiritually high plane, but when they are in a state of spiritual depression. This fact is emphasized in the exodus, again in the days of Elijah and Elisha, and in the days of our Lord and the apostles. The supreme spiritual state is experienced only when men walk by faith and not by sight. The all-sufficient sign for the Christian is found in the resurrection of the Lord Jesus Christ. To believe God, whom we have not seen, is the highest possible compliment the creature can pay to the Creator.

Second, the children of Israel had to be made ready for the wilderness experience that carried with it no visible means of support for them. The moral fiber of the nation had to be strengthened and tested. For example, what would have happened to the three million people, unprepared and undisciplined, if they had been led immediately in the wilderness. Think of this in the light of all the trials, hardships and difficulties that such a journey entailed. Israel had investments in Egypt in flocks, cattle, and homes. In addition, her people had a strong appetite for Egypt's flesh-pots and her condiments. Think of the contrast between Egypt and the trackless wilderness. As far as the flesh is concerned, Egypt offered security, and the wilderness offered uncertainty. The nation had to be prepared and made willing to leave Egypt. This seems to be the main reason for the plagues but not the only reason.

Third, the purpose for the ten plagues was retribution. Judgment fell on the gods of Egypt as well as on Pharaoh and on the Egyptians. "For I will pass through the land of Egypt this night, and will smite all the firstborn in the land of Egypt, both man and beast; and against all the gods of Egypt I will execute judgment: I am the LORD" (Ex 12:12). The plagues struck in judgment at the very things the Egyptians worshiped. What the Israelites offered as sacrifices, the Egyptians considered sacred.

## THE PLAGUES OF EGYPT

In the study of the ten plagues or judgments that came upon Egypt, it is well for us to keep in mind that Egypt is representative of the world—a world-system that seeks to operate upon its own resources, its own power and its own wisdom—apart from God. This world, in spite of its tinsel, glory, pride, position and pomp, constitutes the arena of conflict. It is overshadowed with impending judgments. Pharaoh and Moses are the apparent actors, but behind the scenes stand "the gods of Egypt" on the one hand and Jehovah God, the Creator and Redeemer, on the other.

Conflict described for us in these early chapters of Exodus was in no sense a sham battle consisting of two human forces diametrically opposed to one another. Indeed, it was a conflict between God and Satan—between divine omnipotence and "principalities, . . . powers, . . . rulers of the darkness of this world . . . [and] spiritual wickedness in high places" (Eph 6:12). The failure to comprehend and accept the clear teachings of Scripture with reference to the existence of a personal devil and the reality of demonic forces is to leave oneself in spiritual darkness and to operate blindly on the basis of naturalistic, human philosophy. Following such a line leaves unsolved the greatest of all mysteries—the origin, the nature, and the operation of evil. The conflict in Egypt is only a drama and the shadow of the real, unseen warfare that has raged since the fall of Lucifer. This is an equation that we dare not forget if we are to fulfill our commission as good soldiers of Jesus Christ.

The ten plagues or signs that were experienced by Egypt were merely the outcropping of a subterranean, age-long conflict that will one day find its climax when the Seed of the woman shall bruise the head of the serpent (Gen 3:15). Keeping this in mind, let us examine the first nine plagues as a group and then deal with the tenth plague alone.

## The Nine Plagues Upon Egypt

There are three series of three judgments each. Each series of three begins with "in the morning" (Ex 7:15; 8:20; 9:13).

The first three plagues or signs have to do with "the springs of life." Water is changed into blood, the land of Egypt is filled with frogs, and mankind is contaminated with lice. C. A. Coates, in *An Outline of the Book of Exodus,* has a number of interesting observations along this line. The turning of water into blood includes the rivers, streams, ponds, and reservoirs, all of which constitute the source and refreshment of life. All of these are filled with that which is morally subject to death. Frogs seem to speak of the uncleanliness of man's heart. "And I saw three unclean spirits like frogs come out of the mouth of the dragon, and out of the mouth of the beast, and out of the mouth of the false prophet" (Rev 16:13).

Lice created out of the dust brought a confession from the

magicians that this had to be the work of God (Ex 8:19). There seems to be something here that suggests, in a typical manner, the drama in the agelong conflict. In the Garden of Eden, God delivered to Adam the authority of dominion. In the fall, Adam lost this power, and the rod of authority fell from his hands to rest in the dust. In this picture the rod wielded by Moses brings life out of dust, thus giving us a striking figure of the resurrection power resident in the promise of God.

The distinguishing feature of the second series of plagues is the fact that the land of Goshen, where God's people dwelt, was immune from the flies, the murrain and the boils. As C. A. Coates suggests, these signs could well speak of the things from which the people of God in their normal condition, as redeemed and delivered, should be free. The flies may speak of the small irritations. The murrain among the Egyptian cattle reminds us that man uses all his possessions for himself and not for God. The plague of the boils speaks of the corruption in man's moral nature that is always prone to manifest itself in open sin. From such God has provided deliverance through the new nature that is in Christ.

The last of the three series, including plagues seven, eight, and nine, also begins, "in the morning" (9:13). Here we have hail, locusts, and darkness. These are the last of the ineffectual judgments. Only one more was left, the tenth, and this proved to be the only one that really worked. These in the last series seem to speak of tribulation—such judgments as are described in the book of the Revelation. A judgment of hail is foretold in Revelation 16:21: "And there fell upon men a great hail out of heaven, every stone about the weight of a talent: and men blasphemed God because of the plague of the hail; for the plague thereof was exceeding great." A judgment of locusts is referred to in Revelation 9:3: "And there came out of the smoke locusts upon the earth: and unto them was given power, as the scorpions of the earth have power." Darkness upon the earth is prophesied in Revelation 16:10: "And the fifth angel poured out his vial upon the seat of the beast; and his kingdom was full of darkness; and they gnawed their tongues for pain." Hail, locusts, and darkness all combined "to foreshadow a time when every green thing in which man so delights, that which is so pleasant to the eyes, that which he relies upon for his food, comes under judgment. Darkness, the withdrawing of moral light, seems to characterize this, our day." Men are now closing out the light of revelation, for it was said of God, "The entrance of thy words giveth light" (Ps 119:130). The inspiration of the Scripture is everywhere being denied. Windows are being blocked up. Infidelity and liberalism shut out the light of the divine law and wisdom, leaving nothing but darkness and apostasy. God will leave man for a season to the darkness that he loves.

THE UNIVERSAL JUDGMENT OF DEATH—THE TENTH PLAGUE

"And Moses said, Thus saith the LORD, About midnight will I go out into the midst of Egypt: and all the firstborn in the land of Egypt shall die, from the firstborn of Pharaoh that sitteth upon his throne, even unto the firstborn of the maidservant that is behind the mill; and all the firstborn of beasts. And there shall be a great cry throughout all the land of Egypt, such as there was none like it, nor shall be like it any more. But against any of the children of Israel shall not a dog move his tongue, against man or beast: that ye may know how the LORD doth put a difference between the Egyptians and Israel" (Ex 11:4-7).

Everything comes to a head in this tenth plague. Israel, having been immunized from the previous plagues, now finds herself included in the tenth plague, the death of the firstborn.

The pause between the preceding ineffectual plagues and the last, the effectual one, became ominous. There is always an awful lull in the eye of the hurricane before the last crushing winds break through in their fury, sweeping everything before them. There is silence in heaven before the final peal of thunder. "And when he had opened the seventh seal, there was silence in heaven about the space of half an hour" (Rev 8:1).

The divine sentence of death fell equally upon the Israelites as upon the Egyptians. Yet there was a divine demarcation between the two. "But against any of the children of Israel shall not a dog move his tongue, against man or beast: that ye may know how that the LORD doth put a difference between the Egyptians and Israel" (Ex 11:7). While not even a dog was to move his tongue against man or beast of the Israelites, concerning the death of the firstborn, we read: "There shall be a great cry throughout all the land of Egypt, such as there was none like it, nor shall be like it anymore" (v. 6). This cry would be enough to arouse all the dogs in Egypt. In addition, some three million people were to begin their exodus, and yea, not a dog was to move his tongue against the children of Israel. When God does a job He does it completely.

"The LORD doth put a difference between the Egyptians and Israel." Let us consider the two decrees. The first, the decree of universal death, applied equally to the Egyptians and the Israelites, but note the statement that God put a difference between the Egyptians and Israel. It sounds like a contradiction. In this we find one of the mysterious paradoxes of Scripture that prove so clearly the authenticity of the revelation. The liberals have made much of this seeming contradiction. It does say, "All the firstborn in the land of Egypt must die." It also says "The LORD doth put a difference." Every instructed believer, even though he cannot explain some things, is confident that there are no contradictions in the Bible. Hidden beneath this enigma is to be found one of the great truths of grace. "So then faith cometh by hearing, and hearing by the word of God" (Ro 10:17). The sentence of universal condemnation proceeds from God's righteousness; "the difference" which He put between the Egyptians and Israel was the overflow of His grace. But for the inquirer, there still remains the question as to how God's justice and God's mercy can be reconciled.

The late Dr. Arthur Pink raised the question, "How can justice exact its full due without excluding mercy? How can mercy be manifested except at the expense of justice?" *Gleanings in Exodus*). This is the problem. "For I will . . . smite all the firstborn in the land of Egypt" (Ex 12:12), and yet, the firstborn were delivered from the angel of death. How could that be? Surely both could not be true. Yet, they were, and therein we may discover a blessed illustration of the contents of the gospel. In the death of the firstborn it is a matter of sin that a righteous God must deal with. "For all have sinned, and come short of the glory of God" (Ro 3:23). To quote Dr. Pink again, "It is true that God has purposed to redeem Israel out of Egypt, but He would do so only on a righteous basis. Holiness can never ignore sin, no matter where it is found. When the angels sinned, God 'spared them not' (2 Pt. 2:4). . . . God made no exception of his own blessed Son: when He was 'made sin for us' (2 Cor. 5:21)—He spared Him not (Rom. 8:32)."

The greatest problem that confronts us is the question of how a righteous God can "put a difference between the Egyptians and Israel" when all are sinners, deserving death and hell. It is this question that is raised in Romans 3. In this chapter the seeming impossibilities are reconciled, "that He might be just, and the justifier of him which believeth in Jesus" (v. 26).

We know that a holy God must punish sin. But the Scripture tells us that God is love. If His righteousness acts alone, the sinner must die. If love acts alone, then the holiness of God is violated. His character is impugned. He would be made to appear sentimental, indulgent, and weak.

How then can both God and the sinner be justified? This is the whole story of the gospel. It is by means of substitution. Love found a way. It was in the blood of the lamb that mercy and truth were able to meet together and righteousness and peace were able to kiss each other (Ps 85:10). It was the blood of the paschal lamb that made the difference. It was the paschal lamb that foreshadowed two aspects of the death of Christ. Christ came, as foreshadowed in the whole burnt offering, in complete devotion to the Heavenly Father. He said, "Lo, I come (in the volume of the book it is written of me,) to do thy will, O God" (He 10:7).

Perhaps we can say that the primary aspect of the coming and the death of Christ was first Godward and then manward. It was Godward in that He came to please the Father; it was manward in that He came to redeem. The whole value of the Passover lay in its being a type of Christ. "For even Christ our passover is sacrificed for us: therefore let us keep the feast" (1 Co 5:7-8).

Everything comes to a head in this tenth plague. Egypt was made to realize that the nation was under the judgment of God. "And all the firstborn in the land of Egypt shall die, from the firstborn of Pharoah that sitteth upon his throne, even unto the firstborn of the maidservant that is behind the mill; and all the firstborn of beasts" (Ex 11:5). While the goodness of God did not pronounce the firstborn Israelite safe, He "put a difference between the Egyptians and Israel" (v. 7). He pointed out the way of salvation by blood. This was not a salvation without price. It was not a salvation by prayer and fasting but a salvation by substitution. This is always the divine way. Christ alone is called the Lamb in Scripture. The Lamb in Revelation is always regarded as a substitute or a ransom. Substitution or death was and is the inexorable rule.

The firstborn represents the strength and pride of the flesh—the best the household contains. This speaks of all that would naturally be the pride, boast and strength of the house. All of this is under the judgment of God. In Scripture the firstborn is always rejected and the secondborn received: Cain was rejected, Abel was received; Ishmael was rejected, Isaac was received; Esau was rejected, Jacob was received; the first Adam failed, the last Adam, Christ, succeeded. God rejects our first birth and accepts our second. Israel's firstborn sons, in the beginning, were designated as priests; later the tribe of Levi was substituted. In all of this we find displayed the majesty, the glory, and the grace of God as manifested in redemption by blood through substitution.

# 4

# THE PASSOVER

THE PASSOVER has been called "an early edition of the gospel." First Corinthians 5:7 tells us, "Christ our passover is sacrificed for us." In His death, Christ gave meaning, significance, and amplification to the Passover. The Passover, in turn, gives verification and interpretation to the cross. The Passover is the shadow; the cross is the substance. The Passover is the pattern; the cross is the perfection.

The Passover, the first of the memorial feasts, is a clear, minute, and thrilling foreview of redemption's plan and design. The week-long celebration of the Passover began on the fourteenth of Nisan, a month of the Hebrew calendar which begins in our months of March or April. It marked the deliverance of the Jews from Egypt and the establishment of Israel as a nation by God's redemptive act. The Passover was in every way a divine institution.

## THE IMPORTANCE OF THE PASSOVER

The story of the Lamb that was slain is woven into the texture of practically every book of the Bible. The theme of the slain Lamb runs like a silver thread through the Scripture. In Abel's offering (Gen 4) the Lamb is typified; in the ram caught in the thicket (chap. 22) the Lamb is prophesied; in the Passover (Ex 12) the Lamb is specified; in Isaiah

53 the Lamb is personified; and in John 1 the Lamb is identified: "Behold the Lamb of God, which taketh away the sin of the world" (v. 29). In Revelation 5 the Lamb is magnified, and in Revelation 22 the Lamb is glorified. The Passover was a holy convocation and a sort of perpetual commemoration of Israel's deliverance from death. It was a standing testimonial that their salvation was by the blood of the Lamb. "It was the key note of the Christian system sounding in the dim depths of remote antiquity" (Joseph A. Seiss, *Holy Types*).

The time was "the beginning of months" (Ex 12:2), the Jewish New Year. The place was Egypt, symbolic of the world, where God always meets the sinner. From this memorial feast Christ lifts out the Lord's Supper, the second of the two ordinances of the Christian church.

It is worthy of note that the first ordinance of the Jewish religion was a domestic service, which bespeaks divine wisdom. To quote G. H. Chadwick, "Never was a nation truly prosperous or permanently strong which did not cherish the sanctities of the home. Ancient Rome failed to resist the barbarians, not because her discipline had degenerated, but because evil habits in her homes had ruined the population" (*The Book of Exodus*). In considering the Passover with its profoundly typical analogies, we must not overlook the simple and obvious fact that God built His nation upon families and ordered its great national institutions in a manner that would draw the members of the family together.

In commenting on the value of Israel's sacred-day festivals, her sublime and solemn convocations, Joseph A. Seiss in his book *Holy Types* states it most beautifully. "They served to unite the nation, cemented them together as one people, and prevented the tendency to the formation of separate cliques and conflicting clans or states. Three times a year did these feasts bring vast multitudes together from all sections of the country to meet each other on a common religious ground, requiring of them the acknowledgment of descent from a common father, of consecration to the same God, of heirship to the same promises, and of subjection to the same theocratic system. Persons of different tribes and distant localities thus met on terms of brotherhood and fellowship, fostering old and creating ever new relationships and familiarizing all with each other. They were thus strengthened in unity of faith and interest against internal ruptures, division, and idolatry." For the first time, the term assembly is used: "the whole assembly of the congregation of Israel" (Ex 12:6). It suggests a people called out of the world to be God's possession.

If hostility had sprung up between any of the tribes, the occurrence of these holy convocations required them to lay down their arms and come together as brethren around the altar of their common God. They were to offer the same sacrifices, sing the same grand songs, and bow down with each other before the same almighty Jehovah. It was impossible for a people to obey such regulations and become disunited. The actual split of the ten tribes from Judah, under Rehoboam and Jeroboam, could not and did not become very serious until they set aside the part of the law that related to these national festivals and set up, instead, altars at Bethel and Dan.

"And Jeroboam said in his heart, Now shall the kingdom return to the house of David: If this people go up to do sacrifice in the house of the LORD at Jerusalem, then shall the heart of this people turn again unto their lord, even unto Rehoboam king of Judah, and they shall kill me, and go again to Rehoboam king of Judah. Whereupon the king took counsel, and made two calves of gold, and said unto them, It is too much for you to go up to Jerusalem: behold thy gods, O Israel, which brought thee up out of the land of Egypt. And he set the one in Bethel, and the other put he in Dan" (1 Ki 12:26-29).

Every law of the assembly bore the imprint of a divine origin, and he who disputes these laws calls upon us to exercise a credulity much greater than is agreeable to sober reason. Skepticism may vaunt and boast as it pleases, but it embraces more absurdities than it has ever imputed to the faith of believers. Before the infidel undertakes, on that score, to extract the mote from the Christian's eye, it would be well for him first to remove the beam from his own. "Physician, heal thyself" is rebuttal enough to the arguments and ridicule of unbelief and atheism.

But there was also a direct religious value in the appointment of these festivals. Burning thoughts and holy aspirations there take wings to soar in poetic rhythm, blending sounds of heavenly sweetness to join the songs of the seraphim. Truth revealed therein sends forth its rays to warm, melt, cheer, animate, and bless all who have ears to hear. Earth is thus drawn into fellowship with heaven and invited to think thoughts which please God. In the deep, still intervals of those solemn transactions, the mellowed soul may feel the soft and gentle beatings of the pulse of immortality. Even the silent atmosphere seems to whisper: "God is here."

## Three Epochal Dates

In the first place, the Passover preparation marked the beginning of time with Israel, the actual birth of the nation. It was also the first sacrifice divinely prescribed. "And the Lord spake unto Moses and Aaron in the land of Egypt, saying, This month shall be unto you the beginning of months: it shall be the first month of the year to you" (Ex 12:1-2).

"There is here a very interesting change in the order of

time. The common or civil year was rolling on its ordinary course when Jehovah interrupted it in reference to His people . . . previous history was henceforth to be regarded as a blank. Redemption was to constitute a new step in *real life*" (Charles H. MacKintosh, *Notes on the Book of Exodus*).

It is interesting to observe in Genesis 4 that in Cain's line no ages are given, for "Cain went out from the presence of the Lord" (v. 16). No duration of life is given. This reminds one of what is said about the way of the ungodly: "The ungodly . . . are like the chaff which the wind driveth away. Therefore the ungodly shall not stand in the judgment, nor sinners in the congregation of the righteous. For the LORD knoweth the way of the righteous: but the way of the ungodly shall perish" (Ps 1:4-6). In the line of Seth, ages are recorded.

Walter B. Pitkin has written a book entitled *Life Begins at Fifty*. The Christian knows better—life begins at Calvary. It was so with Israel, and it was so with the redeemed throughout the ages. It is also true of our day that we only begin to live when we live in, with, and for Christ.

Second, the tenth day of the month marked the taking of the lamb—a lamb for a house. The house may have been too small for the lamb, but the lamb was never too small for the house. While actually many thousands of lambs were slain, we hear nothing of "lambs" (plural) but only of one "lamb." The lamb speaks of Christ, the Lamb of God. He too was taken on the tenth day of Nisan. After His triumphal entry into Jerusalem He was for all practical purposes under house arrest for four days.

Third, on the fourteenth day the paschal lamb was to be slain in the evening. "And ye shall keep it up until the fourteenth day of the same month: and the whole assembly of the congregation of Israel shall kill it in the evening" (Ex 12:6). Four days were set aside for the purpose of minute examination so that no defects, blemishes, or diseases might escape detection. These would disqualify the lamb. "Thou shalt not sacrifice unto the LORD thy God any bullock, or sheep, wherein is blemish, or any evilfavouredness; for that is an abomination unto the LORD thy God" (Deu 17:1). The type must be perfect in order to represent the antitype, the Lamb of God, the Lord Jesus Christ.

The lamb was to be killed in the evening (literally, between the evenings—meaning the time between three and six o'clock), before the midnight visit of the angel of death. Little time was left, and haste was required. The blood was fresh, and the whole assembly participated in the death of the lamb. It was no private affair or a thing done in a corner. So it was with the Lamb of God. The whole world shared both in the guilt and in the execution of the Son of God. He was publicly condemned and executed.

### Three Specific Requirements

First, in Exodus 12:5, the lamb was specified: "a male," suggesting strength in unbroken perfection; "of the first year," speaking of tenderness and innocence. "He is brought as a lamb to the slaughter, and as a sheep before her shearers is dumb, so he openeth not his mouth" (Is 53:7). And the lamb was to be "without blemish," bespeaking unrestricted innocence and spotless purity, "And ye know that he was manifested to take away our sins; and in him is no sin" (1 Jn 3:5).

Christ, our Passover Lamb, was without blemish. "And the angel answered and said unto her, The Holy Ghost shall come upon thee, and the power of the Highest shall overshadow thee: therefore also that holy thing which shall be born of thee shall be called the Son of God" (Lk 1:35). Even the demons were made to confess, "I know thee who thou art; the Holy One of God" (4:34).

To the chorus of witnesses are added several voices: Judas declared, "I have betrayed the innocent blood" (Mt 27:4); Pilate affirmed, "I find in him no fault at all" (Jn 18:38); The centurion who watched Him die proclaimed, "Certainly this was a righteous man" (Lk 23:47); the dying thief said, "But this man hath done nothing amiss" (v. 41); and, our Lord challenged His enemies: "Which of you convinceth me of sin?" (Jn 8:46).

Second, the lamb was identified; it had to be taken from the flock. "Your lamb shall be without blemish, a male of the first year: ye shall take it out from the sheep, or from the goats" (Ex 12:5). The lamb had to be identified with the flock. No victim taken unwillingly in a chase was permitted as a sacrifice unto Jehovah.

Prophecy identifies Christ with mankind. "For he shall grow up before him as a tender plant, and as a root out of a dry ground: he hath no form nor comeliness; and when we shall see him, there is no beauty that we should desire him" (Is 53:2). Christ said, "No man taketh [my life] from me, but I lay it down of myself" (Jn 10:18). Our Lamb was identified with the human race. He was, and is, the last Adam (1 Co 15:45).

Third, the lamb had to be killed. "And the whole assembly of the congregation of Israel shall kill it in the evening" (Ex 12:6). Moses wrote, "For the life of the flesh is in the blood" (Lev 17:11). The blood had to be shed. Simply to have tied the appealing, tender lamb to the doorpost would not have availed. To imitate Christ's life will not suffice for sin's guilt. The life of Christ shuts the sinner out from God by revealing that type of manhood a holy God requires.

### The Ritual of the Protecting Blood

Perhaps there were not less than two hundred fifty thousand lambs required to meet the needs of the entire nation. Yet these thousands of lambs are considered as one in the mind of God. Many lambs stood for one Lamb, the Lord Jesus Christ. He was declared by His forerunner, John the Baptist, to be "the Lamb of God, which taketh away the sin of the world" (Jn 1:29).

"And the whole assembly of the congregation of the house of Israel shall kill it in the evening" (Ex 12:6). The lamb had to die, the clean for the unclean, a substitute in death. The living lamb lying before the door would not avail; the blood had to be shed, retained in the basin, and then applied with hyssop to the doorposts and to the lintel. Nothing was left to chance; every detail was minutely outlined. Nothing was left to man's ingenuity. Complete instructions were given. One of the first things a study of the Passover suggests is the fact that it is all of God; very little is left for man to do. This is always the case in the story of redemption. There were no accidents on the day when the Lamb of God, the antitype of the paschal lamb, was crucified.

The blood was applied at the door. It was a seal to the entrance that both kept out the avenging death angel and kept safe those who were thus sheltered. The blood applied by hyssop speaks of the application of the precious blood of our Paschal Lamb by faith.

# 5

# FIVE GREAT FACTS

As we consider the paschal lamb and this feast that was to be annually observed by Israel once they were in the land, we should remember five great truths.

First, the firstborn within the house was sheltered by the blood, for we read, "and when I see the blood, I will pass over you" (Ex 12:13). Deliverance was not based upon the attitude, the state of mind, or the righteousness of the one sheltered but upon the value of the blood on the house. Again, deliverance was not determined by human estimate or appreciation of the blood but by God's evaluation—by what He thought of the blood. We are saved, not because of *what* we are, but because of *where* we are—in Christ. The firstborn was doomed to death by God, not because of his conduct, but because of his birth. The sinner is justly condemned. He must accept salvation by substitution. Remembering this truth, many other things fall in line, and many problems will be resolved.

Someone has depicted for us an imaginary story that carries with it a pungent lesson. There was a young lad, the firstborn in the home, who became restless as the midnight hour drew nigh. He walked the floor, he wrung his hands, he cried, and he appealed to his father for assurance. In so doing he said that he did not feel well; that he had a peculiar feeling, and that he was afraid he would be visited by the death angel. On being invited to eat of the roast lamb, the boy said he had lost his appetite, he could not eat, and he would be so happy when daybreak came and he knew he would be alive.

In the next house was another lad about the same age, who greatly delighted his father by reminding him that he knew the blood was applied, and that God said He would not allow the death angel to cross the threshold. He was jubilant and worshipful in his attitude. He ate the roast lamb with the family, arrayed in the pilgrim's garb.

There is a vast difference in the attitudes of these two boys, but we pause to inquire, Which of the two was the safer? The answer must be that they were equally safe, not because of their disposition of heart or mind, but because they were both sheltered by the blood.

Second, the firstborn was assured by the promise of God. The blood made him safe on the outside. The Word gave him assurance on the inside. Could the family be sure that the death angel would not visit the home? If so, upon what ground? Solely on the ground of what God had promised. "So then faith cometh by hearing, and hearing by the word of God" (Ro 10:17). We have His Word: "Verily, verily, I say unto you, He that heareth my word, and believeth on him that sent me, hath everlasting life, and shall not come into condemnation; but is passed from death unto life" (Jn 5:24).

Again, we would pause to inquire which of the two boys honored God most? Did the first lad, by walking the floor, wringing his hands, and weeping, demonstrate his humility or a lack of faith and assurance? It was the second lad who brought honor to God by taking Him at His word. There are many who tell us we must not say we know we are saved; otherwise we boast. That could be true, but only if we referred to our own state of mind and heart, and we certainly do not. We refer, rather, to our position in Christ, for therein we are sheltered by the blood and assured by the Word.

Third, the people of God were made strong by the feast. The body of the lamb, whose blood made them safe, was prepared and made ready for the feast. The roast lamb suggests that Jehovah had condescended to feast with His people. "That which had become their safety now becomes their food —here we have a symbolism that speaks of joyful participation in the sacrifice and communion with God based upon expiation. Their feast on the first night of the Passover was only an anticipation of that which was to follow in the ages to come" (Alexander MacLaren, *Expositions of Holy Scripture*).

The sacrifice was not to be eaten raw or sodden at all in water but was to be eaten with bitter herbs and roast with fire. In order to be roast with fire, as commanded, the body of the lamb had to be put upon a spit, a symbol of the cross.

The fire and the bitter herbs speak to us of the sufferings of our Lord, who was exposed to the fires of divine wrath as He was made our substitute (2 Co 5:21). The bitter herbs tell of the need for contrition on our part and at least some understanding of what it cost the Lamb of God to provide not only safety but also enduring strength. We gather unto the Lord Jesus Christ, and we feast upon Him as we contemplate His goodness and grace.

The Israelites were also forbidden to eat of the roast lamb that was left over until morning, reminding us of the great truth that the feast and the sacrifice must always be kept close together. Christian fellowship must not be separated from the work that was wrought upon the cross. Those who would take in a wider circle, often including those who have rejected the blood redemption, the deity of the Son of God, and the great cardinal truths of our faith, have widened their circle without scriptural justification. God would have us associate our fellowship with the sacrifice.

Fourth, their attire made them ready to set forth at a moment's notice. We read: "And thus shall ye eat it; with your lions girded, your shoes on your feet, and your staff in your hand; and ye shall eat it in haste: it is the LORD's passover (Ex 12:11). Every symbol here seems to carry with it special meaning. Fire speaks of judgment; bitter herbs, of contrition; the girdle, of separation and service. Shoes speak of joy and testimony; the staff may speak of prayer. People once redeemed by blood are identified as pilgrims and strangers. Therefore we read in 1 Peter 2:11: "Dearly beloved, I beseech you as strangers and pilgrims, abstain from fleshly lusts, which war against the soul."

In summing up, the blood made them *safe,* the Word made them *sure,* the feast made them *strong* and the dress made them *ready.*

Fifth, they were to be in haste. This speaks of readiness and expectancy. They were listening for the heavenly call. They were going somewhere. The attitude of the child of God is herein described. We are looking for the blessed hope, the return of our Lord Jesus Christ. This is a separating hope, a hope which, when practically cherished, brings about separation from sin and a pilgrim attitude. "And every man that hath this hope in him purifieth himself, even as he is pure" (1 Jn 3:3).

Nothing in all this world so separates the believer unto the Lord and from the world as the living hope of Christ's imminent return. Such a hope restores to the individual and the assembly the atmosphere of New Testament Christianity. Attired as travelers, the redeemed were listening for the heavenly shout, a voice, the trump, a command to march. What a thrilling anticipation it must have been for a people who had been so long in bondage. One day we are going to see Jesus Christ, our blessed Lord. Our souls grow weary in the Egypt of this world and cry with John of old, "Even so, come, Lord Jesus" (Rev 22:20).

## The Blood Applied

First, the blood had to be shed. "The life of the flesh is in the blood" (Lev 17:11). "The wages of sin is death" (Ro 6:23). The clean had to die instead of the unclean, the innocent for the guilty.

Second, the blood was to be conserved, by being caught in a basin (Hebrew, *Saph,* meaning a basin or a pounded-out hollow, Ex 12:22). Some are inclined to believe that the usage here refers to the hollowed out threshhold at the door.

> The word rendered "basin" is *sap,* which is an old Egyptian word for the step before a door, or the threshold of a house. The word *is* translated "threshold" in Judges 19:27 and "door" in 2 Kings 12:9—apparently for the sole reason that the sense "basin," favored by lexicographers and translators, could not possibly be given to the word in these passages. . . . No direction was given about putting the blood upon the threshold, for the reason that the blood *was already there.* The lamb was evidently slain at the door of the house which was protected by its blood (Urguhart, as quoted by A. W. Pink, *Gleanings in Exodus).*

We know that once the wilderness tabernacle was established, all sacrifices, by divine decree, had to be slain at the door of the tabernacle. Pink adds,

> The Septuagint gives *"para ten thuran,"* which means along the door-way! While the Vulgate reads, "in sanguine qui est limine"—in the blood which is on the threshold. This point is not simply one of academic interest, but concerns the accuracy of the type. The door of the house wherein the Israelite was protected had blood on the lintel (the cross piece), on the side posts and on the step. How marvelously this pictured Christ on the Cross; blood above, where the thorns pierced His brow; blood at the sides, from His nail-pierced hands; blood below, from His nail-pierced feet!!

The blood applied from the basin to the lintel and two side posts would form a perfect cross. However, this could be pressing Scripture too far.

Third, the blood had to be applied. The blood in a basin, placed in the doorway, would not be sufficient. The blood was potential for all but efficacious only when applied. A bunch of hyssop, insignificant in itself, was used to make the application. Hyssop was an abundant and accessible shrub that grew out of the rocky ground. The blood saved; the hyssop, like our faith, served only to apply the life-giving substance. Alexander MacLaren put it beautifully when he said,

> Compliance with the command to sprinkle the blood gives evidence of faith in the divine command and belief in the broad principle of sacrificial substitution and expiation by blood involving safety by individual application of the blood. In other words, the Passover is the Gospel before the Gospel.
>
> We believe that the whole sacrificial system of Judaism has its highest purpose to shadow forth the coming redemption. Christ is not spoken of as "our Passover" because Mosaic ritual had happened to have that ceremonial; but the Mosiac ritual had the ceremonial mainly because He is our Passover, and, by His blood shed on the cross and sprinkled on our conscience, does in spiritual reality that which the Jewish Passover only did in an outward form. All other questions about the Old Testament are of secondary importance compared with this. Its chief purpose is to prophesy of Christ, His atoning death, His kingdom and church. This was certainly the understanding of the New Testament writers.
>
> Evangelist John finds in the singular swiftness of our Lord's death, which secured the exemption of his sacred body from the violence inflicted on his fellow-sufferers, a

> fulfillment of the paschal injunction that not a bone should be broken; and so, by one passing allusion, shows that he recognized Christ as the true Passover. John the Baptist's rapturous exclamation, "Behold the Lamb of God!" blends allusions to the Passover, the daily sacrifice, and Isaiah's great prophecy. The day of the crucifixion, regarded as fixed by divine providence, may be taken as God's own finger pointing to the Lamb, whom He had provided. Paul's language . . . attests the same truth. And even the last lofty visions of the Apocalypse, where the old man in Patmos so touchingly refers to the earliest words which brough him to Jesus, echo in the same conviction and disclose, amidst the glories of the throne, "a Lamb as it had been slain" *(Expositions of Holy Scripture).*

## Prophetic and Memorial Significance of the Passover

The Passover also speaks of the time when Israel shall be restored to the land and come into her millennial glory or, as the Jews say, "This year, in dispersion; next year, in Jerusalem." During the journey from Egypt to Canaan it is recorded that the Passover was observed three times. The first occasion was in Egypt, which speaks of redemption by expiation from the penalty of death (Ex 12). Next, in the wilderness (Nu 9), after the ordering of the host and the appointment of the Levites instead of the firstborn (chap. 8), it took place on the first month of the second year. The Passover observance in this eighth chapter speaks of deliverance from the power of sin by the blood of the lamb, calling for submission to the leadership of the divine will. Third, the Passover was observed in Canaan (Jos 5), where it speaks of the power of blood redemption to deliver from the satanic forces that hinder possession. MacLaren added:

> What an incomprehensible stretch of authority Christ

puts forth, if He were no more than a teacher, when He brushed aside the Passover, and put in its place the Lord's Supper, as commemorating His own death! Thereby He said, forget the past deliverance; instead, remember me. Surely this was either audacity approaching insanity, or divine consciousness that He himself was the true paschal lamb, whose blood shields the world from judgment and on whom the world may feast and be satisfied. Christ's deliberate intention to represent His death as an expiation, and to fix the reverential, the grateful gaze of all future ages on His cross, cannot be eliminated from His founding of the memorial rite in the substitution for the God-appointed ceremonial, so hoary with age and sacred in its significance. Like the Passover, the Lord's Supper is established before the deliverance was accomplished. It remained a witness at once of the historical fact of the death of Christ, and of the meaning and power which Jesus Himself bade us to see in that death. For us, redeemed by His blood, the past should be filled with His sacrifice. For us, fed on Himself, all the present should be communion with Him, based upon His death for us. For us, freed bondsmen, the memorial of the deliverance begun by the cross should be the prophecy of deliverance that should be completed at the side of His throne, and the hasty meal, eaten with bitter herbs, the adumbration of the feast when all the pilgrims shall sit with Him at His table in His kingdom. (Matthew 26:29).

# 6

# THE FEAST OF THE UNLEAVENED BREAD

THE FEAST OF UNLEAVENED BREAD is the second of the seven annual feasts in Israel's sacred calendar, preceded only by the Feast of the Passover, with which it is closely connected. These two feasts were instituted while Israel was still in the land of Egypt. In a sense, the two form the basis of the other five feasts that were instituted at Mount Sinai more than a year later.

Taken together, the seven feasts outline Israel's national history. Four of these feasts, the Feast of the Passover, the Feast of Unleavened Bread, the Feast of the Firstfruits, and the Feast of Pentecost, have already found their fulfillment. The last three, the Feast of Trumpets, the Day of Atonement, and the Feast of Tabernacles, refer to Israel's future restoration, kingdom, and glory. The first four have to do with the first coming of our Lord; the last three with His second advent.

## ITS PLACE

The Feast of Unleavened Bread is closely associated, not only with the time, but also with the meaning, of the Passover. The former is meant to be a continuation of the topic on which the blood-sheltered people began to meditate at the beginning of the Passover. The two feasts are perhaps best illustrated by the two sides of a coin. As a matter of fact, in Matthew 26:17 and in Mark 14:12, the relationship between these two feasts is carefully spelled out. The evening of the Passover marked the beginning of the Feast of Unleavened Bread.

The Passover was the cause of the Feast of Unleavened Bread. In the Passover we behold Christ *for* us; in the Feast of Unleavened Bread we see Christ *in* us. In the Passover we find the topic of our redemption; in the Feast of Unleavened Bread we have the ground rules governing our fellowship with Christ.

God led the Israelites out of Egypt so that they might be a separate people among whom He could dwell. A sanctified people are called upon to be holy in their walk, and thus they were told, "Ye shall put away leaven [a type of evil] out of your houses" (Ex 12:15). Unleavened bread would continually remind them of God's demands.

"This feast is typical of what a particular separation from evil can accomplish for those who have been washed in the blood of the Lamb and have taken their place among those who are willing to have fellowship in His sufferings. The Israelite did not put away leaven in order to be saved, but because he was saved; if he failed to put away leaven, it did not raise a question of security through the blood, but simply of fellowship with the assembly . . . salvation and communion are not the same thing" (Charles H. MacKintosh, *Notes on the Book of Exodus*).

Many are under the blood who know but little of communion with God because leaven remains unrecognized and unjudged in their lives. It is the blood, and the blood alone, that makes us safe; it is the separation from evil that makes possible our feast and our enjoyment of all that the blood has accomplished for us.

## Its Provisions

Just as Jehovah sets the terms and specifications of the Passover, leaving nothing to human judgment, ingenuity, or taste, in the Feast of the Passover, nothing is left to the whims or emotions of man. There are six provisions set forth for the observance of the Feast of Unleavened Bread.

First, the feast was to last seven days. This speaks of a complete period and serves as a reminder that certain basic truths should govern the child of God throughout the whole sojourn on earth. This fact is transplanted from the Old Testament economy to the New Testament order of things. Paul advised the Corinthian church: "To deliver such an one unto Satan for the destruction of the flesh, that the spirit may be saved in the day of the Lord Jesus" (1 Co 5:5).

This passage reminds us what leaven, like evil, can do when it is tolerated in the assembly. If leaven remains unjudged, it will ultimately contaminate the whole body of believers. In the light of this passage it is easy to see one of the weaknesses that characterizes Christendom today. Church discipline is passé in the great majority of our churches. The church is so deeply involved and mixed with the world that it has rendered itself intimidated and unwilling to tackle the question of discipline. In the final analysis, one has to make a choice between two fellowships that are mutually exclusive. He must choose either fellowship with God in the assembly of believers or fellowship with the world, which is enmity with our Lord.

Second, the unleavened bread speaks of "sincerity and truth" (1 Co 5:8). "Old leaven" signifies that which remains from one's former history, such as "the leaven of malice and wickedness."

This feast is not for the foreigner or for the hired servant (Ex 12:45). The same is true of the counterpart of this feast—the Lord's Supper. There were no unconverted individuals present when this New Testament ordinance was instituted (Jn 13). Judas Iscariot went out before it began.

Third, there are severe penalties attached to the failure to observe the feast. "Seven days shall there be no leaven found in your houses: for whosoever eateth that which is leavened, even that soul shall be cut off from the congregation of Israel, whether he be a stranger, or born in the land" (Ex 12:19). It is important to keep in mind the meaning of the expression "cut off from the congregation of Israel." It meant for the Israelite the loss of participation in the feast and in religious services as long as he remained unclean (Lev 7). To be unclean affects the fellowship but not the relation of the saved. It has been well said, "Relationship is by blood and cannot change: fellowship is by obedience and may change." It is a fearful thing for a child of God to live in a state of broken fellowship. Such a state can bring upon the believer the corrective judgements and the discipline of our heavenly Father (Heb 12.)

Fourth, the Feast of Unleavened Bread is to be kept forever. Moses wrote, "Therefore shall ye observe this day in your generations by an ordinance for ever" (Ex 12:17). God grants no indulgences to sin. Just as "seven days" speaks of the duration of the feast, carrying with it the idea of the entirety or completeness of one's obligation toward consecration, "in your generations . . . for ever," carries with it the idea of perpetuity and endurance throughout Israel's history. "No leaven" means separation at the time the Passover and the Feast of Unleavened Bread were initiated. It means substantially the same thing when we view the New Testament and the believer's present obligation. There is no need for a revision of divine truth. There is a heavenly wisdom displayed in the consistency of typology. Languages are variable and are subject to change, but types, like music, constitute the universal, stabilizing vehicle of thought. What leaven symbolizes in one place, it symbolizes in another. What leaven means in the Old Testament it means in the New Testament. Unleavened bread in the Old Testament was a memorial; in the New, it represents an experience—a continuous walk of separation to the Lord.

"Because we are saved by grace, through the sprinkling of the blood of Christ, it is not that we may now indulge in sin without fear of its consequences, or that grace may abound. Not so. Redemption by the blood of Christ imposes upon us an additional responsibility to separate ourselves from all evil, that we may now walk forth in the praise of Him who has called us out of darkness into His marvelous light. Carelessness of walk, evil associations, worldliness, fleshy indulgence and things which hinder us from keeping the Feast of the Passover are wrong" (Pink, *Gleanings in Exodus*).

Fifth, the Feast of Unleavened Bread begins with a feast and ends with a feast. "And in the first day there shall be an holy convocation, and in the seventh day there shall be an holy convocation to you; no manner of work shall be done in them, save that which every man must eat, that only may be done of you" (Ex 12:16). The Christian's fellowship, while it is a continuous feast as he feeds upon Christ through His Word, in no sense means immunity from sorrow, warfare, trial, or hardship. The feast spoken of in this verse is an inward peace. We rejoice in the Lord, and at the same time we glory in tribulation. This is the paradox of our Christian walk.

Sixth, the Israelite was to do no servile work. Just as it is with the believer today, serving the Lord was a full time job. "Either He is Lord of all or not Lord at all."

## Its Prohibitions

Since the reference to leaven in Exodus 12 is the first

mentioned, the prohibition is interesting and profitable. The "law of first mention" is always important. To follow the lesson learned here throughout all Scripture would save from much confusion. An example of this confusion is found in the general interpretation of the parable of leaven in Matthew 13:33. An attempt is often made to interpret "leaven" in this passage as the gospel, the meal as the mass of humanity, and the woman as the church. The results, the leavening of the whole lump, would indicate the gospel's success, a phenomenon that is contrary to the whole teaching of the New Testament, to history, and to experience.

A further examination of the use of leaven in the New Testament reveals that it stands for:

1. The hypocrisy of the Pharisees, or formalism. "In the mean time, when there were gathered together an innumerable multitude of people, insomuch that they trode one upon another, he began to say unto his disciples first of all, Beware ye of the leaven of the Pharisees, which is hypocrisy" (Lk 12:1).

2. Rationalism, or "the leaven ... of the Sadducees." "Then Jesus said unto them, Take heed and beware of the leaven of the Pharisees and of the Sadducees . . . Then understood they how that he bade them not beware of the leaven of bread, but of the doctrine of the Pharisees and of the Sadducees" (Mt 16:6,12. The Sadducees did not believe in spirits or angels, and they denied the resurrection. They were the materialists and rationalists of Christ's day.

3. Worldliness, the leaven of Herod. "And he charged them, saying, Take heed, beware of the leaven of the Pharisees, and of the leaven of Herod" (Mk 8:15).

4. Evil conduct. "Your glorying is not good. Know ye not that a little leaven leaveneth the whole lump?" (1 Co 5:6).

5. Evil doctrine. "A little leaven leaveneth the whole

lump" (Gal 5:9). Here it was the doctrine of legalism, sometimes referred to as "Galatianism," that threatened to corrupt the whole church, and against which Paul fought so ardently.

The Feast of Unleavened Bread was to be kept by Israel throughout their generations as a memorial of the deliverance of an earthly people from death and bondage in Egypt. The Lord's Supper commemorates the call and redemption of a heavenly people.

### Its Prophecy

The Feast of Unleavened Bread, like all the unexplained ceremonies in the Old Testament, was appointed with a view to its future counterpart, the memorial of the Lord's Supper. "For as often as ye eat this bread, and drink this cup, ye do shew the Lord's death till he come" (1 Co 11:26). The believer feasts on Christ when his mind is nourished by the Word, his heart is filled with the love of Christ, his conscience is taken up with His peace, his will esteems God's Word above "necessary food," and Christ manifests Himself in a sweet sufficiency that meets the deep longing of the human soul.

# 7

# SATAN'S COMPROMISES

THE IMPORTANCE of recognizing the character of Pharaoh, the adumbration (shadow) of Satan, cannot be overemphasized. Next in importance to recognizing the existence of God, His nature, and His character, is the recognition and knowledge of Satan, his identity, his subtlety, and his devices, as typified in Amenhotep II, the Pharaoh that did not know Joseph. Sad to say, the average professing Christian is, in spite of Scriptural warning, ignorant of Satan's devices. Pharaoh is typical of the "god of this world" (2 Co 4:4). From a careful study of the conflict that existed between Pharaoh and Moses we gain an insight into the secrets of the believer's warfare. Here again we come face to face with the importance of faith in the Word. Is the account given "written for our admonition" (1 Co 10:11), or is it merely a highly dramatized record of some irritating happenings to an ancient people? The approach here is of supreme importance.

Now let us view Pharaoh's proposed compromises as typical of Satan's devices.

### REPUDIATION OF AUTHORITY

When God's demand to let Israel go was first presented to Pharaoh, the king replied with haughtiness, "Who is the LORD, that I should obey His voice to let Israel go? I know not the LORD, neither will I let Israel go" (Ex 5:2). Herein is revealed the basic sphere of conflict. It is man's will against God's will. The two poles in the moral universe are not goodness and evil but the human will and the divine will. Christ said to the Pharisees, "Ye will not come to me, that ye might have life" (Jn 5:40).

There may be many excuses offered by individuals as to why they do not accept Christ, but only one reason lies underneath—the rebellious human will that has its orbit about self. Even though the unregenerate person may not recognize it, his main enmity is against God. Out of such awful depravity grows the rebellion of man's heart.

God saved the firstborn in Egypt by blood, but the moment each individual thus saved came under the blood, God's command to him was to get out of Egypt. Pharaoh, typifying Satan, anticipated this demand and offered four compromises. A study of these compromises alerts believers to Satan's devices.

The Pharaoh of the Exodus is believed to have been Amenhotep II (1439—1406 B.C.), son of Thutmose III (1490—1436 B.C.), who was the Pharaoh of the Oppression.

## Jehovah's Demand and Pharaoh's Refusal

"Let my people go" (Ex 5:1). God demanded an absolute break with Egypt. He would redeem in Egypt, but He would agree to no fellowship in the land. There were no altars in Egypt, only servitude and oppression.

Something had to happen. Somebody had to give in, so the contest began. "And Pharaoh said, Who is the Lord, that I should obey his voice to let Israel go? I know not the Lord, neither will I let Israel go" (5:2). At first he refused to even recognize God, much less submit to His claims.

How much like Satan this is in his dealing with the convicted sinner! In his view, the whole matter of divine claims and the question of salvation are absurd, things to be quickly dismissed from the mind. Pharaoh's recommendation was more labor; in his opinion, too much time was being allowed for the slaves to think. Take away their straw, he said, and increase their misery. How characteristic this is of the working of Satan. As long as sinners are asleep in Satan's grasp, they experience little resistance. Matters seem to go comparatively smoothly. It is when man's conscience is aroused before God that the real battle begins.

## The Hardening of Pharaoh's Heart

There seems to be a great problem here for some who cannot quite reconcile the divine judgment visited upon one whose heart the Lord hardened. We do well to remember that three terms are used in this respect: (1) Pharaoh's heart was hardened (Ex 7:22); (2) The Lord hardened Pharaoh's heart (4:21); and (3) Pharaoh hardened his own heart (8:32).

In his *Studies in the Book of Exodus,* George Henderson says,

> It should be carefully noted that God's providential dealings as described in these chapters were not the reason for, but merely the occasion of, the hardening of Pharaoh's heart. The Word of God makes abundantly clear man's moral freedom and consequent responsibility; and in a matter of this sort we must be guided by its testimony as a whole. In this connection the words of Dr. John Anderson are eminently wise. "Historically," he says "the facts are clear: Pharaoh, a bad man, is made worse and worse by his own actions. Theologically, the doctrine is clear: God retained command of the situation and carried out His purpose in His own way. Speculatively, we cannot fathom it: Paul could not. Practically, those who receive this doctrine are in the van of the world's progress."

However great the intellectual difficulties, one can always take refuge in faith. Abraham found such a situation when Jehovah announced He was about to destroy Sodom and Gomorrah. "That be far from thee to do after this manner, to slay the righteous with the wicked: and that the righteous should be as the wicked, that be far from thee: shall not the Judge of all the earth do right?" (Gen 18:25). When we cannot understand God's way, we can believe in God Himself.

A very blessed passage is found in Psalm 103:7: "He made known his ways unto Moses, his acts unto the children of Israel." Israel knew His acts and murmured. Moses knew God's ways and was meek and faithful. Sin against that which is light brings with it the judgement of blindness. Undue exposure of the eyes to the sun, even though the eyes are designed to perceive light, will destroy the retina, the light-sensitive part of the eye. Truth resisted is more destructive than unharnessed radioactivity.

Opportunity is fleeting and will not tarry. Time must be taken by the forelock. Because of his persistent self-will, his sin against the light, and his neglect of opportunities when he was faced by the great Moses and the miracles of judgment, Pharaoh's doom was forever sealed. Moses and Aaron, commissioned of Jehovah, proclaimed God's message and demanded the deliverance of His people. As we have seen, they were met with an absolute refusal.

John Ritchie, in his book *From Egypt to Canaan,* reminds us:

> This is Satan's way; it is the first of his plans to hinder the deliverance of a poor sinner. Here, there is no disguise. It is the roar of the lion of hell, and open hostility to God and His truth. So long as he can keep his slaves at peace, quietly serving him, he does it. But let God begin to deal with the sinner for his deliverance, and immediately hell is let loose to hold him. Satan never gives up his prey with-

out a struggle. At this point the sinner's state is worse (See Exodus 5:15-23) than before, for his conscience is awake, and his chains are felt. Eternity is revealed, and like the prodigal (Luke 15:17), he has "come to himself."

The plagues that follow are thick and severe, but they have temporary effects on Pharaoh. He stated that he did not know God. The implication is that he was concerned only with the gods of Egypt and not with the tribal God of the despised Hebrews. Since he did not know God, he was to have a rude introduction to Him. The ten plagues were judgments against Egypt and her gods, but they were the means of deliverance for Israel.

### Second Compromise—Sacrifice in the Land

"And Pharaoh called for Moses and for Aaron, and said, Go ye, sacrifice to your God in the land" (Ex 8:25). It sounded reasonable; Pharaoh made quite a concession. He did not offer religious freedom but religious toleration. There is quite a difference between the two. This subtle suggestion concealed one of Satan's masterpieces.

Egypt is typical of the world, this cosmos, this orderly arrangement or world-system. God demanded a three-day journey out of Egypt. The world, the flesh, and the devil say, "Why be so peculiar? Be pracitcal, modernize your methods, and give a new message for a new age." All too many are sacrificing in the land, bringing the world into the church, and knowing nothing of the three days' separation—the death and resurrection of the Lord Jesus Christ. Theirs is a worship before the cross. God demands worship after the cross.

Having failed to stifle the sinner's desire for deliverance, the devil uses his wiles to suggest a compromise—adapt a religion in keeping with decent living in the world. "Worldly religion embraces everything and condemns nothing but wholeheartedness for Christ." George Henderson put it well when he said, "Historically, Nero is the illustration of the one, Constantine of the other; and the testimony of the centuries clearly shows that while Nero's persecution and violence only had the effect of driving the early Christians to new lands to preach the Word, Constantine's patronage inflicted on the church of God a blow from which she has never recovered."

John Wesley said, "I have long been convinced from the whole tenor of ancient history that this very event, Constantine's calling himself a Christian, and pouring a flood of wealth and honor upon the Christian church, was productive of more evil to the Christian church than all the ten persecutions put together."

There is nothing Satan hates like out-and-out separation to God. He cares little about how many things men are separated *from,* but he does care about whom they are separated *to.* God's call is clear, "Come out from among them, and be ye separate, saith the Lord" (2 Co 6:17).

### Third Compromise—Go, But Not Far

"And Pharaoh said, I will let you go, that ye may sacrifice to the Lord your God in the wilderness; only ye shall not go very far away: intreat for me" (Ex 8:28). In other words, Pharaoh was telling them to go but stay in reach of luxury. Journey into the wilderness, with its dependence upon God's supply, only briefly; but live in Egypt—hurry back!

Pharaoh's suggested compromise has its counterpart in those who profess Christ but who alter their way of living little—those who live on the border and try to face two ways at the same time. How many efficient businessmen are there who are capable, personable, keen in mind, and shrewd in business, but who seek to blend politics with religion and service for God and His church with a carnal absorption in worldly affairs. Lot tried such a life. He tried to blend politics and piety while living in Sodom. Lot vexed his soul, lost his testimony, saw his daughters marry Sodomites, witnessed the burning up of his worldly possessions, and the sudden, tragic death of his wife. He ended his life in a lonely cave with a blighted testimony.

The fear of those who say "Don't go far" is that of being overly zealous, slightly extreme, dangerously fanatical, and a bit peculiar. Satan would have the saints to be "regular fellows" who offer no discomfort to the unsaved and no rebuke to the godless. Satan says, "Don't go far." God says, "Go three days' journey" (Ex 8:27). Which will it be?

### Fourth Compromise—Let the Men Go

"Go, serve the Lord your God: but who are they that shall go? And Moses said, We will go with our young and with our old, with our sons and with our daughters; . . . for we must hold a feast unto the Lord. And he said unto them, . . . Not so: go now ye that are men, and serve the Lord" (10:8-11).

The hand of God was heavy on Pharaoh, but the king was a poor loser. His defense was liquid; defeated on one line he fell back on another, still fighting. He was reluctant to lose his slaves and the economic advantage derived from their labors. He wanted to send the men to sacrifice while leaving the women and children behind, knowing that the men would soon return. We have seen the modern equivalent of this: Families move to the city, leaving the old country church where both parents and youngsters were faithful. We have seen parents delay in making church connections in the city, and when they did, their children were going the way of the world. The older folk were saved, but their children went into sin. They did not feel it was quite right to "force" their children to go to church, since they were young only once.

How many pious parents are satisfied to educate their children in terms of worldly principles—to send them to schools that denature their faith, alter their lives and neutralize their influence for good—for purely secular ends.

God trusted Abraham with the secrets of judgement because, He said, "I know him, that he will command his children and his household after him" (Gen 18:19). Joshua said, "As for me and my house, we will serve the LORD" (Jos 24:15). Paul said to the Philippian jailer, "Believe on the Lord Jesus Christ, and thou shalt be saved, and thy house" (Act 16:31). Doubtless there are exceptions, but in general, there is no greater test of a man's true piety than the reflection of that piety in his family. Pious people who know little or no discipline in the home reveal a weakness that is far more serious than commonly judged. Modern psychology and education are gradually undermining the stability of the American home, where everything is run by a switch except the kids. Eli was high priest in Israel, but he reared two impious sons who broke their father's heart and brought judgment upon themselves and upon the nation. Young college graduates often build their home on the fallacy that you must not break a child's will. If they fail to break a child's will, that child will break their hearts.

Moses refused to compromise for less than God's demand. "And Moses said, We will go with our young and with our old, with our sons and with our daughters, with our flocks and with our herds will we go; for we must hold a feast unto the LORD" (Ex 10:9).

### FIFTH COMPROMISE—GO, BUT LEAVE YOUR WEALTH

"And Pharaoh called unto Moses, and said, Go ye, serve

the LORD; only let your flocks and your herds be stayed: let your little ones also go with you" (v. 24). This was Pharaoh's trump. He was getting down to where men live when he spoke of their possessions. This is Satan's last opportunity and Israel's last battle before victory. How many people, however sincere, stumble here! They consecrate all but their wealth to the Lord.

Pharaoh knew the importance of this last stroke and he played it well. "Go," he told them, "but leave your cattle behind." But he failed to reckon with the principle of Matthew 6:21: "Where your treasure is, there will your heart be also." Many Christians are deceived into believing they are consecrated, while they fail to take God into the most important sphere of their lives. The devil gets us here as at few other places. The outward test of an inward state can well be determined by one's attitude toward tithing. God claims it, man owes it, joy awaits it, the world needs it! There is one real reason why instructed Christians will not tithe—they do not want to!

God's demands, as delivered by Moses, were, "There shall not a hoof be left behind" (Ex 10:26). Why? The answer is in the remainder of this verse: "For thereof must we take to serve the LORD our God; and we know not with what we must serve the LORD, until we come thither."

When all the proposed compromises failed, Pharaoh threatened to kill Moses. This was the final act. No more interviews were necessary. The tenth plague followed immediately. Nothing was left but the full execution of the divine decree of judgement upon the firstborn. On this night, therefore, there was the culmination of a long struggle. One subterfuge after another had been swept away. God acted in righteousness after He had made an offer of mercy. There was nothing more to be done than to achieve Pharaoh's overthrow through righteous judgment. What might have been accomplished with less hurt by cooperation! The curtain descends and the scene hastens to a fearful climax for Pharaoh and Egypt, as it always must when men harden their hearts against God.

# 8

# TRAVELING THE LONG ROAD

"And it came to pass, when Pharaoh had let the people go, that God led them not through the way of the land of the Philistines, although that was near; for God said, Lest peradventure the people repent when they see war, and they return to Egypt: but God led the people about, through the way of the wilderness of the Red Sea: and the children of Israel went up harnessed out of the land of Egypt" (Ex 13:17-18).

There were evidently many surprises and perplexities that came to Israel during the forty years of journeying, but none was more strange than the direction of God as they departed from Egypt. Certainly there was no geographical necessity for taking the more circuitous route up through the wilderness by way of Sinai. Indeed, without explicit command from God, it would have been the height of folly for any leader, even Moses, to have attempted to conduct such a large number of people, who had no visible means of support, into a wilderness so vast and barren. Without doubt, after they had been released from bondage, the children of Israel naturally looked forward to a speedy occupation of the promised land. But in this they were doomed to disappointment. They were not permitted to go directly and immediately to their inheritance.

There were two ways to the land of promise. "God led them not through the way of the land of the Philistines, although that was near; for God said, Lest peradventure the people repent when they see war, and they return to Egypt" (v. 17). One was a highway, the other was a way through the wilderness. The direct road which led from Rameses, generally identified with the ancient Tanis or Zoan, to Canaan, lay along the coast of the Mediterranean. It was over this caravan route that Jacob traveled when he went down to Egypt and by which the funeral procession went up to bury him in the sepulcher of his fathers. The Mediterranean route, we are told, could be traversed, under ordinary conditions in eight or ten days. This road led through a populated area; it was easy, rapid and safe. But it was not the road selected by Jehovah. The one deterrent was Philistia, which stood across this pathway. Instead of following the ordinary caravan route, the Israelites were led southeastward into a wilderness toward the Red Sea. Here there were no highways, no bridges, no resources to supply their needs, and no signs to direct their path. Two years were spent in journeying to Mount Sinai and later reaching the border at Kadesh-barnea. Then they were turned back to spend thirty-eight more years in the wilderness.

### The Providence of the Long Way

God led them. It is encouraging and refreshing to learn that Jehovah took full responsibility for the redemption of His covenant people—first by blood and then by power, including the selection of their pathway. There are no accidents for those who walk in the will of God.

"When Pharaoh had let the people go, . . . God led them" (v. 17). How blessed is this thought! There is sweet assurance in this passage. Israel was delivered from Egypt's bondage and slavery to enter into another slavery—the slavery of love and grace. God's providential dealings are in sequence and always timely. There was no intervening period of uncertainty or waiting. It is always true, in life and in death. "Absent from the body . . . present with the Lord" (2 Co 5:8).

As we meditate upon the divine providence of the long road, we are reminded of love's forethought. This is seen everywhere in the plan of redemption. "According as he hath chosen us in him before the foundation of the world" (Eph 1:4). This section of the long road gives us another example of God's infinite plan that reaches back into eternity. Love has forethought; love anticipates. Like an expectant mother, who prepares for the unborn child, or like the provident father, who makes plans for his children with reference to their education and training as well as their physical and moral welfare, the Lord provides for His children.

Once the Christian comes to understand this great truth concerning God's forethought of love, there is added to life a new dimension. Once in Christ, one is found in the mainstream of eternity. This forethought of love is beautifully brought out in Jeremiah 31:3: "The LORD hath appeared of old unto me, saying, Yea, I have loved thee with an everlasting love: therefore with lovingkindness have I drawn thee."

To understand the divine purpose in choosing for Israel the long road, we do well to remember that the sons of Jacob were little better than slaves. They were undisciplined in the art of welfare. They were ill prepared to face a formidable enemy like the Philistines. In loving forethought God chose the long way for His ancient people. This tender and loving care is exemplified throughout Scripture. "Like as a father pitieth his children, so the LORD pitieth them that fear him. For he knoweth our frame; he remembereth that we are dust" (Ps 103:13-14). On reaching Kadesh-barnea at the end of the second year, God reminded His people, "Ye have seen what I did unto the Egyptians, and how

I bare you on eagles' wings, and brought you unto myself" (Ex 19:4).

## THE PRINCIPLES

In dealing with this passage, the late Dr. F. B. Meyer said, "These words expound the whole philosophy of human life."

In discussing the principles of the long road, it might be profitable to approach the thought from a negative point of view and consider first the principle of the "short way." This is the way of the world—the way of human judgment and acceptance. The way that God rejected is known by the world as a shortcut, the way of quick dividends, the way of human appeal, and the way of sight. In nearly every instance where man is left to his own inclination, this principle is followed. Following this philosophy many are ensnared by the appeal of getting something for nothing, as manifested in gambling and lottery and in the fascination people have for taking a chance.

One of the most characteristic quirks of human nature is man's assumption that he can drown his troubles in drink and dope. He gains an artificial thrill of success, an aura of fake happiness, and a pseudo sense of self-importance. In order to escape from the humdrum of life, some seek refuge in gambling or in giving free reign to lust and dissipation.

Esau provided a good example of the quick-and-easy way when he sold his birthright for a mess of pottage. Esau mortgaged the future for present gains. Man, in striving to get rich quickly, often cheats and steals, hoping thereby to get things now for which he is unwilling to work and wait.

On the other hand, the true philosophy of the long road reverses the order and is based upon the principle of a walk by faith rather than sight. It is characterized by a willingness to wait, to trust God, and to be patient. We cannot always understand God's present providential workings, but we believe and trust God Himself. His way is best. Centuries have always justified themselves when compared with mere hours. Every child of God must learn that there is no success without sacrifice and no reward without labor. There must be obedience before blessings are bestowed.

## The Purposes of the Long Road

One of the greatest mysteries of divine grace is found in the fact that a holy and righteous God, who is rich in everything, cares to have a people like the sons of Adam, including these sons of Jacob, identified with Himself. The all-sufficient reason must lie within the mystery of the divine will and love. The mystery still remains beyond human comprehension; the benefits of such grace must be appropriated through faith. God seems to have wanted Israel, and in like manner He wants us—for much the same reason that a childless couple looks for an heir. The couple desires to have someone upon whom they may lavish their love and perpetuate their hopes—someone in whom they can see the reflection of their own likeness and the realization of their cherished aspirations. In this connection, one of the most blessed of all passages in Scripture is to be found in the second chapter of Ephesians: "And hath raised us up together, and made us sit together in heavenly places in Christ Jesus: that in the ages to came he might show the exceeding riches of His grace in his kindness toward us through Christ Jesus" (vv. 6-7). Think of that!

The wilderness way was the way of self-discipline. First, Israel needed to know God. Therefore God led the nation alone into the solitude of the barren places, where a people were wholly and completely dependent upon divine resources. Men seldom come to know God in the days of prosperity. The darker the night, the brighter the stars. The mystery and purpose of God's providence may best be seen through the prism of tears. Often, "the longest way around is the shortest way home." Someone has also written, "He that goes straight across may have to carry the cross. He that goes around about may have the chance to go without." God's thoughts are not man's thoughts, and His ways are not man's ways (Is 55:8-9). How wonderful it is to be under His guidance.

As A. W. Pink said in *Gleanings in Exodus*:

> God's purpose in leading Israel to Canaan through the wilderness instead of via the land of the Philistines was manifested in the sequel. In the first place, it was in order that His marvelous power might be signally displayed on their behalf in bringing them safely through the Red Sea. In the second place, it was in order that Pharaoh and his hosts might be destroyed there. In the third place, it was in order that they might receive Jehovah's laws in the undisturbed solitude of the desert. In the fourth place, it was in order that they might be properly organized into a Commonwealth and Church-state (Acts 7:53), prior to their entrance into and occupation of the land of Canaan. Finally, it was in order that they might be humbled, tried, and proved (Deuteronomy 8:2, 3) and the sufficiency of their God in every emergency might be fully demonstrated.

There is a very blessed purpose made evident as we look back upon Israel's experience. The Lord shields from His infant people trials that may be the lot for His adult children. For He knows our frame and balances His trials according to what the saints are able to endure. Then He mercifully orders their course. "The Lord, in His condescending grace, so orders things for His people that they do not, at their first setting out, encounter heavy trials which might have the effect of discouraging their hearts and driving them back" (C. H. MacKintosh, *Notes on the Book of Exodus*).

This is well exemplified in the four great surrenders of Abraham. He was not called upon at first to sacrifice his son. This was the final test. First, he was called upon to surrender his life—to separate himself from his people and from his land. Next, he was to surrender his rights by permitting his nephew to make the first choice. Later, he surrendered the opportunity to become rich when he rejected the wealth of the king of Sodom. The final test came when Abraham was called upon to offer his son Isaac as a sacrifice. It has often been said, "God tempers His wind to a shorn lamb." God's dealings with His children are seasonable and in proportion to their endurance. "There hath no temptation taken you but such as is common to man: but God is faithful, who will not suffer you to be tempted above that ye are able; but will with the temptation also make a way to escape, that ye may be able to bear it" (1 Co 10:13). This was true in the case of Israel. Later they were to fight many battles in Canaan. However, in the beginning, He led them away from the way of the Philistines, for that would have involved immediate warfare. God had respect for the tender weakness of His children.

The purpose of the long road is further discerned as one follows Israel's history through the wilderness. There are two basic lessons Jehovah wanted Israel to learn in this wilderness experience. "And thou shalt remember all the way which the LORD thy God led thee these forty years in the wilderness, to humble thee, and to prove thee, to know what was in thine heart, whether thou wouldest keep his commandments, or no" (Deu 8:2). The two lessons were to know self and to know God.

Paul wrote, "For I know that in me (that is, in my flesh,) dwelleth no good thing" (Ro 7:18). The first lesson for Israel and for us to learn is to have no confidence in the flesh. Israel learned this the hard way. So does everyone else. It is never easy. This was the purpose of the Law as given at Sinai. "Now we know that what things soever the law saith, it saith to them who are under the law: that every mouth may be stopped, and all the world may become guilty before God. Therefore by the deeds of the law there shall no flesh be justified in his sight: for by the law is the knowledge of sin" (3:19-20).

The second lesson was to know God. "And he humbled thee, and suffered thee to hunger, and fed thee with manna, which thou knewest not, neither did thy fathers know; that he might make thee know that man doth not live by bread only, but by every word that proceedeth out of the mouth of the LORD doth man live" (Deu 8:3).

Jehovah led Israel in the wilderness so that He might meet with them, speak with them, reveal Himself to them, and teach them to know themselves and to know Him.

When the sons of Jacob left Egypt, they were undisciplined. They had to be trained, and the wilderness was a training school. Israel could never know God on man's highway. This training had a purpose: the Israelites were destined to be a priestly nation among nations. This destiny will yet find its culmination. "They shall look upon [Him] whom they have pierced" (Zec 12:10), and they will acknowledge Him as David's greater Son.

## THE PRIVILEDGE OF THE LONG ROAD

The long road has its companions of the way. The passage that tells of the long road also tells us twice that God led the people (Ex 13:17-18). God had to lead the children of Israel through the trackless wilderness in order to make them dependent upon Himself. This is so often true in the believer's daily experience. God has a way of turning "disappointments" into "His appointments." It is everlastingly true that our losses, our loneliness, our sorrows, our disappointments, and our sicknesses turn out to be within the loving providence of God. These are the means used by God to enrich the lives of His own children and bring them closer to Himself. There is no part of life from which He withholds Himself. How refreshing it is to know that there is no dark night of earthly misery, whether bodily suffering, disappointment, deep sorrow, or loneliness, from which He withdraws Himself.

Nonetheless, He desires to share the brightness of spiritual glory and heavenly success with those who are willing to walk with Him and trust Him. In our walk with Him there are bright places as well as shadows, joys as well as sorrows, sunshine as well as rain. In all of these, believers are privileged to know Him better and to share by faith the glory that shall be theirs in the hereafter.

Often God must lead His children through the deep, dark valleys to teach them the blessedness of divine fellowship. The apostle Paul understood this when he cried out, "That I may know him, and the power of his resurrection, and the fellowship of his sufferings, being made conformable unto his death" (Phil 3:10).

Those who have visited Mammoth Cave in Kentucky, or a similar cavern, can vividly recall the inward urgency to keep close to the guide. Even the thought of being left behind in the oppressive darkness of a vast cave is bone-chilling. Oftentimes God must lead us through the deep valley to teach us the blessedness of divine fellowship. "Yea, though I walk through the valley of the shadow of death, I will fear no evil: for thou art with me; thy rod and thy staff they comfort me" (Ps 23:4). Wilderness and valley experiences here prepare us for the road ahead.

The children of Israel also gained a fellowship with the redeemed. These wilderness children gained comradeship through suffering. Suffering rightly endured brings a blessed compensation. There can be life, but little or no virtue, apart from the frostbite and chilly winds of adversity.

The writer was a lad of nine when his mother died. It was a terrible experience, and he was left indescribably lonely. The older brothers had left home. The days the youngest son spent with a suffering father did something in the way of knitting the two together that could not have been experienced otherwise. The relationship between those with whom the Christian is privileged to suffer is always unique. The price that must be paid for a blessed and sacred intimacy is the same, whether it is human or divine.

## The Persons of the Long Road

This narrative exemplifies a principle of general application in connection with the Lord's dealing with His children in every age. Joseph was led the long way to the place near the throne of Pharaoh—through a pit at Dothan, a period of servitude in Potiphar's house, and prison. The apostle Paul had a great ambition, "to preach the gospel to you that are at Rome also," but he tells us that he was "hindered hitherto." When he did arrive in Rome he came in bonds. The apostle Paul had to travel the long road. What a strange, but blessed providence! Strange then but not now. Out of his prison experience came the prison epistles. Christ Himself traveled the wilderness way—the Via Dolorosa.

The prophet Daniel was called upon to travel the long way in faraway Babylon. In loneliness and in anguish of soul he waited and prayed for the redemption of his people, which he was privileged to see only in prophetic vision. This was the way trod by all the heroes of faith, by our blessed Lord, and by the apostle Paul. John Bunyan's pathway led through Bedford's jail; David Livingstone's led through the jungles of Africa; and tens of thousands of unnamed saints, whose records are kept in heaven and whose glory will be revealed in eternity, have journeyed the same pathway.

That which God would employ must be subject to arduous trial. "God had one Son without sin, but none without sorrow." Since Israel was to be trained for a priestly ministry among the nations, she had to be brought low in order to learn dependence and obedience. There are few people that can bear responsibility and authority thrust suddenly upon them. We see this illustrated in a thousand ways in everyday life. Rarely are we permitted to walk straight ahead. Most often we are called upon to follow the zigzag pathway. Those who climb must travel the hard way.

God has promised to take His children to heaven, but He had not promised to take them the short way. The Christian life, in fact, is characterized by protracted trying experiences. In our Lord's high priestly prayer of intercession, He prayed, "I pray not that thou shouldest take them out of the world, but that thou shouldest keep them from the evil" (Jn 17:15). Applying this to ourselves, we have the answer as to why God's children are left in the world.

Certainly we must all agree that the saint is saved and safe. Why then doesn't God take His redeemed ones to heaven the moment they are saved? It is reasonable to believe, had there been any chance of losing salvation, that He never would have prayed for such but would have snatched them out before the devil could get them. The risk of going to hell would have been too great. There has to be another reason.

We know the Christian is left here to go through the school of experience; to learn to have no confidence in the flesh; to be a witness to the world, and in every way to represent God as His ambassador.

# 9

# THE PILLAR OF CLOUD AND FIRE

"And the LORD went before them by day in a piller of a cloud, to lead them the way; and by night in a pillar of fire, to give them light; to go by day and night: he took not away the pillar of the cloud by day, nor the pillar of fire by night, from before the people" (Ex 13:21-22).

As we trace the travels and the trials of God's ancient people, we are overwhelmed with the fact of God's tender care for His own. Nothing is lacking where God is given His rightful place. In this wilderness experience we are privileged to behold the continuity, the symmetry, and the agreement of the Scriptures. This consistency is maintained both in the types and shadows of the Old Testament and in the substance in the New. Nowhere is this consistency more in evidence than in the constantly recurring story of salvation. As we reach this important juncture, marked by the appearance of the cloud, we are brought face to face with the wonderful presentation of the unfolding redemptive story. As a sinner, Israel needed a savior; as a captive, Israel needed a deliverer; as a pilgrim, Israel needed a guide. The predominant function of the pillar of cloud and the pillar of fire was that of *guiding* the nation through a barren wilderness.

## A GIFT

All of God's gifts are timely and suitable. Here again

grace was manifested in the giving of the cloud, as in all God's former dealings. God is a great giver. How keen must have been the astonishment of the children of Israel when, for the first time, they looked upon this spreading cloud of glory, which was indicative of Jehovah's presence. Only God could provide such a gift. Both for Israel and for ourselves it is a gift of grace and power. "Every good gift and every perfect gift is from above, and cometh down from the Father of lights, with whom is no variableness, neither shadow of turning" (Ja 1:17).

## A Gateway

The appearance of the cloud marked a turning point in their journey. It proved to be a gateway into an incomparable experience. It is here that we notice two basic truths.

We read in Exodus 13:20: "They took their journey." Here the initiative is with the people themselves. They left Succoth under their own power. They were still in Egypt, and they were traveling a paved highway. They naturally sensed no need of a supernatural guide. It was a different matter when they came to Etham, where they encamped at the edge of the wilderness. This was the road's end. The wilderness spread out before them. As long as Israel was in the pathway that was well trodden by human feet, they needed no guide; the way was clear. But the edge of the wilderness marked a change.

In the next verse we read: "And the Lord went before them" (v. 21). The ancient pilgrims arrived at the end of self-reliance; "Man's extremity is God's opportunity." This is not a comfortable place for the flesh to be found. Sad to say, the majority of professing Christians would rather play it safe, walking by sight, than venture into a so-called wilderness where all natural resources are cut off and man becomes totally dependent on his Maker. There are a few rare souls who reject the easy way—the man-made road—to walk with God by faith.

There is romance in this wilderness walk because God is there, present in the cloud. Salvation from Egypt's bondage is but the beginning. The child of God has never fully lived or felt deep joy, abiding peace, and security of soul until he has taken the first step beyond the place where the road ends. It is here that man is privileged to enter into a venture with God.

Our hearts often thrill as we read the stirring words found in Psalm 107:23-24: "They that go down to the sea in ships, that do business in great waters; these see the works of the LORD, and his wonders in the deep." Those who dare to walk in the dangerous wilderness where God leads will find His presence manifested and His power assured. In this path all the heroes of faith in every age have walked.

Our Lord commanded His weary disciples, who had toiled all night and had caught nothing, "Launch out into the deep, and let down your nets for a draught" (Lk 5:4). Verse 6 tells us the result: "And when they had this done, they inclosed a great multitude of fishes: and their net brake." It is those who venture into the deep waters with God who discover the tingling delight of an abundant success. Timid souls would rather wade in the surf than fish in the deep waters, where spiritual success is found.

### A Guard

In this thirteenth chapter of Exodus the statement is made concerning the giving of the pillar of cloud and fire. The fourteenth chapter opens with the account of Moses leading the children of Israel to Pi-hahiroth "between Migdol and the sea, over against Baal-zephon" (v. 2). From the human point of view Israel was trapped in the wilderness. The sea was before them. Pharaoh realized this and, even though he had permitted them to go, he changed his mind, arrayed his army of chariots, and set out to recapture his former slaves.

It is here that we have stated for us the first real work of the piller of cloud and fire. "And the angel of God, which went before the camp of Israel, removed and went behind them; and the pillar of the cloud went before their face, and stood behind them: and it came between the camp of the Egyptians and the camp of Israel; and it was a cloud and darkness to them, but it gave light by night to these: so that the one came not near the other all the night" (Ex 14: 19-20). Thus the cloud became a guard for Israel. The conflict was no longer betwen the Egyptians and the Israelites but between Jehovah and Pharaoh.

Among the first great needs of those who have been redeemed by the Pascal Lamb, the Lord Jesus, is to find security in realizing that God has put Himself between His blood-bought children and the enemy. Redemption with uncertainty has little joy. Redemption with assurance brings peace and invigoration. Along with guidance which was the primary function of the pillar of cloud and fire, there was need for a shield. The good Shepherd of Psalm 23 had both the rod and the staff. Likewise Israel experienced the two aspects in her journey.

The cloud protected the people not only from their human enemy, but also from the heat of the sun in the daytime and from the fear of the shadows in the night. Likewise, in the fullest sense, God has placed Himself between us and our sins; it is our blessed privilege to find Him protecting us from all things that could be against us. It is the true way to find peace of heart and peace of conscience. "The angel of the LORD encampeth round about them that fear him, and delivereth them" (Ps 34:7).

## A Guide

We read, "And the LORD went before them" (Ex 13:21). Think of the glory of such an experience—the experience of walking in the light of His countenance! Even here the Christian's privilege is greater. It is to serve Him whom we have not seen, yet love. The late Dr. Arthur Pink, in his book *Gleanings in Exodus,* had this to say in his description of the pillar of cloud and fire. "This 'pillar' was the visible sign of the Lord's presence with Israel. It is called 'a pillar of cloud' and 'a pillar of fire.' Apparently its upper portion rose up to heaven in the form of a column; its lower being spread out cloudwise, over Israel's camp. . . . The two descriptive terms are combined, showing that the 'pillar' did not change its form, as a 'cloud' by day and a 'fire' by night as is popularly supposed; but, as stated . . . [Ex 14:24] it was one—a 'pillar of fire' in its upper portion, a 'cloud' below."

Israel had two guides in the wilderness. The first was the pillar of cloud and fire, which seems to speak of the Holy Spirit. The second guide is described for us in this passage: "Make thee two trumpets of silver; of a whole piece shalt thou make them: that thou mayest use them for the calling of the assembly, and for the journeying of the camps. And when they shall blow with them, all the assembly shall assemble themselves to thee at the door of the tabernacle of the congregation" (Num 10:2-3).

One guide was heavenly, and the other was earthly. The two trumpets were made of one piece of silver. To the anointed eye and ear these two trumpets spoke a marvelous message. Israel was guided by these—the cloud and the blowing of the trumpets. Israel was required to remain in camp as long as the cloud stood still, but it was to move with the moving of the cloud. So Israel had the cloud above and the trumpet below.

In a true sense, the Christian has two similar guides—the

Holy Spirit and the Word of God. Do we not have, in the two trumpets made out of one piece of silver, the Old and the New Testaments? The two Old Testament guides, the cloud and the trumpets, had to be synchronized. Likewise, the two New Testament guides must be kept together—the Word and the Spirit.

There are many sincere people, devout and pious, who make the mistake of watching the cloud while neglecting the trumpet. There are those who state that they are led by the Spirit by means of impressions, intuitions, feelings, and the dry and wet fleece. They claim that the Lord speaks to them, tells them what to do and what not to do. In such a position they seem to have a certain advantage over the average Christian, since they can apparently get their message fresh every morning through contemplation while others have to rely upon the Bible that was written two thousand years ago. We are exhorted to try the spirits to see what sort they are, for there are many false prophets (1 Jn 4:1).

Only in the Bible do we have the formula for trying true and false spirits. It is a dangerous thing for one to put up his antenna and wait for a message if his antenna is not grounded in the Word of God. On the other hand, we are told that the letter kills, but the spirit makes alive. It is equally as dangerous to handle the Word without the Spirit as it is to magnify the Spirit without the Word. "But the natural man receiveth not the things of the Spirit of God: for they are foolishness unto him: neither can he know them, because they are spiritually discerned" (1 Co 2:14).

## A Guest

Returning to the passage relative to the giving of the cloud, we read, "And the Lord went before them by day in a pillar of a cloud, to lead them the way" (Ex 13:21). Jehovah not only chose Israel's paths but also He came down to sojourn with His people in spite of their unworthiness. They were grand witnesses not only to the presence of God as manifested in the cloud but also as to His power, His patience, and His loving care. "The Spirit itself [Himself] beareth witness with our spirit, that we are the children of God" (Ro 8:16).

### A Grandeur

One can hardly imagine any event more glorious than the appearance of the pillar of cloud and fire which gave evidence that God was in the midst of His people. This earth of ours has experienced some marvelous scenes in the past, and it is destined to witness others even more wonderful.

It must have been a supreme moment when God laid the foundation of creation, "when the morning stars sang together, and all the sons of God shouted for joy" (Job 38:7). It was a stupendous hour when the Spirit of God brooded over the chaotic earth, "and God said, Let there be light: and there was light" (Gen 1:3). It must have been a great moment when Noah and his family finally stepped out of the ark and looked upon the rainbow that God had placed upon the shoulders of the dying storm. It was a great experience for the shepherds who watched their sheep by night to hear the angelic host proclaim the birth of the Saviour. It was a glorious experience for Peter, James, and John when they were with Christ in the holy mount and were privileged to witness the out-flashing of the glory of their wonderful Lord. "While he yet spake, behold, a bright cloud overshadowed them: and behold a voice out of the cloud, which said, This is my beloved Son, in whom I am well pleased; hear ye him" (Mt 17:5). It was a great moment when the disciples stood on the Mount of Olives and witnessed the ascension of the glorified Son of God as a cloud received Him out of sight.

It will certainly be a great moment when "we which are

alive and remain shall be caught up together with them in the clouds to meet the Lord in the air" (1 Th 4:17). It will be a great moment when the shout shall be heard, "Behold, he cometh with clouds; and every eye shall see him, and they also which pierced him: and all kindreds of the earth shall wail because of him. Even so, Amen" (Rev 1:7). What a moment it will be! "And I saw a great white throne, and him that sat on it, from whose face the earth and the heaven fled away; and there was found no place for them" (20:11).

The appearance of this pillar of cloud and fire ranks among God's greatest wonders of divine, providential dealing with the sons of men. This cloud is mentioned nearly fifty times in the Pentateuch alone, and it is found throughout Scripture. In Exodus 14:24 God is said to have "looked unto the host of the Egyptians through the pillar of fire and of the cloud, and troubled the host of the Egyptians." In Exodus 16:10, "The glory of the LORD appeared in the cloud." In Exodus 19:9 the Lord appeared in "a thick cloud" on Sinai. In Exodus 24:15-16 the cloud of glory covered the mount. In Exodus 34:5 the "LORD descended in the cloud" and spoke on the occasion of the giving of the second tables of the law. In Leviticus 16:2, "I will appear in the cloud upon the mercy seat." Upon completion of Solomon's temple, the cloud of glory filled it (1 Ki 8:10-11).

In Ezekiel 10:3-4 the cloud was taken from the temple and the city. In Ezekiel 43:4 the glory of the Lord returns to dwell in the new millenial temple. It is interesting to note that the cloud introduced at Etham continued to play an important part in the destiny of the children of God.

## A Glorious Prototype

The similarity between the pillar of cloud and of fire and the Holy Spirit is very striking. The pillar of cloud was not given until Israel had been delivered from Egypt. This is the order of the New Testament: the death of God's Lamb, the resurrection and the ascension, and then the public descent of the Holy Spirit on the day of Pentecost. In 1 Corinthians 10:1-2 we read, "Moreover, brethren, I would not that ye should be ignorant, how that all our fathers were under the cloud, and all passed through the sea; and were all baptized unto Moses in the cloud and in the sea."

This similarity between the pillar of cloud and of fire and the Holy Spirit is further seen in the threefold position that tells us God is *for* us, God is *with* us, and God is *in* us. At the Red Sea He stood between them and their foes (Ex 14:19); as they walked along the desert the cloud went before them to seek out a resting place (Num 9:17); and in the tabernacle it rested in their midst (Ex 40:34). These three positions very beautifully illustrate the threefold chain of the New Testament: God for us, God with us, and God in us. All of God's pictures agree with God's purposes.

# 10

# BAPTIZED IN THE CLOUD AND IN THE SEA

Since we are told, "All these things happened unto them for ensamples: and they are written for our admonition, upon whom the ends of the world are come" (1 Co 10:11), let us look again at Israel's passage through the sea.

## The Cloud and the Sea

In 1 Corinthians 10:6 we are told that this experience of Israel's passage through the sea and her wilderness experiences were our examples. More literally, they were typical of Christian experiences.

Notice where the apostle Paul began his summation of this wilderness experience. He wrote, "Moreover, brethren, I would not that ye should be ignorant, how that all our fathers were under the cloud, and all passed through the sea" (1 Co 10:1). Paul was writing to Christians, and he used Christian baptism as a type of the believer's position in Christ: "Therefore we are buried with him by baptism into death. . . . If we have been planted together in the likeness of his death, we shall be also in the likeness of his resurrection" (Ro 6:4-5). The believer's position in Christ declares the truth dramatized in baptism—death to the world, death to the flesh, and death to self. Romans 6 is a declaration of emancipation, serving notice that the believer now stands on resurrection ground.

Paul, in 1 Corinthians 10, argued for a life on resurrection ground. He was writing to saved people to warn them and to challenge them to victorious living. He was not speaking of the Passover, which tells of salvation from the penalty of sin. This was past. He was dealing with salvation from the power of sin, as set forth in Christian baptism. Israel had already been delivered by blood from death in their passage through the sea. Now they were about to be delivered from the bondage of sin or slavery in Egypt. These Israelites were saved before they left their blood-sprinkled doors, but their emancipation was not complete. They were still in enemy territory, subject to bondage.

We often wonder how many people today are under the blood—saved—but are still in Egypt. They are saved but defeated. They hold a passport to victory, but they refuse to travel. They are hungry, and rather than eat manna, they long for "the fleshpots of Egypt." It is God's purpose that we shall experience victory over this world. We are still in the world, but must not be of it (Jn 17:14).

It is the recognition of our identification with Christ in Romans 6 that brings victory over sin. It is the baptism of the children of Israel unto Moses, as it were, in the cloud and in the sea, that became an example for the saints in Christ—both as a warning against presumption and as a challenge to push on to their inheritance.

The Christian, while secure in his salvation, can come under chastisement and die in the wilderness. The apostle Paul introduces this truth in 1 Corinthians 9:27: "But I keep under my body, and bring it into subjection: lest that by any means, when I have preached to others, I myself should be a castaway." The word *castaway* is a translation of the Greek work *adokimos,* a word that means "disapprove." Paul was not afraid of losing his salvation; he feared being set aside or disqualified in the race.

For Israel the power of sin was broken. First, there was death to the penalty of sin in the Passover. In the passage through the sea and through victory over Egypt (a type of the world) we see death to the power of sin. To have been redeemed by the blood, and then to have remained in Egypt, would have been slavery, oppression, and defeat. But that was over now. The wilderness was before them.

Our Passover experience as believers is past. We were saved from the penalty of sin at the cross. We are now being saved from the power, the habit, the thralldom of sin. Our victory, as we see in Romans 6, is set forth in four words: "knowing" (v. 6), "reckon" (v. 11), "yield" (v. 13, and "obeyed" (v. 17).

J. H. Todd, in his book *Prophetic Pictures of Christ,* has this to say:

> The cloud is a type of the Holy Spirit, who dwells with God's people today, manifesting God's presence with and in them, guiding, teaching, and controlling them in all their ways. They were all baptized unto Moses in the cloud. So all believers are baptized by the Spirit into one body (1 Corinthians 12:13). This is one of the two places in the epistles where the baptism with or in the Spirit is mentioned, the other being Romans 6:3. The latter passage refers to the union of individual believers with Christ in death and resurrection; whereas in 1 Corinthians 12:13 it is the union of all believers with Christ and with one another, as members of the body of which He is the head. The baptism in the Spirit is the action of Christ in uniting to Himself and to one another all who believe on Him as their Saviour, and at the moment of their putting their trust in Him. That is a matter of Christian position, and not of experience. Being filled with the Spirit according to Epesians 5:18 is quite a different matter, and is an experience which every believer should have and know by the grace of God. Such experience comes by faith, and by faith alone. The baptism in the Spirit is an act done once and forever, whereas

the filling of the Spirit should be a constantly recurring experience, for the literal rendering of Ephesians 5:18 is "be being filled with the Spirit."

They were baptized both in the cloud and in the sea. Our baptism shows our identification with Christ in death and resurrection and speaks of our separation unto Him to walk in newness of life. Only one form or mode will fit the picture here, and that is baptism by immersion. Any other mode distorts and destroys the entire picture. In Romans 6:17 we read, "But ye have obeyed from the heart that form of doctrine which was delivered you." Immersion in water is only a picture, but it is a picture of an important fact—the truth and the heart of the gospel. Try any other mode and see how it fits.

The two ordinances, baptism and the Lord's Supper, both speak of death, burial, and resurrection. They involve the past in that they point back to Calvary's transaction. They involve the present in that they point to the believer's experience in that spiritual resurrection known as regeneration. They point to the future by expressing the Christian's hope of the resurrection of the body at the Lord's coming.

We are told in 1 Corinthians 11:23-30 that many come under condemnation, not discerning the Lord's body in the Lord's Supper, and "for this cause many are weak and sickly among you, and many sleep" (v. 30). It seems that many fail to discern the Lord's death in baptism, with sad results. The believer's baptism by immersion is not, by its nature, very complimentary to man's state, for it carries with it the stigma of the cross.

### Man's Extremity, God's Opportunity

The people, on coming out of Egypt, were not led directly north along the caravan route but through the way of the wilderness. They were brought to the banks of the Red Sea, where there was neither bridge nor ferry. Through Moses, God told them to "encamp before Pi-hahiroth, between Migdol and the sea, over against Baal-zephon" (Ex 14:2). The sea was in front of them, and there were mountains on either side. What a strange place for God to lead His people!

The setting was complete. Pharaoh hardened his heart once more. He was unwilling to lose his labor batallion, so, gathering a mighty army with six-hundred chariots, he pursued the children of Israel and overtook them, "entangled in the land" (v. 3). Pharaoh and his fast-moving army were behind the children of Israel, and God's people were forced to depend on divine help. They had to look up; there was no other direction from which help could come. But they did not look up. They looked forward, visualizing death for themselves, their children, and the cattle. To the rear was a rising dust cloud created by the charging armies of Egypt.

### What the Flesh Saw and Did

"And when Pharaoh drew nigh, the children of Israel lifted up their eyes, and, behold, the Egyptians marched after them; and they were sore afraid: and the children of Israel cried out unto the Lord. And they said unto Moses, Because there were no graves in Egypt, hast thou taken us away to die in the wilderness? Wherefore hast thou dealt thus with us, to carry us forth out of Egypt? Is not this the word that we did tell thee in Egypt, saying, Let us alone, that we may serve the Egyptians? For it had been better for us to serve the Egyptians, than that we should die in the wilderness" (Ex 14:10-12).

Consternation reigned, bedlam broke loose, panic seized the people. They jumped on Moses, grew sarcastic, and initiated a wave of murmuring that lasted for forty years. It was a sad picture indeed for a people who had only a short time earlier come under the blood.

## What Moses Said

"And Moses said unto the people, Fear ye not, stand still, and see the salvation of the Lord, which he will shew to you to day: for the Egyptians whom ye have seen today, ye shall see them again no more forever. The Lord shall fight for you, and ye shall hold your peace" (Ex 14:13-14).

"Stand still!" How can the flesh stand still in the face of such odds? The flesh must do something, but what? Nothing is left. The strength of the flesh has come to an end. "Man's extremity is God's opportunity!"

There is a vast difference between "surrender" and "relaxation." Many Christians surrender but do not relax. Every wife who has been taught to drive a car by her husband can readily understand the difference. He surrenders the wheel, but does he relax? "Watch out. Didn't you see that other car? Don't drive off the highway!" He grabs the wheel again. If he truly relaxes, he surrenders the wheel, folds his arms, and trusts his wife.

Many people treat God the same way. They may say they surrender, but when a crisis comes, they immediately get excited and grab the wheel. Their attitude is: "Watch out, Lord! I trust you, but I am afraid." How dishonoring this is to God! What if we should really trust Him? If we surrender and then relax, we can be like a friend of mine who had just completed a new church building. When he was asked if he had any insurance on the wooden structure, he replied, "No, it belongs to the Lord. If He wants to burn it down, it is all right with me." This sounds extreme, but if you knew the man who spoke the words, you would readily understand. He was the greatest man of faith it has been my privilege to know. He lived that way.

Most of us are really afraid to relax with the Lord. We feel we must help Him out! How little faith we have! Remember that if the boat had gone down during the night of the storm, Jesus would have been in it. "Master, carest thou not that we perish?" (Mk 4:38) is the voice of those Jesus described with the words, "Oh, ye of little faith" (Mt 8:26). Oh, that we might trust the Lord!

## What God Said

"And the Lord said unto Moses, Wherefore criest thou unto me? speak unto the children of Israel, that they go forward" (Ex 14:15).

The children of Israel were forced to exercise faith. This is the situation where God wants to have all of His children. "Forward" is the only command given to those who are in the will of God. God's people realized that if it meant death in the Red Sea, that was God's responsibility.

When it was all over the waters of death rolled between the Israelites and the place of bondage—Egypt, the land of death. Pharaoh and his army were no more; the arm of the Red Sea had been crossed. A three-day journey in the wilderness would have placed them on resurrection ground if they had continued to exercise their faith.

# 11

# THE PASSAGE THROUGH THE SEA

"The LORD shall fight for you, and ye shall hold your peace" (Ex 14:14). The Lord is sufficient for every emergency. The cloud that provided light for the people of Israel shifted to the rear. "And the angel of God, which went before the camp of Israel, removed and went behind them; and the pillar of the cloud went from before their face, and stood behind them: and it came between the camp of the Egyptians and the camp of Israel; and it was a cloud and darkness to them, but it gave light by night to these: so that the one came not near the other all the night" (vv. 19-20).

God threw Himself between Israel and death, as exemplified in the Passover. He also puts Himself between the believer and circumstances. We often make the same mistake that Israel made when her people interpreted God in the light of circumstances instead of interpreting circumstances in the light of God. This was the difference between Joshua and Caleb and the other ten men who were sent to spy out the land of Canaan. The ten saw walled towns and giants, and saw God in the light of these things—a little God and big circumstances. Joshua and Caleb saw God first, and they interpreted the walled towns and giants in the light of God's greatness. Caleb said, "Let us go up at once, and possess it; for we are well able to overcome it" (Num 13:30).

## God's Miracle and Israel's Experience

"And Moses stretched out his hand over the sea; and the LORD caused the sea to go back by a strong east wind all that night, and made the sea dry land, and the waters were divided. And the children of Israel went into the midst of the sea upon the dry ground: and the waters were a wall unto them on their right hand, and on their left" (Ex 14:21-22).

Miracles in Scripture authenticate the work of God. Extract the miracles and you have just another religion. Miracles do not violate natural law; they transcend it. To lift a book off a table is to act contrary to the law of gravity that holds the book in place. The intervention of the superior power of your hand, in this particular instance, does not violate the law but introduces a superior force. Men say, "Where is the promise of his coming? for since the fathers fell asleep, all things continue as they were from the beginning of the creation" (2 Pe 3:4).

Peter goes on to give the reason for their question: "For this they willingly are ignorant of, that by the word of God the heavens were of old, and the earth standing out of the water and in the water: whereby the world that then was, being overflowed with water, perished" (vv. 5-6).

God did intervene in behalf of His children. How wonderful is His mercy and power!

Try to put yourself in Israel's place. Walk with God's people through the sea. See the walls on either side. Come out on the other side with them.

"But the children of Israel walked upon dry land in the midst of the sea; and the waters were a wall unto them on their right hand, and on their left. Thus the LORD saved Israel that day out of the hand of the Egyptians; and Israel saw the Egyptians dead upon the sea shore. And Israel saw that great work which the LORD did upon the Egyptians: and the people feared the LORD, and believed the LORD, and his servant Moses" (Ex 14:29-31). Could they ever forget? You would hardly think so, but they did.

## ISRAEL'S FIRST SONG

Born out of this experience—their passing through the Red Sea and watching the destruction of Pharaoh and his army—the children of Israel burst into a song of praise. True praise is always born of a great experience. Someone has said that praise is like the mist that rises from Niagara. Doubtless much of our singing today carries with it little praise because there is much lack of a great experience. We do not venture far with the Lord. We play it safe. For us, it is the paved highway rather than reckless faith in the wilderness and the glory cloud of His presence.

The Jewish people of old were not seafaring people. To them, the sea was the great unknown. Yet we read: "They that go down to the sea in ships, that do business in great waters; these see the works of the LORD, and his wonders in the deep" (Ps 107:23). Such a word challenges the soul. Is such ecstasy reserved for missionaries or for some rare soul alone? No! It is for us if we are willing to "do business in great waters." It is wonderful to see His work and to learn the wonders of the deep! Or would we rather play safe and leave the launching into the deep to others? There is adventure with God for all who dare to embark on it.

We read concerning this experience: "Israel saw that great work which the LORD did . . . and believed the LORD. . . . Then sang Moses and the children of Israel" (Ex 14:31—15:1). "Then believed they his words; they sang his praise" (Ps 106:12).

And this is the place for praise—after salvation, not before it. Note the sequence in Psalm 40:2: "He brought me up also out of an horrible pit, out of the miry clay, and set my feet upon a rock, and established my goings. And he hath put a new song in my mouth, even praise unto our God." The prodigal first received his father's kiss of love, and then "they began to be merry" (Lk 15:24). Philip went down to Samaria and preached Christ. The people believed the Word, "and there was great joy in that city" (Ac 8:8). The Ethiopian in the desert of Gaza believed and then "went on his way rejoicing" (v. 39). Both the story and the order of activity are the same in every case.

The song is all about Jehovah, His workings, and His glory. There is no word of self here: "The LORD . . . hath triumphed gloriously. . . . The LORD is my strength and song. . . . The LORD is a man of war" (Ex 15:1-3). When we see grace, all boasting is gone. How distasteful much of our so-called praise must be to God. John Ritchie wrote:

> The most daring insults are offered to the God of heaven under the pretence of praise. The most solemn scenes of the 'Messiah's' sufferings are set to music, and sung by hundreds of careless sinners, and applauded by thousands more! The death agonies of the Son of God are brought forth in a popular form, to please the revolted tastes of wicked men and soothe their consciences into forgetfulness of the day when the murdered One and the murderers shall meet. The scenes of the 'judgment day' are turned into song, accompanied by strains of music; and God's redeemed ones are not clear of the open shame, nor are they separate from it. Oh, if they would only think of the tenderness of the heart they so rudely pierce by this unhallowed work! If they but remembered the depth of the darkness and the woe that He passed through to make them His, and to separate them from the world that cast Him out, how different all this would be *(From Egypt to Canaan)*.

# 12

# MARAH—THE BITTER WATERS

"So Moses brought Israel from the Red sea, and they went out into the wilderness of Shur; and they went three days in the wilderness, and found no water. And when they came to Marah, they could not drink of the waters of Marah, for they were bitter: therefore the name of it was called Marah. And the people murmured against Moses, saying, What shall we drink? And he cried unto the LORD; and the LORD shewed him a tree, which when he had cast into the waters, the waters were made sweet: there he made for them a statute and an ordinance, and there he proved them" (Ex 15:22-25).

"From the Red sea . . . into the wilderness of Shur." Surely it must have seemed strange to the children of Israel to leave the place of victory and song, and to come so soon into the wilderness of Shur. Redeemed by blood from the penalty of sin and redeemed by power from the slavery of Egypt, why should not these people, who had been so highly favored by heaven, have expected smooth sailing ahead? This may seem all the more reasonable to us as we remember that they were in the path of divine leadership, directed by God. Yet we read, "And they went three days . . . and found no water." With a great deal of disappointment they must have inquired, "Has God forgotten?" Indeed, we read, "And the people murmured against Moses, saying, What shall we drink?" (v. 24).

## The Wilderness of Shur

We may desire to be very harsh and severely critical of these children of Israel, but if we were, we would find ourselves a bit embarrassed by our own experience and by that of others. This picture is characteristic of God's people in all ages. Once saved and dedicated, the redeemed expect to walk an easy pathway. We seem to be totally unprepared to accept the wilderness way and bitter waters. How often have we heard young Christians, filled with confidence and radiant in experience, say, "I am saved, I'm happy in the Lord, and I never expect to turn back." There are lessons ahead which may first shake that confidence and then strengthen it.

The divine purpose, though often misunderstood, is always the same: Character is developed through difficulty. Where can the loving heavenly Father walk with His children except in the wilderness? Free from Egypt's distractions, self-help, and supply, they are wholly dependent on Him. This is a blessed experience, but not for the flesh. Men often spend their lives trying to avoid such dependence. Human philosophy and divine wisdom seldom agree. God's Word and our experience teach us that there is no other place where men may learn the divine lesson.

The wilderness experience serves two purposes: First, we discover, as these Israelites did later, the way of God. He knows how to sweeten bitter waters. His method at that time was neither apparent nor reasonable, but it worked. It always does! Their first great lesson was to learn to trust God, and to believe in Him in spite of circumstances and apparent conflict.

Where could they learn the lessons they needed to know but in the place of utter dependence? There was none to trust but God. The flesh can think of many better things. To live "from hand to mouth," even from God's hand to our mouths, can only be painfully endured. In our weakness we look for better assurance and more tangible evidence.

Second, we learn that God meets our emergencies and shames us when we fail to trust Him. To wait is often our greatest cross, while patience should be our greatest virtue.

### Bitter Waters

The taste of bitter waters was the tangible manifestation of one of the first lessons the children of Israel had to learn.

God hath not promised skies always blue,
Flower-strewn pathways all our lives through;
God hath not promised sun without rain,
Joy without sorrow, peace without pain.

God hath not promised we shall not know
Toil and temptations, trouble and woe;
He hath not told us we shall not bear
Many a burden, many a care.

God hath not promised smooth roads and wide,
Swift, easy travel, needing no guide;
Never a mountain, rocky and steep,
Never a river turbid and deep.

But God hath promised strength for the day,
Rest for the labor, light for the way,
Grace for the trials, help from above,
Unfailing kindness, undying love.

Annie Johnson Flint

God has His way of sweetening life's bitter waters. "And he [Moses] cried unto the Lord; and the Lord shewed him a tree, which when he had cast into the waters, the waters were made sweet: there he made for them a statute and an ordinance, and there he proved them" (Ex 15:25). They had their tree, which seems to have been a foreshadow of the believer's. When we see our sufferings, disappointments, heartaches, privations, and losses through the prism of the cross, we are able to read the meaning of our tears. This seems to be the great lesson in Romans 5:1-5: "Therefore being justified by faith, we have peace with God through our Lord Jesus Christ: by whom also we have access by faith into this grace wherein we stand, and rejoice in hope of the glory of God. And not only so, but we glory in tribulations also: knowing that tribulation worketh patience; and patience, experience; and experience, hope: and hope maketh not ashamed; because the love of God is shed abroad in our hearts by the Holy Ghost which is given unto us."

These are mighty expressions—"justified," "peace," "access," "hope of the glory,"—but Paul could still say, "We glory in tribulations" (v. 3). How can anyone glory in tribulation? The apostle outlines these steps: "Knowing that tribulation worketh patience; and patience, experience; and experience, hope" (vv. 3-4).

The young fellow on the football field with a desire to make the team and to reap the glory faces a similar experience. He is tackled, jumped upon, and roughly treated. Why does he take all this rough treatment and the exacting discipline that goes along with a football player? He will be involved in the combat of a real game soon, and there is no other way to qualify. The boxer says to his sparring partner, "Hit me again!" Why? The answer again is clear—there is a big bout ahead.

We must view our tribulations in the light of the cross and answer the question as to why Christ suffered: "Who for the joy that was set before him endured the cross, despising the shame, and is set down at the right hand of the throne of God" (Heb 12:2). The cross is the tree for bitter waters. Our hope is for the glory of God. The great day that is coming is spoken of in Romans 8: "And if children, then heirs; heirs of God, and joint-heirs with Christ; if so be that we suffer with him, that we may be also glorified together" (v. 17).

We stand amazed at the words, "Suffer with him, that we may be also glorified together." But we read Paul's next statement: "For I reckon that the sufferings of this present time are not worthy to be compared with the glory which shall be revealed in us" (Ro 8:18). When our Lord comes there will be a glorious procession led by the great Captain of our salvation. We should desire not only to be saved, but also to share with Him in His glorious celebration, when all the intelligent beings of the universe will be the spectators. There will be glory, and "it doth not yet appear what we shall be: but we know that, when he shall appear, we shall be like him; for we shall see him as he is" (1 Jn 3:2).

Salvation is a free gift, but glory is commensurate with suffering. "Therefore I endure all things for the elect's sakes, that they may also obtain the salvation which is in Christ Jesus with eternal glory. It is a faithful saying: For if we be dead with him, we shall also live with him: if we suffer, we shall also reign with him: if we deny him, he also will deny us" (2 Ti 2:10-12).

Calvary's tree, cast into our bitter waters, transforms them into sweet waters. None are so bitter that He cannot make them sweet. George Henderson gave the following illustration: "A beautiful incident occurred a few years ago at a meeting which was held in London. The hall was crowded, and just under the platform was a carriage in which lay a paralyzed woman. Before the meeting proper began, one of the missioners took the audience through a singing practice, during which he asked one and another to choose a hymn. Eventually he stooped over the side of the platform and said to the poor paralytic: 'Sister, will you choose a hymn? What shall it be?' With a smile of heavenly sweetness, she replied, 'Count Your Blessings.' For her the waters had been made sweet" (*Studies in the Book of Exodus*).

## Elim

Not all the pilgrim journey is taken up with Marahs. There are also Elims along the path of His leading. "And they came to Elim, where were twelve wells of water, and threescore and ten palm trees: and they encamped there by the waters" (Ex 15:27). There were "twelve wells of water," a well for every month; and there were seventy palm trees, a tree for every year.

God will not suffer us to be tempted above that which we are able to bear (1 Co 10:13). He remembers that we are dust (Ps 103:14). He knows when we have had enough. Close to Marah was Elim, the place of refreshing. The transformation of Marah made the waters sweet. Our Lord said to His weary disciples: "Come ye yourselves apart into a desert place, and rest a while" (Mk 6:31).

There is a place of quiet rest,
Near to the heart of God,
A place where sin cannot molest,
Near to the heart of God.

There is a place of comfort sweet,
Near to the heart of God,
A place where we our Saviour meet,
Near to the heart of God.

There is a place of full release,
Near to the heart of God,
A place where all is joy and peace,
Near to the heart of God.

O Jesus, blest Redeemer,
Sent from the heart of God,
Hold us, who wait before Thee,
Near to the heart of God.

C. B. McAfee

# 13

# THE MANNA

"And they took their journey from Elim, and all the congregation of the children of Israel came into the wilderness of Sin, which is between Elim and Sinai, on the fifteenth day of the second month after their departing out of the land of Egypt" (Ex 16:1).

Israel was on the move; every day brought a new crisis. This is always true of those who journey with God in a wilderness and refuse to be entangled with the things of this world. At Marah and Elim the Israelites had witnessed God's willingness and power to meet emergencies and to abundantly supply their temporary needs; in the giving of the manna God had revealed His sufficiency in meeting man's protracted and sustained needs. "And the children of Israel did eat manna forty years, until they came to a land inhabited" (v. 35).

## Murmuring

"And the whole congregation of the children of Israel murmured against Moses and Aaron in the wilderness" (v. 2).

How characteristic it is that "the whole congregation . . . murmured." Even though we know human nature, we are shocked that a people so recently delivered by blood, led through the Read Sea, guided by the cloud, relieved by the waters made sweet, and refreshed at Elim, could believe that their God had led them out of the land of Egypt to die of hunger and thirst in the wilderness. How difficult it is for man to trust the Lord and to give God credit for pure and perfect love. Few things are more lamentable than the failure to cultivate the spirit of gratitude and thanksgiving. Mankind is quick to murmur against the Lord in the face of ten thousand mercies, yet he never utters a word of complaint against Satan, the author of sorrow, suffering, and servitude.

We are told in 1 Corinthians 10:11, "Now all these things happened unto them for ensamples: and they are written for our admonition, upon whom the ends of the world are come." On our wilderness journey, we have spiritual truth in solution—the unrefined ore which contained the rare silver of New Testament revelation.

In dealing with manna we can be sure that we are on safe scriptural ground in applying manna as a type of Christ. He Himself made this application. "Which had the golden censer, and the ark of the covenant overlaid round about with gold, wherein was the golden pot that had manna, and Aaron's rod that budded, and the tables of the covenant" (Heb 9:4). If one of the three articles kept as a memorial before the Lord in the ark of the covenant was the "golden pot of manna," how significant this type must be to the Holy Spirit. This truth is further emphasized in Revelation 2:17: "He that hath an ear, let him hear what the Spirit saith unto the churches; to him that overcometh will I give to eat of the hidden manna, and will give him a white stone, and in the stone a new name written, which no man knoweth saving he that receiveth it."

In Exodus 16, manna is provided and explained; in Numbers 11:4-9, manna is despised; in Deuteronomy 8:3, manna is instructive; in John 6:22-59, manna is personified; in Hebrews 9:4, manna is preserved; in Revelation 2:17, manna is hidden.

## MANNA, A TYPE OF CHRIST

*Manna was from heaven, a gift of God.* The Lord told Moses, "I will rain bread from heaven for you" (Ex 16:4). Manna was heavenly in origin, a product which man had no part in producing. He could not work for it since it was a gift of free grace. Man's only part was to recognize and appropriate it. Therefore Christ chose manna to represent Himself. To fail to see Christ in the manna is to fail to see Him in His heavenly aspect and is thus to miss the typical significance of the manna. It was this claim of our Lord that so offended the Jews: "I am the living bread which came down from heaven: if any man eat of this bread, he shall live for ever: and the bread that I will give is my flesh, which I will give for the life of the world. The Jews therefore strove among themselves, saying, How can this man give us his flesh to eat?" (Jn 6:51-52).

"Many therefore of his disciples, when they had heard this, said, This is an hard saying; who can hear it?" (v. 60). Upon the basis of this claim, Jesus lost many of His disciples. "From that time many of his disciples went back, and walked no more with him" (v. 66). The world is willing and anxious to receive a human Christ, but is unwilling to receive the Christ of God. If He were to give up His heavenliness, and His deity, the natural man would applaud Him. As the true manna from heaven, He must always remain. There must be no surrender here or all is lost. It may take time, but surrender at this point will ultimately result in the loss of all.

*Manna was miraculous.* "And when the dew that lay was gone up, behold, upon the face of the wilderness there lay a small round thing, as small as the hoar frost on the ground" (Ex 16:14).

Men have tried to explain away the miraculous nature of manna, saying it was the gum of the tamarisk tree .Bees, they say, punctured the leaves of this tree, and a gum was exuded which hardened and fell to the ground. They admit that the possibility of such a phenomenon lasted for about two months in the year. When we realize that about three million people were fed manna daily for forty years while they traveled through mountains, over sandy wastes, and across rocky plains, we are forced to say with Dr. John J. VanGorder, "Some trees, some bees, some lies!"

This scientific, naturalistic, rationalistic age attempts to manufacture from its own imagination a fictitious Christ who is less embarrassing to sinful man. Herein lies the battleground of this and all ages. Here Christianity stands or falls! We had better not deceive ourselves.

*Manna was mysterious.* Manna came in the dewdrop. "And when the children of Israel saw it, they said one to another, It is manna: for they wist not what it was. And Moses said unto them, This is the bread which the LORD hath given you to eat" (v. 15).

Dr. Robert L. Moyer said, in *The Savior in the Shadows,* "We are told of its appearance, its shape, its color, its size, its taste, but after all, what is it? There is so much about it that cannot be understood, so many questions that may be asked that cannot be answered. The very word, 'manna,' means 'what is it?' When the Israelites went out and looked upon the manna as it lay round about the camp, they said, '*Man-hu?*' 'What is it?' So when our Lord was here, men said, 'Who is this?' 'What manner of man is this?' "

The very simplicity of our Lord's unique humanity constitutes one of the great mysteries of His incarnation. "For he shall grow up before him as a tender plant, and as a root out of a dry ground: he hath no form nor comliness; and when we shall see him, there is no beauty that we should desire him" (Is 53:2).

In Revelation 2:17 it is called "hidden manna." This spiritual food is called "hidden manna" because the source of our spiritual life is invisible. "Ye are dead, and your life is hid with Christ in God" (Col. 3:3).

Here we are reminded of the words of the apostle: "But if our gospel be hid, it is hid to them that are lost" (2 Co 4:3). Manna was desert food, food for the redeemed, God's people. The manna came during the night. Likewise, our Lord came at a time of deep moral darkness. The manna fell while men slept. Christ's own people, Israel, were given over to formalism and ritualism with little life or love. The pagan nations were morally bankrupt. The shadows were deep and dark when He came.

*How the manna was given.* It came at night while the people were asleep. "This is the thing which the LORD hath commanded, Gather of it every man according to his eating, an omer for every man, according to the number of your persons; take ye every man for them which are in his tents" (Ex 16:16). The manna had to be gathered personally, according to each man's need. God gave it, the people gathered it. It had to be appropriated in order to be enjoyed. Even so it must be with us; we must personally feed upon Christ, the true bread from heaven.

Christ's blood is both the ground of our redemption and the source of our life, sustaining us throughout this wilderness journey. Not only are we saved by Christ; we are sustained by Him. The source of our spiritual energy is found in Him as we feed on the true bread from heaven. We contemplate Him, behold Him in the Word, meditate upon Him, and commune with Him. He is accurately depicted in the Bible, In our anxiety for the mystical, we dare not worship a Christ that is but the figment of our own imagination. He is, and must ever be, the Christ of revelation. There is safety here. The Word incarnate and the Word written must be faithfully identified by the believer.

John Ritchie said, in *From Egypt to Canaan,*

> The low state of spiritual life among the people of God, the lack of divine power in the service of the Lord, and the sadly uneven walk of many who profess to be the Lord's are things deplored and mourned over among us. But is there not a cause? Most undoubtedly there is; and we would humbly suggest that the chief cause is this—neglect of the soul's nourishment, through a lack of meditation on the Word, alone with God. This is a busy age. Things go at a great rapidity, and everything tends to draw the saints from their closets and their Bibles. Controversies in the church, and upheavings in the world are engrossing the attention of many of the saints, and the devil is making capital of the occasion in quietly alluring saints from the solace of the "secret place." Troubles and perplexities are abroad in the commercial world, and from early till late, Christian men are occupied, scheming how those difficulties are to be met. It is perfectly right that the Christian merchant should have his business so ordered that the world will not be able to point the finger of scorn at any inconsistency therein, but nothing on earth can justify the habitual neglect of communion with God in meditation on His Word, nor will God's blessing rest upon the man who attempts it. It may be that such seasons will at times be necessarily short, but the Lord knows all our circumstances, and He can make a little gathering go a long way, "for he that gathered little had no lack." Every man gathered according to his eating, some more, some less, but the manna was adapted to the requirements of all; so little children, young men, and fathers, all find their portion in the Word (1 Jn 2:12-17).

*How the manna was to be gathered.* God gave definite rules for gathering the manna:

1. Manna had to be gathered personally and individually (Ex 16:16).

2. Manna could only be gathered by stooping. This is an abiding truth. Religion that prefers manna which requires no bending of the will, no stooping, and no repentance is but a counterfeit. Most men want their religion served in smorgasbord fashion—they like it standing up.

3. Manna had to be gathered early. "And when the sun waxed hot it melted" (v. 21). This principle vitally affects the quality of our daily devotions. It is our privilege to commune with God while the day is young and the morning is fresh. This habit can well sanctify the entire day.

4. Manna was to be gathered daily. One day's portion would not suffice for the next. Manna spoiled easily when stored. "And Moses said, Let no man leave of it till the morning. Notwithstanding they hearkened not unto Moses; but some of them left of it until the morning, and it bred worms, and stank: and Moses was wroth with them" (Ex 16:19-20). Testimonials by individuals are wonderful, but these must be fresh. We have all heard the same story told year after year until it stank. To relate to others what we ourselves have never experienced cannot be a blessing.

5. Manna satisfies. In giving the manna, the Word tells us, "Then said the LORD unto Moses, Behold, I will rain bread from heaven for you; and the people shall go out and gather a certain rate every day, that I may prove them, whether they will walk in my law, or no" (v. 4).

"That I may prove them"—what solemn words these are! Later this truth is brought out in bold relief. At Kibroth-hattaavah the manna was despised, as we shall see later when we come to the chapter on the mixed multitude. Nothing reveals what we really are in our spiritual state so much as our attitude toward the manna. Does Christ satisfy? Are we taken up with Him? We could ask ourselves the question, What is the formula that would satisfy me? Would it be Christ plus? Is He enough?

Is the bride satisfied with the love, affection, and devotion of her husband? Or does she have to have her husband plus? Perhaps we were satisfied when we were first saved—when we were enjoying the unbroken fellowship of our spiritual honeymoon. But the years have brought a change. Romance has gone. Now it is Christ plus the world, Christ plus possessions, Christ plus pleasures. After all, it is not a sacrifice to be separated unto the one you love. It is our choice, even our greatest joy.

I am satisfied with Jesus.
He has done so much for me,
He has suffered to redeem me,
Can He always count on me?

# 14

# THE SMITTEN ROCK

"And all the congregation of the children of Israel journeyed from the wilderness of Sin, after their journeys, according to the commandment of the LORD, and pitched in Rephidim: and there was no water for the people to drink" (Ex 17:1).

"And" connects with chapters 15 and 16 (Marah and Elim). Why? The late Dr. Pink says it is to show "the unexcusableness on man's part, and the infinite mercy on God's part."

## HUMAN DEPRAVITY

If we did not know something of the depravity of our own hearts, we could easily be astounded at Israel's exhibition of such carnality, ingratitude, and insensibility to all the Lord's goodness, faithfulness, and mighty acts. Since we are more prone to see evil in others than in ourselves, we still marvel that a people who had so recently experienced such wonders could so soon forget.

Recall for a moment what these people had gone through in less than three months (Ex 19:1). Since they had left Egypt, they had experienced the redemption of the firstborn, the appearance of the pillar of cloud, the passage through the sea, the miracle of God's judgment that destroyed Pharaoh's army in one night, the glorious time of praise on the far side of the Red Sea, the sweetening of the waters of

Marah, and the partaking of heavenly manna and the quails. With all of this, they are ready to stone Moses, their leader. Someone has well said, "Nothing can exceed the desperate unbelief and wickedness of the human heart save the superabounding grace of God."

In arguing with Moses and demanding "Give us water," the people were displaying a human characteristic. Was Moses not responsible? Was he not under obligation to them? Had he not brought them out of Egypt? Criticizing Moses was really criticizing God. Mankind has been slow to learn this sad truth. Moses, instead of replying, sought the Lord. "What shall I do unto this people? They be almost ready to stone me" (Ex 17:4). God's answer is found in the instructions concerning the smiting of the rock.

## The Divine Pathway

"And all the congregation of the children of Israel journeyed from the wilderness of Sin, after their journeys, according to the commandment of the Lord" (v. 1). From the viewpoint of the natural man, Israel up to this time had experienced many mysterious difficulties. At the Red Sea it was what the eyes saw—the approaching army of Pharaoh. At Marah it was what they tasted—the bitter waters—that produced disappointment. In the wilderness of Sin it was what they felt—hunger—that produced dissatisfaction. And at Rephidim it was ravishing thirst that generated rebellion against God and against Moses. It is well to keep in mind that these children of Israel were in the pathway of divine leading.

We may be tempted to ask, Does God intentionally lead His children along the pathway that is strewn with sorrows, difficulties, and privations? Yes, very often He does. This is the way His Son went. The path of faith is in the path of trial. As someone has said, "Those who are led by God must expect to encounter that which displeases the flesh. Those whom God would greatly use He must expose to hardship and trial." Here is a paradox.

While walking in the immediate presence of the pillar of fire and pillar of cloud and under their light and shadow, the redeemed people of Israel were experiencing hardships. We hear some say, I thought that if I obeyed God, I would be happy. Another will inquire, Why did God do this to me? The answer to all of this is found in what God did to His beloved Son. The cross is the answer. Suffering seen through the prism of the cross is reckoned as a part of the divine economy which is ordered for our good and for His glory. "Beloved, think it not strange concerning the fiery trial which is to try you, as though some strange thing happened unto you: But rejoice, inasmuch as ye are partakers of Christ's sufferings; that, when his glory shall be revealed, ye may be glad also with exceeding joy. If ye be reproached for the name of Christ, happy are ye; for the spirit of glory and of God resteth upon you: on their part he is evil spoken of, but on your part he is glorified" (1 Pe 4:12-14).

## Natural Thirst

"And the people thirsted there for water" (Ex 17:3). Many of God's trials come in the sphere of the legitimate and the ordinary. The most natural and dominant yearning of the human body is for water. Men can live remarkably long without food but only a very short time without drink. Dehydration is always perilous. Those who have experienced the deep pangs of thirst tell us that this desire is beyond compare—often turning normal men into maniacs. This thirst is but a picture of the deeper soul-thirst so often described in Scripture. "O God, thou art my God; early will

I seek thee: my soul thirsteth for thee, my flesh longeth for thee in a dry and thirsty land, where no water is" (Ps 63:1).

Thirst is natural, and water saves the body from dehydration. Denial of water drives men to despair and ruin. How wonderful it would be if thirsty men would turn from the broken cisterns of religious form and ceremony, ornate worship in which the flesh delights, to drink at the living fountains of divine truth. The true heaven-born soul will have a strong desire for God. "As the hart panteth after the water brooks, so panteth my soul after thee, O God. My soul thirsteth for God, for the living God: when shall I come and appear before God?" (Ps 42:1-2). There is within man a thirst that knows no satisfaction until it is filled at the fountain of God's presence.

The experience recorded in the early verses of Exodus 17 serves to remind us of that which is so prevalent in human nature. We can almost hear the murmuring of the people—some three million of them! With no water in sight, miracles are forgotten. The divine presence is overlooked, and despair reigns. These Israelites saw with the eyes of men. There was no thought of God's presence. Losing sight of God, they attacked the human leadership. "And Moses cried unto the LORD, saying, What shall I do unto this people? They be almost ready to stone me" (v. 4). This attitude is being repeated in many of our churches today. When men lose sight of a divine call, they attack the human leader. Those whom they can "hire" they can "fire." This attitude is prevalent among us.

In spite of their murmurings, God was ready to satisfy the thirst of His needy people. God's supply was Israel's commissary.

## A Revelation of Divine Grace

"And the LORD said unto Moses, Go on before the people,

and take with thee of the elders of Israel; and thy rod, wherewith thou smotest the river, take in thine hand, and go. Behold, I will stand before thee there upon the rock in Horeb; and thou shalt smite the rock, and there shall come water out of it, that the people may drink. And Moses did so in the sight of the elders of Israel" (Ex 17:5-6).

As always, man's extremity becomes God's opportunity. Grace operates where nothing else can serve. The cause of grace is found only in God Himself. Upon the dark background of man's murmuring, rebellion, and complaint are exhibited the highlights of divine benevolence. The greater the malady, the more astounding is the divine cure. Moses, as we have seen, was told to take with him the elders of Israel as well as the rod, with which he had smitten the river of Egypt, and to smite the rock in Horeb. This proposal did not then, and does not now, lend itself to human reasoning. To the worldly-wise, the direction given by Jehovah must have sounded exceedingly foolish, but it worked. Our God appeals to faith and not to natural reasoning.

The act was to be a public performance. The smiting of the rock was to be done in the presence of the elders of Israel. All of God's activity is open for inspection to all who are willing to be convinced. Following the smiting of the rock, the waters came out and the people drank. It was an abundant supply. We read in Psalm 105:41, "He opened the rock, and the waters gushed out; they ran in the dry places like a river." All of this Moses did in the sight of the elders of Israel.

## The Typical Meaning

We do well to learn some of the lessons of the Horeb experience:

1. It's location, Horeb, means "dry, desert, barren." How much this is like the world about us!

2. Its designation, "Behold, I will stand before thee there upon the rock" (Ex 17:6), was one of divine selection. "And that Rock was Christ" (1 Co 10:4). See Deuteronomy 32:15; 2 Samuel 22:2-3; Psalm 95: 1.

3. Moses speaks of the law.

4. The rod, "wherewith thou smotest the river" (Ex 17:5), speaks of divine judgment.

5. The smiting, "And thou shalt smite the rock" (v. 6), speaks of the judgment that fell upon Christ, our substitute, at Calvary. While the manna speaks of Christ's incarnation, the smitten rock speaks of His crucifixion. Smitten in the presence of the elders of Israel, the act emphasized the governmental character of Christ's death. God stood upon the Rock—"Behold, I will stand before thee there upon the rock in Horeb" (v. 6). God was there. "Surely he hath borne our griefs, and carried our sorrows: yet we did esteem him stricken, *smitten of God,* and afflicted. But he was wounded for our transgressions, he was bruised for our iniquities: the chastisement of our peace was upon him; and with his stripes we are healed" (Is 53:4-5).

6. The water, "And there shall come water out of it" (Ex 17:6), tells of benefits that accrue to the believer as result of the death of Christ. Running water in Scripture speaks of the Holy Spirit's presence. "In the last day, that great day of the feast, Jesus stood and cried, saying, If any man thirst, let him come unto me, and drink. He that believeth on me, as the scripture hath said, out of his belly shall flow rivers of living water. (But this spake he of the Spirit, which they that believe on him should receive: for the Holy Ghost was not yet given; because that Jesus was not yet glorified)" (Jn 7:37-39).

To the Samaritan woman at Jacob's well our Lord said, "If thou knewest the gift of God [Christ] . . . thou wouldst have asked of him, and he would have given thee living water [the Spirit]" (Jn 4:10).

Israel's thirst could not be satisfied by simply looking upon the rock in Horeb. Nor could it be slaked by standing and admiring its magnificence. Such action, persisted in, could only have brought death. It is not enough for man to gaze upon, admire, and worship Christ in the flesh. It is not enough for man to speak well of Christ's manhood, to compliment His character, or to strive to emulate His example or to follow His teachings. The unsmitten rock could not avail.

The rock must be smitten. No smiting, no water; no smiting, no satisfaction and no means of appropriation. There was no means of entry into the blessedness of God's Son or the benefits of His grace before He was smitten. His earthly life shuts us out from God by revealing the type of righteousness that God requires and what no man of himself can furnish. It is in the cleft rock that we find a hiding place—a place of refreshing and strength.

This is the third type of death that we have witnessed so far in the wilderness journey. There are five in all, each giving, like the five levitical offerings, a different aspect of Christ and Calvary. Through the Passover God speaks to us of redemption by blood from the penalty of sin. In the passage through the Red Sea God speaks to us of redemption by power from the slavery of sin, of separating men from bondage, and of making them victorious over the world by virtue of what He has wrought. In the smitten rock we behold the death of Christ providing new life through the Spirit. First, we behold redemption provided through the smiting, and then we see regeneration symbolized by drinking from the gushing waters that came forth as a result of the stroke. Both Calvary and Pentecost are seen here. The two must always be kept together.

7. The rock followed them. It is verified in 1 Corinthians 10:4 that that rock was Christ. Earlier we noted, in the same verse, "They drank of that spiritual Rock that followed them." Have you ever faced the question of how the benefits of the death of Christ, an event that transpired more than nineteen hundred years ago, could affect you and me at this present hour, removed as we are by the centuries? The answer is found in the crystal stream that followed this event. This stream first issued from Calvary. It manifested itself in the upper room (Jn 20:19-23) and at Pentecost, and it comes down to us as fresh as it was the day the Spirit was given. This crystal stream bears life-giving and redemptive powers that are as potent as when it issued from the cleft rock of Calvary.

There is nothing said in Exodus 17 about the people drinking, but in 1 Corinthians 10:4 we read, "They drank of that spiritual Rock." Of us it can be equally said that we "have been all made to drink into one Spirit" (12:13). "All" leaves no room here for a second work of grace. This is a serious error. To drink of one Spirit is the birthright and the heritage of every born-again believer. There is no such thing as a believer in Christ who has not received the Spirit. "Now if any man have not the Spirit of Christ, he is none of his" (Ro 8:9). Receiving the Spirit depends not upon our attainments but upon the finished work of the Son of God: "But as many as received him [Christ], to them gave he power to become the sons of God" (Jn 1:12). "Because ye are sons, God hath sent forth the Spirit of his Son into your hearts, crying, Abba, Father" (Gal 4:6).

There is a difference between receiving the Spirit, the heritage of all the children of God, and being filled with the Spirit, the privilege of those who are found fully in His will. All Christians have the Spirit indwelling them, but not all Christians are filled with the Spirit. The filling of the Spirit is open to all believers, but it is not appropriated by all. This fullness belongs to those who recognize the Spirit's presence and yield to His directing authority. The life is the same in all, but the manifestation of that life in terms of spiritual development is different in each believer.

John Ritchie reminds us that the Spirit of God dwells in every son of God, but that the manifestations may be varied in measure. The new-born babe in Christ has life in Christ. Every necessary organ is given at birth and needs only development. Such terms as "the higher life" and "the holy life" are misnomers. They convey unscriptural thoughts. The life is the same character in all. However, it can and does develop in different persons in varying degrees. There are carnal Christians and there are spiritual Christians. Paul describes the carnal Christian in 1 Corinthians 3:1-4: "And I, brethren, could not speak unto you as unto spiritual, but as unto carnal, even as unto babes in Christ. I have fed you with milk, and not with meat: for hitherto ye were not able to bear it, neither yet now are ye able. For ye are yet carnal: for whereas there is among you envying, and strife, and divisions, are ye not carnal, and walk as men? For while one saith, I am of Paul; and another, I am of Apollos; are ye not carnal?"

In 1 Corinthians 2 the apostle describes the spiritual Christian: "But God hath revealed them unto us by his Spirit: for the Spirit searcheth all things, yea, the deep things of God. For what man knoweth the things of a man, save the spirit of man which is in him? even so the things of God knoweth no man, but the Spirit of God. Now we have received, not the spirit of the world, but the spirit which is of God; that we might know the things that are freely given to us of God. Which things also we speak, not in the words which man's wisdom teacheth, but which the Holy Ghost teacheth; comparing spiritual things with spiritual. But the natural man receiveth not the things of the Spirit of God: for they are foolishness unto him: neither can he know them, because they are spiritually discerned. But he that is spiritual judgeth all things, yet he himself is judged of no man. For who hath known the mind of the Lord, that he may instruct him? But we have the mind of Christ" (vv. 10-16).

It is clear from these passages that there is no difference of character as far as the life is concerned; the difference appears in the development and growth of that life. The carnal Christian is called a babe. The spiritual Christian is called a mature man. "For every one that useth milk is unskilful in the word of righteousness: for he is a babe. But strong meat belongeth to them that are of full age, even those who by reason of use have their senses exercised to discern both good and evil" (Heb 5:13-14). Stephen was "a man full of faith and of the Holy Ghost" (Ac 6:5; cf. 7:55; 11:24). We are commanded, "Be filled with the Spirit" (Eph 5:18), and "Walk in the Spirit" (Gal 5:16). This is not optional; it is a command from the throne of God. How tragic it is for anyone to live in the shadows of a restricted life when God has made for us the wide ocean of His grace and power!

# 15

# THE BATTLE WITH AMALEK

As a person reads and studies the Scriptures with an open mind, there must surely come the abiding conviction that the book we call the Bible is none other than the Word of God. Only God could have written such a book; it is a revelation from heaven. Like the watermark of identification often seen in the best of stationery, particularly in evidence to those who scrutinize with discretion, so the Bible carries within its own texture adequate credentials of its authenticity, genuineness, and claims of inspiration. The very sequence of Israel's experience in their battle with Amalek furnishes another proof of the incomparable wisdom of the Bible.

How significant and instructive are the happenings in Exodus 17! As soon as Moses had provided water for the children of Israel, they discovered the presence of an unsuspected enemy, Amalek, who was kinsman in the flesh. This is where the Christian's battle begins. All saved persons are indwelt by the Holy Spirit, but not all realize this, and thus they fail to reckon upon the fact. The moment the believer discovers this truth concerning the personality and power of the Holy Spirit as symbolized by the water which sprang from the smitten rock, he not only experiences the deep satisfaction that quenches the thirst of his deepest needs, he is likewise aware of a new enemy, symbolized by Amalek. This enemy symbolizes our kinsman, the flesh.

## Amalek's Identity

Amalek was a grandson of Esau (Gen 36:12), named as one of the dukes in verse 16. The name "Esau" (Edom) means "ruddy." He was like Adam, that is, of the earth. He stands for the man after the flesh. Over against him stood Esau's twin brother, Jacob, who became Israel, and who represents the spiritual man. These twin brothers represent the two elements that are found here. In this battle with Amalek, we can see the beginning of a mortal combat. Family feuds are the most bitter. The struggle was intense between Israel and Amalek. Amalek's attack was without warning; it was sneaky, subtle, and treacherous. The Amalekites attacked Israel in the rear, pounced upon the weakest of the camp—those who fell behind through weakness, weariness, or illness. The devil also knows how to catch us off our guard.

The connection between this experience with Amalek and the earlier provision of water for Israel's needs is most marked and instructive. In 1 Corinthians 10:4 we learn: "That Rock was Christ." In John 7:37-39, we are told the running water is a type of the Holy Spirit. Just as soon as Israel discovered the new source of refreshing, the place for satisfying its thirst, the nation was brought face to face with a new enemy, "the flesh." This is obviously similar to the believer's conflict with his evil nature that resides within.

Apparently there was no strife in the home of Abraham as long as Ishmael dwelt alone in the house. But after Isaac had been born and weaned, we are told that Ishmael mocked Isaac and a crisis was created. This crisis found no abatement until Abraham had obeyed God's orders by putting Hagar, the mother of Ishmael, who symbolized the flesh, out of the house. No house is big enough for two wives or for two sets of offspring; therefore, when we discover the new nature that is given as a result of the new birth, the flesh rises up to mock us. In Romans 7 there is a description of what many believe to be Paul's own experience. Some fifty-nine times in this chapter we find the personal pronouns used: I, me, my, we, and our. Here is a portion of this chapter of conflict:

> For that which I do I allow not: for what I would, that do I not; but what I hate, that do I. If then I do that which I would not; I consent unto the law that it is good. Now then it is no more I that do it, but sin that dwelleth in me. For I know that in me (that is, in my flesh,) dwelleth no good thing: for to will is present with me; but how to perform that which is good I find not. For the good that I would I do not: but the evil which I would not, that I do. Now if I do that I would not, it is no more I that do it, but sin that dwelleth in me. I find then a law, that, when I would do good, evil is present with me. For I delight in the law of God after the inward man: but I see another law in my members, warring against the law of my mind, and bringing me into captivity to the law of sin which is in my members. O wretched man that I am! who shall deliver me from the body of this death? I thank God through Jesus Christ our Lord. So then with the mind I myself serve the law of God; but with the flesh the law of sin (Ro 7:15-25).

When we move into Romans 8, we come into the sphere of victory. The Holy Spirit was not mentioned even once in chapter 7, but He is mentioned eighteen times in chapter 8. It is the victory that the believer experiences where struggle ceases and there is complete dependence upon Christ. Here is a quotation from C. H. M.'s *Notes on the Book of Exodus:*

> Israel's conflict began when they stood in the full power of redemption, and had tasted "that spiritual meat, and drunk of that spiritual Rock." Until they met Amalek, they

> had nothing to do. They did not cope with Pharaoh; they did not break the power of Egypt, nor snap asunder the chains of its thraldom; they did not divide the sea, nor submerge Pharaoh's hosts beneath its waves; they did not bring down bread from heaven, nor draw forth water out of the flinty rock. They neither had done, nor could they do, any of these things; but now they are called to fight with Amalek. All the previous conflict had been between Jehovah and the enemy. They had to "stand still" and gaze upon the mighty triumphs of Jehovah's outstretched arm and enjoy the fruits of victory. The Lord had fought *for* them; but now he fights *in* or *by* them.

It has been the experience of nearly every true child of God that the real Christian struggle did not start until after he or she was brought somehow into the truth concerning the blessed presence, power, and function of the Holy Spirit within. The moment a person drinks deeply of this truth, "Amalek" shows his enmity: "For the flesh lusteth against the Spirit, and the Spirit against the flesh: and these are contrary the one to the other: so that ye cannot do the things that ye would" (Gal 5:17). When the Holy Spirit took up His abode in us, in consequence of the accomplished work that was wrought upon Calvary's cross by the Holy One of God, then we began to abhor ourselves and to see ourselves as the chiefest of sinners.

The war in Rephidim with Israel foreshadows that conflict known only to those who have been redeemed to God, delivered from the authority of darkness, and severed from the present evil world.

## The Source of Victory

"Then came Amalek, and fought with Israel in Rephidim. And Moses said unto Joshua, Choose us out men, and go out, fight with Amalek: tomorrow I will stand on the top of the hill with the rod of God in mine hand. So Joshua did as Moses had said to him, and fought with Amalek: and Moses, Aaron, and Hur went up to the top of the hill. And it came to pass, when Moses held up his hand, that Israel prevailed: and when he let down his hand, Amalek prevailed. But Moses' hands were heavy; and they took a stone, and put it under him, and he sat thereon; and Aaron and Hur stayed up his hands, the one on the one side, and the other on the other side; and his hands were steady until the going down of the sun. And Joshua discomfited Amalek and his people with the edge of the sword" (Ex 17:8-13).

Israel's source of victory lay in two things, namely, warfare and intercession. The warfare was in the valley; Joshua led the armies against his kinsman Amalek and those identified with him. His weapon was the sword that reminds us of our weapon in such a warfare—the Word of God, which is the "sword of the Spirit" (Eph 6:17). On the hill was Moses, who was making intercession. Moses' hands grew heavy as he held up the rod that insured victory in the valley. When his hands went down, Amalek prevailed; when his hands stayed up, Israel prevailed. It was a seesaw battle; victory and defeat came intermittently. Therefore, the real source of victory rested with the man on the hill. This is an important lesson and one that we would all do well to learn. The victory of the believer rests not in his own dexterity, boldness, or weapons, but upon the man on the hill, the man in glory, even our High Priest, the Lord Jesus Christ. His arms never grow weary. The victory of Israel was assured by the act of Aaron and Hur; they stayed the hands of Moses until sundown. How grateful we are that our High Priest's hands never grow heavy. He constantly remains the same.

How many of our acquaintances, who have been otherwise sincere and struggling Christians, have been led astray as a result of a misunderstanding concerning the great truth of the indwelling Spirit. All too many make the mistake of considering regeneration an act of eradication or a total change of the old nature. Nothing could be further from the truth. The old man remains, and he will remain as long as we remain in the flesh.

This mistake of eradication is accompanied by a false belief that when one is born again, the Holy Spirit purifies and makes him ready for heaven. Were he to die at that moment, he would go straight to heaven; but if he were to sin, he would have to have a new "sterilization." Otherwise, he could not be a fit subject for heaven. One fault leads to another; the second grows out of the first.

Advocates who believe that one is made fit for heaven by regeneration find it necessary to maintain perfection in this state, and for them, to sin means apostasy. From their point of view, sin would make a Christian unholy and therefore unfit for heaven. It must be done all over again. We need to learn the fact, so clearly set forth in Scripture, that our redemption rests not in our regeneration and not in our new birth but in the blood of the Lord Jesus Christ. We need to put our faith where God put our sins. We need to look away from self and realize that the act of God, not our act, is the source of assurance. The Holy Spirit comes in to interpret and to make real and effective in the lives of believers the benefits that were accomplished for us on Calvary's cross.

Our warfare is a real one; it is not shadow-boxing or an imaginary fight. Our victory is in Him, the man in glory, through the blessed Holy Spirit within us. In Scripture, we are told that we have, as believers, two Advocates. The first Advocate is the Lord Jesus Christ at God's right hand; The other is the Paraclete (Holy Spirit) within who makes intercession with groanings that cannot be uttered (Ro 8:26). In other words, we have two Advocates or Paracletes; one is in the court of heaven, keeping up our reputation before God. "He ever liveth to make intercession" (Heb 7:25). The other Advocate, who lives within, struggles in His attempt to move our state up to our standing. "In like manner the Spirit also helpeth our infirmities . . . the Spirit himself maketh intercession for us" (Ro 8:26, ERV).

Another mistake that is often made along this line is that, since we have a perfect man in glory who intercedes for us before the throne of grace, and we have a perfect Spirit within us, and we recognize and surrender to the Spirit, all struggles and fighting must cease. This doctrine is quite similar to the doctrine of eradication of the flesh that has done such harm.

## The Decree Against Amalek

"And the Lord said unto Moses, Write this for a memorial in a book, and rehearse it in the ears of Joshua: for I will utterly put out the remembrance of Amalek from under heaven. . . . The Lord hath sworn that the Lord will have war with Amalek from generation to generation" (Ex 17:14-16).

In this Christian warfare, which is but a segment of the battle of the ages, there must be no compromise. One cannot spare the flesh. It will be remembered that Saul was commanded to smite the Amalekites, and to utterly destroy all, together with their possessions. This is the same generation, the descendants of Amalek. Did Saul carry out the command of the Lord? No, he feared the people, we are told, and spared King Agag for the sake of displaying the victory. He had captured a real, live king! He spared also the fat cattle. Keep in mind that it was the Amalekites that eventually slew Saul (2 Sa 1:6-10). We are not to spare the flesh. We are told to make no provision for the flesh to fulfill the lusts thereof.

The decree against the flesh is the decree of death.

> Mortify therefore your members which are upon the earth; fornication, uncleannesses, inordinate affection, evil concupiscence, and covetousness, which is idolatry: for which things' sake the wrath of God cometh on the children of disobedience: in the which ye also walked some time, when ye lived in them. But now ye also put off all these; anger, wrath, malice, blasphemy, filthy communication out of your mouth. Lie not one to another, seeing that ye have put off the old man with his deeds; and have put on the new man, which is renewed in knowledge after the image of him that created him (Col 3:5-10).

The flesh can never be tamed; its nature is incorrigible. "The carnal mind is enmity against God: for it is not subject to the law of God, neither indeed can be" (Ro 8:7). All through Israel's history we are made aware of this unconquered enemy; even Haman, in the book of Esther, who secured the decree of death for all Jews, was a descendant of Amalek. We must never underestimate the strength of our enemy; neither should we forget the strength of the Captain of our salvation. "Greater is he that is in you, than he that is in the world" (1 Jn 4:4).

# 16

# THE GIVING OF THE LAW

In the battle with Amalek, Israel discovered the closeness of its enemy. It was among the nations related to it by blood. Amalek's defeat was temporary, for God said, "The Lord will have war with Amalek from generation to generation" (Ex 17:16). Since the truth concerning Amalek's character, power, and temporary defeat had been demonstrated, God had to reveal the one instrument that could deal with "sin in the flesh," namely, the law. "The sting of death is sin; and the strength of sin is the law" (1 Co 15:56).

The flesh is the enemy exposed and opposed in the wilderness. How often we hear the voice of the flesh, murmuring, chiding, complaining, and finding fault with Moses, Aaron, and God. "And in the morning, then ye shall see the glory of the Lord; for that he heareth your murmurings against the Lord; and what are we, that ye murmur against us? And Moses said, This shall be, when the Lord shall give you in the evening flesh to eat, and in the morning bread to the full; for that the Lord heareth your murmurings which ye murmer against him: and what are we? Your murmurings are not against us, but against the Lord. And Moses spake unto Aaron, Say unto all the congregation of the children of Israel, Come near before the Lord: for he hath heard your murmurings" (Ex 16:7-9).

Up to this time God had dealt with Israel on the ground of pure grace. Their complaints, their murmurings, and their unfaithfulness were met with divine graciousness. "And Moses went up unto God, and the LORD called unto him out of the mountain, saying, Thus shalt thou say to the house of Jacob, and tell the children of Israel; Ye have seen what I did unto the Egyptians, and how I bare you on eagles' wings, and brought you unto myself. Now therefore, if ye will obey my voice indeed, and keep my covenant, then ye shall be a peculiar treasure unto me above all people: for all the earth is mine: and ye shall be unto me a kingdom of priests, and an holy nation. These are the words which thou shalt speak unto the children of Israel" (19:3-6). This covenant of grace made with Abraham four hundred years earlier was of unmingled grace. It proposed no conditions, it made no demands, it put no yoke on the neck, and it laid no burden on the shoulder.

Now God had to deal with them harshly. Up to this point, He had dealt with them as sons; now He had to deal with them as hired servants under the law, because of their disobedience. They had asked for it. Their self-righteousness and their darkened minds in this disastrous moment met Jehovah's offer of a covenant of works with these words, "And all the people answered together, and said, All that the LORD hath spoken we will do. And Moses returned the words of the people unto the LORD" (v. 8).

## THE SHIFTING OF COVENANTS

While the Israelites were brought under a temporary covenant of law or works, we are strongly reminded in Paul's letter to the Galatians that the introduction of this covenant in no sense annulled, set aside, or abrogated the covenant of pure grace made with Abraham, Isaac, and Jacob. This covenant involved the promise of a seed and a land. "And this I say, that the covenant, that was confirmed before of God in Christ, the law, which was four hundred and thirty years after, cannot disannul, that it should make the promise of none effect. For if the inheritance be of the law, it is no more of promise: but God gave it to Abraham by promise" (Gal 3:17-18).

From the moment that the unanimous chorus, "We will do," was heard (Ex 19:8), a new order was invoked. Instead of being as sons on a father's bounty, the nation is now reduced to the status of servants on the basis of merit and demerit. Jehovah spoke from the mount, covered in a thick cloud, with thunderous tones, warning the people to remain at a distance. "Whosoever toucheth the mount shall be surely put to death" (v. 12). The people quaked; the law filled them with fear. It was terrible, "and so terrible was the sight, that Moses said, I exceedingly fear and quake" (Heb 12:21). God was moved at a moral distance, and these sinful people were too close for their own good.

### The Nature of the Law

The law is tailor-made for the flesh; it fits the natural man. "For what the law could not do, in that it was weak through the flesh, God sending his own Son in the likeness of sinful flesh, and for sin, condemned sin in the flesh" (Ro 8:3). The law does not fit the "new man," the spiritual man, any more than buggy harness fits an automobile or a locomotive coalstoker fits a jet plane. The law is concerned with external acts of obedience; grace involves internal motives. The law commands a person who has no strength to comply with its demands, and then inflicts a penalty on him for failure; grace entreats a person who is supplied with merit and strength not his own, and rewards him for the display of these virtues. The law bids man to "do," grace says, "It is done"; the law bids us to be taken up with self-weakness and failure; grace asks only that we be taken up with God—His Person, His work, and His glory. Under the law, God demands righteousness which man cannot produce; grace bestows righteousness as a free gift through faith upon the unworthy.

## The Ministry of the Law

The purpose of the law as set forth in Scripture is to make sin "break out," just as our grandmothers used to give a certain "tea" to make the measles come to the surface. "Wherefore then serveth the law? It was added because of transgressions, till the seed should come to whom the promise was made; and it was ordained by angels in the hand of a mediator" (Gal 3:19). The expression "because of transgressions" means "to give to sin the character of transgression." The law is like a thermometer—it detects fever but does not treat it. Or it is like a looking glass—it reveals blemishes, but it does not wash or cleanse.

The law in itself, we are told, is holy, just, and good (Ro 7:12). The trouble is not with the law but with man. "Was then that which is good made death unto me? God forbid. But sin, that it might appear sin, working death in me by that which is good; that sin by the commandment might become exceeding sinful" (v. 13). "The law . . . was weak through the flesh" (8:3).

The law was given as a stopper for man's mouth! "Now we know that what things soever the law saith, it saith to them who are under the law: that every mouth may be stopped, and all the world may become guilty before God" (Ro 3:19).

One hot summer day in Alabama some years ago, when the writer's wife was expecting company and needed some extra ice, a dispatch was made to the nearby ice plant. The writer's three-year-old daughter insisted on going along for the ride. Twenty-five pounds of ice was purchased and placed on the running-board of the car, and the return trip was completed. The ice, now weighing a little less than twenty-five pounds, was lifted from the running-board, whereupon the three-year-old daughter insisted on carrying it into the house. The father said, "No," but the daughter said, "Yes, Daddy, let me show you." "You cannot carry the ice," insisted the father. "Yes," said the daughter, so down went the ice on the sidewalk, and the three-year-old daughter began to pull this way and that way, but could not move it. Finally, looking a little sheepish, she said, "Daddy, you take it." The father did not put down that ice expecting his daughter to carry it, he put it down to stop her mouth. Man continues to boast about what he can do, like the Israelites in the wilderness. But God handed his chosen people the law and said, "See how you can get along with this!"

The law neither justifies the sinner nor sanctifies the believer (cf. Gal 3:2-3, 11-12, 16). Ritchie puts it this way:

> To the believer, the law with its demands, has no terror. He knows that in Christ its claims have all been met for him. "What the law *could not* do, in that it was weak through the flesh, God sending His own Son in the likeness of sinful flesh, and for sin, condemned sin in the flesh" (Romans 8:3). "Christ is the end of the law for righteousness to every one that believeth" (Romans 10:4). In Christ the believer is judicially dead to the law: it has no further claim upon him. He is able to look at it full in the face, and say, "I through the law died to the law, that I might live with God" (Galatians 2:19 RV). "I have been crucified with Christ" (Galatians 2:20 RV). The law cannot apprehend or condemn a dead man; and the believer has become "dead to the law by the body of Christ" (Romans 7:4). He stands now in Christ, risen and possessed of a new life, united to a new husband,

and controlled by a new power. "The *law* of the Spirit of life in Christ Jesus hath made me free from the *law* of sin and death," (Romans 8:2) is the language and experience of his soul.

But it has been said, the law is the believer's "rule of life." This was what the Galatians were seeking to make it. They had begun with grace but had returned to the law as a "rule of life." "Ye are not *under* the law but under grace" (Romans 6:14) is God's answer to this. The believer is a child in the Father's house (Luke 15:32; 1 Jn 3:1), a subject of its rule. He is in the Kingdom of God's dear Son (Colossians 1:13): he confesses and acknowledges Jesus as His Lord (1 Corinthians 12:3; Philippians 3:8), and all this brings with it responsibility. But his obedience is prompted by love. His subjection is not in the spirit of a slave, but of a son. He serves in the liberty of one who has access and welcome to the innermost circle of Divine favour and love. He is not a lawless person; neither is he a legalist; he walks and serves in "the liberty wherewith Christ made him free" (Galatians 5:1). This honour belongs to all the saints. See that you do not let it slip then, dear fellow-believer, or lose it by worldliness, or in the mists of human tradition. Let Christ be your object. Set Him before you as your example. Honour Him only as your Lord. Let His Word alone be as your rule and guide (*From Egypt to Canaan*).

## Law and Grace Contrasted

The quaint words of John Bunyan express the basic difference between law and grace:

Run, John, run, the Law commands,
But gives me neither legs nor hands.
Far grander news the gospel brings;
It bids me fly, and gives me wings.

# 17

# THE GOLDEN CALF

In unmistakable terms, the New Testament sets forth the seriousness of the golden calf incident with these words, "Neither be ye idolaters, as were some of them; as it is written, The people sat down to eat and drink, and rose up to play" (1 Co 10:7). This tragic affair, found in Exodus 32, demonstrates a new low in Israel's rebellion against God. We shudder with the thought of a sin so heinous as to provoke Moses to cast down the two tablets of the Decalogue, which he had just received from the hands of God. In addition to this, twenty-three thousand perished in one day (v. 28). Since "all these things happened unto them for ensamples: and they are written for our admonition, upon whom the ends of the age are come" (1 Co 10:11), we find in Exodus 32 certain pertinent and profitable lessons.

## A Picture in Contrast

In the preceding twelve chapters of Exodus, we have been taken up with the scene of Moses in the mountain surrounded by the tokens of the majestic presence of Jehovah. The lightning flashed, the thunder rolled, and the mountain trembled. Moses worshiped while the people in the valley reveled. Divinely sustained, Moses spent forty days alone with God on Mount Sinai. It was there that he received the law and the pattern of the things in heaven—the wilderness tabernacle that was to speak of the incomparable Christ.

Then suddenly the scene shifts from the mount of God to the valley below, there to behold the melancholy wreck which man makes of everything his hand touches. "And when the people saw that Moses delayed to come down out of the mount, the people gathered themselves together unto Aaron, and said unto him, Up, make us gods, which shall go before us; for as for this Moses, the man that brought us up out of the land of Egypt, we wot not what is become of him" (Ex 32:1). It is difficult for us to believe that such degradation and display of depravity could be possible on the part of a people who, during a three-month period, had been sheltered by blood, redeemed by power, overshadowed by the guiding cloud, fed by the manna, and privileged to drink from the smitten rock. Even while they were debauching themselves, there towered above them the smoking Mount Sinai. With all of this we hear the people demand of Aaron, "Make us gods" (v. 1), thereby revealing, amid such sublime surroundings, their demand for gods which could neither hear nor speak nor see.

In such a picture we have set before us the moral distance that separates man from God. This is, as we know, a distance that only infinite grace can span. Here again we see the emphasis of the two great lessons that God wanted to teach Israel in the wilderness as well as those disposed to hear: to know God, and then to know man in the flesh.

## A Potential in Leadership

Viewing this scene before us, we are made aware of the importance of leadership. This is illustrated in the contrast between the two men, Moses and Aaron. Prior to this time, the people had made known their preference for a mediator.

They did not want to come into the near presence of God. Whether we are willing to admit it or not, most of us are just as close to God as we want to be. In response to the people's suggestion, Moses took himself up the side of Mount Sinai, where he spent forty days. The seventy elders accompanied Moses part of the way, but they too were content with having seen the sapphire stone beneath God's feet and to have eaten and drunk in his presence (Ex 24:10-11). It did not take much to satisfy even the best.

In the absence of Moses, the great leader, the people became restless and impatient. They complained,—"We wot not what is become of him" (32:1). They were soon ready for a new leader—one of their own choosing, namely, Aaron.

How pertinent this lesson is! Once Moses was out of sight, the smoldering passions that burned within the souls of the people who had so recently left Egypt burst out in an open and consuming flame. Here again we are reminded of the restraining influence exerted by the presence of a great and noble leader. The golden calf incident could never have transpired if Moses had been present. It was the very absence of leadership that broke the heart of our Lord as He looked upon the multitude and beheld them as sheep without a shepherd—a confused multitude without a leader (Mt 9:36).

Recognizing the potential that rests in leadership as exemplified in Moses, our attention is now called to the perils of weak leadership as exemplified in Aaron and his conduct in the first crisis he faced. Aaron became the time-saver, the compromiser, the situation-adapter, the servant of the people rather than the servant of God. A further weakness of Aaron was manifested in his excuse-making when confronted by Moses. He told Moses the people had given him gold. "Then I cast it into the fire, and there came out this calf" (Ex 32:24). Someone has said that an excuse is the skin of a reason stuffed with a lie. The classic in this category is found in the New Testament: "He, willing to justify himself" (Lk 10:29). Few things are more ridiculous than an attempt at self-defense when no defense exists.

## The Petulance of Impatience

"And when the people saw that Moses delayed to come down out of the mount, the people gathered themselves together unto Aaron, and said unto him, Up, make us gods, which shall go before us; for as for this Moses, the man that brought us up out of the land of Egypt, we wot not what is become of him" (Ex 32:1). Perhaps the highest grace in the New Testament is that of patience, the ability to wait without wavering, the disposition to trust the Word in the face of adverse circumstances.

Notice the proximity of the two incompatible events—Moses was in the mount with God while the people were committing lewdness in the valley. These were not pagans; remember, those who "sat down to eat and drink, and rose up to play" (v. 6) were the same people who had just been redeemed by the blood in Egypt. They are the same people who had been sustained by the miracles in the wilderness and led by the pillar of cloud.

Impatience is the enemy of faith. Abraham, in a moment of impatience, took Hagar to wife and begat Ishmael. Saul, before battle, became impatient because of the delay of Samuel. He took upon himself the function of a priest, offered a sacrifice, and thereby lost the kingdom. Impatience can well be defined as an attempt to do for oneself that which God has not done or has delayed in doing.

## The Portents of Idolatry

"Neither be ye idolators, as were some of them; as it is

written, The people sat down to eat and drink, and rose up to play" (1 Co 10:7).

The golden calf incident is a clear illustration of the nature of the sin of idolatry. The Greek word for "idolatry" is *eidōlolatreia,* from *eidōlon,* "idol" (that which is seen). Fallen human nature is not nonreligious; only the carnal man by nature is "incurably religious." The religion of the carnal man demands something upon which his eyes can feast—something tangible. Even the saved and enlightened individual must be aware of the gravity that is constantly exerted, pulling toward the earth things material, touchable, and visible. Moses had gone up on high, and because he delayed to return, Israel made a god that they could see. So it is today. Christendom prefers a human priest, a little piece of bread that may be seen and handled, to the divine Priest who has passed into the heavens.

Moses was in the mountain, Aaron was left alone with the people, and the golden calf was the outcome. Here is exemplified the moral tendency of those who want to worship but who will not wait for the divine instruction concerning the method of approach. In other words, we have a priest without a prophet. The prophet is one who goes in before God and receives a divine message and then goes out to speak to the people on behalf of God. The priest, on the other hand, reverses the order. He begins with sinful man. He is supposed to proceed along a divinely prescribed course of sacrifice and cleansing, finally reaching the presence of God. He thus represents man before God.

The whole procedure is set before us in the wilderness tabernacle with its sacrifices, its priesthood, and its offerings. At the very time Moses was receiving the law and instructions concerning the tabernacle, that so plainly tell the way of approach, the children of Israel were devising their own method of worship. At the moment the golden calf was being set up in the valley, Moses was being given instructions in the mountain. But the impatient people could not wait. They had to set up their own humanly devised systems, mostly copied from Egypt. A prophet without a priest is a way without implementation; like the law, it is a demand without ability to perform; a worship without knowledge. Zeal without knowledge is worship run riot, worship that knows no blood redemption, and worship according to human taste and opinion. Like the spider that spins her web out of herself, priestcraft spins its plans out of carnal minds. The women broke off their ornaments, an offering in which the flesh delighted, and gave them to Aaron to cast into the furnace. According to Aaron, "There came out this calf" (Ex 32:24). We have had the calf with us ever since.

In the study of this incident of the golden calf, one is struck by the irresistible fascination of idolatry. It is always so where there is a priest without a prophet. That howling, leaping crowd tells what sort of religion men would evolve if left to themselves. In its individual application, idolatry is anything that comes between God and the human soul. Any thing, any person, or any institution that holds first place, the place reserved for God, is the object of idolatry. The New Testament refers to covetousness as idolatry. Idolatry in its corporate sense, as we see here, not only places emphasis on emotionalism and things but on emotionalism run riot. A religion without a prophet is a religion that substitutes sincerity and enthusiasm for doctrine and correctness before God.

Roman Catholicism is built on a system of priestcraft without a prophet. This system of priestcraft was initiated about the time of the supposed conversion of the emperor Constantine in the fourth century. Christianity was made popular, and whole armies were baptized. The influx of multitudes fresh from paganism into the churches, people who know nothing of regeneration, made it necessary to devise plans of worship that would actually be an adaptation of worship to the heathenism from which they had so recently come. Bibles were scarce, and services were held in Latin. The whole order grew out of a pagan expedient. This system of priestcraft brought on a thousand years of the Dark Ages. Liberalism in our day is an attempt to worship without the Word. This produces a worship that excludes the idea of man's need for redemption and atonement. The whole elaborate, liturgical system, with its forms, altars, and ceremonies, is but the revival of the golden calf technique.

## The Pretense of Piety

The Israelites did not propose to forsake the worship of Jehovah but only to make an adaptation by the introduction of an Egyptian expedient. Aaron shouted, "These be thy gods, O Israel, which brought thee up out of the land of Egypt" (Ex 32:4). Aaron, in order to make it appear more orthodox, built an altar and offered burnt offerings and brought peace offerings (v. 6). The sin offering was noticably absent.

The greatest enemy of Christianity today is not pure paganism but the introduction of pagan methods into the worship of the true and living God. The idea of the golden calf was brought from Egypt; this was the chief symbol of Egyptian worship. God speaks of glory, but there was no blood. All the world will join the believer in worshiping the God of glory and even the Christ of Bethlehem, but most find repugnant even the mention of the cross. The golden calf worship combined hypocrisy and lewdness: "And the people sat down to eat and to drink, and rose up to play" (v. 6). It was a way that augmented man's pleasure and suited his natural taste. Today we see a repetition of this lewdness and hypocrisy by the introduction of pageantry and play into the worship of the Lord Jesus Christ.

The children of Israel, in worshiping the calf, had a piety without purity and a pretext without substance. The rankest liberals are great worshipers. Their buildings are often ornate, their robes elegant, and their liturgies beautiful in sequence and impressive to the natural religious instincts of mankind. It has been rightly said that "all men are religious." This is true. There is no real virtue in worship. Worship becomes virtuous only when it is exercised in spirit and in truth.

The children of Israel were extravagant in their gifts of gold to a cause that was wholly degrading. Their enthusiasm ran riot as the noise of their revelry fell upon the ears of Joshua and Moses. They attributed to the golden calf, made by hands, the works of Jehovah in leading them out of Egypt. They built an altar, proclaimed a feast, and offered burnt offerings and peace offerings. This erratic and impious procedure seemed not to shock their sensibilities or produce within their souls a sense of horror. Only the contrary is true: "They sat down to eat and to drink, and rose up to play."

## The Perils of Judgment

One of the strangest features of the golden calf episode is Aaron's seeming unawareness of the fact that his participation in such horrible idolatry would call down upon himself and the people immediate and severe divine retribution. The question arises, How could Aaron, who had witnessed the plagues in Egypt, and who had seen the lightning flash and heard the thunder roll about Sinai's brow, be so forgetful? The answer is to be found in the fact that sin carries its own deadening opiate and blinding effect. It is everywhere evident that only in the light of divine judgment and a consciousness of one's accountability before God is the hideousness of sin comprehended.

Upon Israel came the awesome and fearful judgments of Jehovah. Even while the children of Israel were participating in their religious orgy, God was making known to Moses what was transpiring in the valley below. In righteousness, God was ready to consume the people. He said, "Let me alone, that my wrath may wax hot against them, and that I may consume them: and I will make of thee a great nation" (Ex 32:10). Moses became an intercessor in behalf of his people and made a plea for mercy on the grounds of the divine covenant and the holy name of God. We need to remember that this was before Moses had looked upon the scene about which God had spoken; however, it occurred as soon as Moses had turned and gone down the mountain with the two tablets. "And it came to pass, as soon as he came nigh unto the camp, that he saw the calf, and the dancing: and Moses' anger waxed hot, and he cast the tablets out of his hands, and brake them beneath the mount" (v. 19). This drastic and dramatic scene of the broken covenant has through the intervening centuries served to arrest and warn mankind in his idolatrous descent.

Moses, after having looked upon the scene before him, agreed with God and initiated judgment by burning the golden calf, grinding the remains into powder, casting the powder upon water, and making the people to drink the shame and humiliation of the nation. Judgment did not stop here. "Then Moses stood in the gate of the camp, and said, Who is on the LORD's side? Let him come unto me. And all the sons of Levi gathered themselves together unto him" (v. 26). Sin against the person of God, as in all cases of idolatrous worship and practice, calls for drastic measures. The sons of Levi gathered themselves to Moses, each with a sword by his side. "And there fell of the people that day about three thousand men" (v. 28). There had to be judgment in the camp first and then a call for consecration (vv. 29-30). Moses cast himself in the breach, atonement was found, and grace prevailed.

# 18

# THE MIXED MULTITUDE

"And the mixt multitude that was among them fell a lusting: and the children of Israel also wept again, and said, Who shall give us flesh to eat? We remember the fish, which we did eat in Egypt freely; the cucumbers, and the melons, and the leeks, and the onions, and the garlick: but now our soul is dried away: there is nothing at all, beside this manna, before our eyes" (Num 11:4-6).

There is something strangely familiar in the term *mixt multitude* (v. 4). It is significant that we read in Exodus 12, on the occasion of Israel's departure out of Egypt: "A mixed multitude went up also with them" (v. 38). Nearly two years passed, during which we hear nothing of this motley group. When next we do hear, it is that they rebelled against the manna, the heavenly diet. Israel was on the march, and God had mightily undertaken for His people.

Under the judgment of the plagues God had "put a difference between the Egyptians and Israel" (11:7). This difference had finally been manifested in the judgment of death against the firstborn and the redemption by blood that followed. The second stage of redemption was about to take place—redemption by power. Israel was being led out, separated from the land of bondage and death. Having first been sheltered by the blood of the Paschal Lamb, they were now being led out of Egypt for the stated purpose that they might hold a feast unto the Lord. "Let my people go" (Ex 5:1). This is always the divine command. There were no altars in Egypt. The people were being led out so that God might lead them in.

It strikes us as a bit odd, as we read the account of this dramatic exodus of a nation, to discover that which seems at the time parenthetical: "And a mixed multitude went up also with them; and flocks and herds, even very much cattle" (12:38). It was a glorious affair, and God was delivering His people with a mighty hand. But right in the midst of the account is found a reference to a mixed multitude. Why did the near perfection of the picture have to be marred by this reference to the mixed multitude?

This is true in life. In the parable of the sower, first the field was sown with good seed and then was sown again, this time with tares, by the evil one. The very nature of Satan and evil is to work confusion and to mix matters. God separates: "And God divided the light from the darkness . . . God . . . divided the waters which were under the firmament from the waters which were above the firmament" (Gen 1:4,7). Men are great mixers. We often hear pulpit committees, selected to find a pastor, state that they are looking for a young man who is a good mixer. Someone has reminded us that what most of our churches need is not a good mixer but a good separator. Already there has been entirely too much mixing. We are living in an age that has gone beside itself in the art of mixing creeds and mixing the church and the world. There is an unholy mixture everywhere of things that should be separated.

According to the standard of our present order, if you can get a Jewish rabbi, a Catholic priest, and a Protestant minister to meet together in the town hall for a program, you have moved the world appreciably further on the road to a new order. Many loose-jointed, world-minded religionists would have us believe that tolerance is better than righteousness. We are witnessing the mixing of the saved with the unsaved, believers with infidels, the church with the world, and light with darkness. As a result, there is much calling of evil, good and good, evil. Moral confusion is all but complete. Without doubt the failure to recognize and to deal scripturally and effectively with the mixed multitude in Christian churches serves as a great deterrent to both spiritual power and scriptural orthodoxy, to say nothing of true fellowship and effective service. There are two laws in the spiritual world that must never be divorced, namely, creation and separation. This is clearly exemplified in the creation story: "And God said, Let there be light: and there was light. And God saw the light, that it was good: and God divided the light from the darkness" (Gen 1:3-4).

## The Identity of the Mixed Multitude

The mixed multitude that accompanied Israel out of Egypt should be accounted for. Who were they and why did they come? They were certainly not Israelites; neither were they said to be Egyptians. They were a mixed multitude. They were camp followers, perhaps attracted by the excitement which accompanied the exodus. They were disgruntled and dissatisfied with Egypt, and they were ready for anything that promised a change. They had been caught up in the current of a great movement, like trash and driftwood lifted and moved by a swollen stream. Others were probably attracted by their love for the spectacular. Some perhaps had intermarried with the Israelites and came for family reasons. This same mixed multitude is with us today. They have been caught in the fine meshes of an overwrought desire to count members—a movement that is sometimes substituted for evangelism.

Like the soldiers who gambled under the cross for the garments of Christ, this mixed multitude desires the benefits and blessings of Christianity without caring in the slightest for the truth of our Lord. They refuse Christ, but they accept the garments of Christianity. Some of the mixed multitude that went up with Israel were most likely drawn by Israel's characteristic peculiarity. There are many people with us today who take delight in being peculiar. The Lord knows that we have them in our churches. They are not "a peculiar people" (Titus 2:14); they are just peculiar. Again some of the mixed multitude have been drawn by the marching millions. To many, this pageantry offers irresistible temptation. They know nothing of the cause, but they are thrilled to be with the crowd.

It is a pretty sure guess that many who went along when Israel moved out of Egypt did so for no other reason than that of a desire for a change. There are lots of folk who do not know what they want. They only know that they do not want what they have.

## The History of the Mixed Multitude

Very little, if anything, had been heard from this mixed multitude for more than eighteen months. God had led the hosts of Israel through the Red Sea dry-shod. For them He had sweetened the bitter waters of Marah and rained down manna from heaven. A rock smitten by divine command had yielded water to break their thirst. The sloping heights of Mount Sinai had witnessed the giving of the Law and the instructions for building the tabernacle, and the tabernacle itself had been set up. At last the cloud lifted, and Israel moved toward Kadesh-barnea, the borderland of Canaan, the place of testing. A crisis arose over the rations. A food riot was on. Insurrection was inevitable. "And the mixt multitude that was among them fell a lusting: and the children of Israel also wept again, and said, Who shall give us flesh to eat? We remember the fish, which we did eat in Egypt freely; the cucumbers, and the melons, and the leeks, and the onions, and the garlick: but now our soil is dried away: there is nothing at all, beside this manna, before our eyes. And the manna was as coriander seed and the colour thereof as the colour of bdellium" (Num 11:4-7).

The secret long hidden finally comes out in the fourth verse. The mixed multitude must have been the starting point of much of the trouble and complaining that has occurred since the children of Israel left Egypt. "And the mixt multitude . . . fell a lusting" (v. 4). If it had only stopped there, it would not have been so bad. But we read on: "And the children of Israel also wept again, and said, "Who shall give us flesh to eat?" The mixed multitude started the complaining, but it did not end with them. The people of God have the flesh in them. This flesh can be activated by carnal influences emanating from others. "A little leaven leaveneth the whole lump" (1 Co 5:6). It does not take a large group to disrupt a congregation. The bark of a dog can arouse a whole pack of hounds. Many pastors' hearts have been broken and the work in their churches greatly hampered by the vociferous voice of a disgruntled few.

In regard to the mixed multitude, what went wrong? When God was about to rain down manna, He told Moses: "Behold, I will rain bread from heaven for you; and the people shall go out and gather a certain rate every day, that I may prove them, whether they will walk in my law, or no" (Ex 16:4).

The mixed multitude was being tested by their reaction and attitude toward the manna. Here in this passage we have the results. They despised the manna, the bread that came down from heaven, and longed for cucumbers, melons, leeks, onions, garlic, and the fleshpots of Egypt. How revealing indeed! In truth, they had accompanied Israel but had never lost their Egyptian appetite. They remembered and longed for Egypt's highly flavored, spicy, and aromatic food—food that had but little nutritive value. Because of this they grew weary of the divinely provided manna. First, it tasted like "wafers made with honey" (Ex 16:31); later it tasted like "fresh oil" (Num 11:8). But when they remembered the fleshpots of Egypt, they lost their taste for manna. Too many of the mixed multitudes within our churches have grown weary of the food of the saints. Christ is not enough for them. They are calling for Christ *and* the world. There is too much sameness in the gospel of God's grace. Notice that, as the manna grew to be despised, the people attempted to add variety:

"And the people went about, and gathered it, and ground it in mills, or beat it in a mortar, and baked it in pans, and made cakes of it: and the taste of it was as the taste of fresh oil" (Num 11:8).

Once the mixed multitude had brought to mind the fleshpots of Egypt, they said, "We remember the fish, which we did eat in Egypt freely; the cucumbers, and the melons, and the leeks, and the onions, and the garlick: but now our soul is dried away" (Num 11:6). Thoughts of onions and cucumbers at once destroyed their appetites for heavenly manna.

C. A. Moates, in *An Outline of the Book of Numbers,* reminds us, "The food of the world is tasty to the natural man, and if we have known it in the times past of our lives, we have to watch against influences which tend to revive old lusts. We may be sure that the flesh will hanker after what suits it, so that our only security is to walk in the Spirit. If we drop down from that, we are at once on the level of the flesh, and nothing suits the flesh but Egypt's food—despising the manna brings out that the flesh has no inward appreciation of Christ."

## "Doctoring" the Manna

With thoughts of Egypt's food in mind, we hear a new and strange thing: "And the people went about, and gathered it, and ground it in mills, or beat it in a mortar, and baked it in pans, and made cakes of it: and the taste of it was as the taste of fresh oil" (Num 11:8). Here we behold an attempt to "doctor" or to season the heavenly food, grinding it in mills or beating it in mortars. This is very different from what we read in Exodus 16:23, where God told the people: "Bake . . . and seethe." Since the manna in its natural state was despised, the people resorted to a variety of methods of serving it. Evidently the attempt was to make the manna more palatable for those who had little or no appetite for the manna as it came from heaven.

The mixed multitude, both then and now, must be served with a variety program in music and entertainment. They must have interpretive dancing, drama, and religious pageantry, which become the counterpart of the fleshpots of Egypt. It is a deplorable fact that the mixed multitude led others astray. The presence of such a group creates dissension and dissatisfaction with God's own people. Unity is destroyed and confusion reigns.

The mixed multitude is always found among God's children. For instance, consider the revival under Nehemiah, which included the rebuilding of the wall of Jerusalem under adverse circumstances. There were difficulty and opposition without and within. Next we hear of the reading of the book of the Law during the first part of the day. Then the people stood, confessed their sins, and worshiped during the second part of the day. Among the results that grew out of the revival were the putting away of the heathen wives and the voluntary separation of Israel from the mixed multitude: "Now it came to pass, when they had heard the law, that they separated from Israel all the mixed multitude" (Neh 13:3).

## What Shall Be Done with the Mixed Multitude?

Shall we give them what they desire? Being a mixed multitude they want worldly entertainment. They long for the onions and the garlic. It is true that these foods are high in flavor qualities, but not one of them is rich in nutritive value. Shall we give them their desire and bring the fleshpots of Egypt into our churches? Many have already succumbed to this temptation. It is certainly not uncommon today to hear of church dances, bingo, and card parties. What a sad commentary this is on professed Christianity in this modern day. In the record of the mixed multitude we learned that God gave them flesh. He gave it to them until it came out their nostrils, and rotted in their teeth. On the other hand, are we going to leave the mixed multitude alone? They are our problem. We must do something about them.

It is evident that a large crowd of non-attending church members, who are godless, worldly minded, and indifferent to spiritual things, could not possibly prosper us. They are in the mixed-multitude classification. They are in our churches, but they are not saved; they are professing Christians, but they are not born again. This mixed multitude discredits the church and hinders her work. Either the church must reach these people with the gospel, or it must dissociate itself from them. Otherwise they will tend to corrupt the whole church. To ignore them or to adopt a program suited to their appetites would most surely lead to impotence and ruin. It is apparent that much of our present-day problems root themselves in a mixed multitude who have crowded our church roll, introduced worldly methods, and sought the world's peace. Now there is so much of the church in the world and so much of the world in the church that only judgment can disrupt such an unholy union.

# 19

# KADESH-BARNEA—ISRAEL'S LOST OPPORTUNITY

AFTER A STAY of nearly a year at Sinai, where Israel had been brought under a covenant of Law, the cloud lifted and some 2 or 3 million people resumed their journey northward. The experience at Sinai had wrought many changes. The nation had been molded into a commonwealth. The economy had shifted from one of pure grace, where God had borne them on eagles' wings, to a covenant of Law. Under this covenant, though the covenant of grace made with Abraham was not nullified, the possession of the land of Canaan was conditioned upon obedience. Up to now God had met their murmurings with patience and overflowing grace. But from this time onward, such sins would be met with appropriate and summary judgments.

This change was soon to evidence itself as the children of Israel came to Taberah.

"And when the people complained, it displeased the LORD: and the LORD heard it; and his anger was kindled; and the fire of the LORD burnt among them, and consumed them that were in the uttermost parts of the camp. And the people cried unto Moses; and when Moses prayed unto the LORD, the fire was quenched. And he called the name of the place Taberah: because the fire of the LORD burnt among them" (Num 11:1-3).

It was here that the people of the mixed multitude revealed their true identity in lusting after the fleshpots of Egypt and proclaiming their dislike of the heavenly manna. At Kibroth-Hattaavah God answered their lustful prayers and sent the quails that were consumed with such greed as to bring on sickness and a devastating plague (vv. 31-35).

"[They] lusted exceedingly in the wilderness, and tempted God in the desert. And he gave them their request; but sent leanness into their soul" (Ps 106:14-15).

At Hazeroth, Miriam and Aaron murmured against Moses for marrying an Ethiopian woman. Immediately Miriam was stricken with leprosy, but as a result of Moses' intercession she was finally cured (Num 11:35—12:16).

The next movement on the part of the children of Israel was to pass through the wilderness of Paran and then on to Kadesh (13:26). At last the very border of the promised land had been reached.

Some two years had elapsed since the redemption of this people from Egypt by blood and by power. At long last it looked as though their hopes would be realized. The land long dreamed of was before their eyes.

It was an hour of crisis, an hour of opportunity. There was given to this nation a moment to decide. To go forward would have meant immediate possession. There would have been no Jordan to cross, no thirty-eight years of wandering, and no death in the wilderness to the generation before whom lay the glories of the land that flowed with milk and honey.

Once to every man and nation
  Comes the moment to decide.
In the strife of Truth with Falsehood,
  For the good or evil side.

—James Russell Lowell

Shakespeare reminds us, "There is a tide in the affairs of

men, which, taken at the flood, leads on to fortune; omitted, all the voyage of their life is bound in shallows and in miseries."

Whether we will it or not, life is interspersed with imperative hours of decision, and moments pregnant with undreamed-of opportunities. As John Greenleaf Whittier said, "For of all sad words of tongue or pen, the saddest are these: 'It might have been!' "

The nation Israel stood at the moment of destiny with a potential that could require age upon age to tell about. A mistake here could well cast the die and mark the course of uncounted generations.

## The Opportunity Anticipated

About 420 years earlier, God had promised Abraham a seed and a land. We hear repeatedly about the seed and the land. From a very small beginning and what appeared to be a precarious providence, Abraham's seed had at last reached an astounding number of 600,000 fighting men. Adding to this figure the women, children, and adult men unfit for fighting could easily make the total about three million.

The seed and the land had been separated for four generations. The sojourn in Egypt had been used of God as the furnace of affliction to prepare a nation for the world destiny to which He had called it. As Israel's children labored and suffered under the taskmasters, the darkness of their night and the seeming hopelessness of their plight caused them to revive the ancient hope that had been kept alive from generation to generation—the hope of a land that would be their very own, the land of promise.

We may safely surmise that this hope had been kept alive as father told son the intriguing story of the land of promise. Young hearts had burned and wide-eyed children had listened to their grandfathers, who would again and again tell the favorite story of a homeland that flowed with milk and honey. Restless dreams interspersed the night until hopes deferred made the heart sick. Often some new form of cruelty in their slave experience made them even more eager to be in the favored generation that would one day, according to divine promise, be led out of Egypt to Canaan's fair and happy land.

At last the day had arrived! The power of Pharaoh had been broken. At Sinai the Law had been given. It was at Sinai that the children of Israel had remained while the wilderness tabernacle had been prepared and set up. At the end of the second year, after many trials and failures, they came to Kadesh-barnea.

## The Opportunity Presented

At Kadesh-barnea hopes long deferred were about to find fruition. The eyes of the people could, for the first time, view what their hearts had longed for. The experience must have been breathtaking, the scene magnificent beyond description. A nation stood at its moment of crisis. One bold thrust and their feet would be touching the homeland. What would they do?

The answer was ready at hand. Unbelief had characterized the people since the time they left Egypt. This same unbelief asserted itself in this crucial hour. Instead of pushing forward with the assurance that God's promises were trustworthy, they faltered. At first sight, it may have appeared as if the sending forth of the twelve spies to search out the land of Canaan had had the approval of God, but when we turn to Deuteronomy 1, we learn that the idea originated in the heart of man: "And ye came near unto me every one of you, and said, We will send men before us, and they shall search us out the land" (v. 22). As is often the case, God allowed an action which was compatible with His permissive will. He permitted Israel to send out the spies. God had appeared to Moses in Egypt and had made clear His purpose in leading Israel into its inheritance. "And I am come down to deliver them out of the hand of the Egyptians, and to bring them up out of that land unto a good land and a large, unto a land flowing with milk and honey" (Ex 3:8).

Ritchie, in *From Egypt to Canaan, says,* "They had the first and second part of this definite promise fulfilled to them. They had been delivered from the Egyptians and brought up out of the land. They might well have counted on the faithfulness of God to fulfill what remained and gone forward, depending on Him to do it. But instead of their trusting God and believing His word, they demanded that spies be sent to 'see the land, what it is . . . whether it be good or bad, . . . whether it be fat or lean' (Num 13:18-20)." This was the equivalent of saying, "We cannot accept God's description of the land of Canaan. We must have it confirmed by man." Men have always found it hard just to rely upon the Word of God where human experience and human vision dictate otherwise. True faith is not a faith that interprets God through circumstances but a faith that interprets circumstances through a vision and a realization of God. Weak faith must be bolstered by human investigation and visible proof.

Twelve spies were chosen, a spy from each tribe, and commissioned to go forth and spy out the land. Scripture gives us this sad account:

"And Moses sent them to spy out the land of Canaan, and said unto them, Get you up this way southward, and go up into the mountain: and see the land, what it is; and the people that dwelleth therein, whether they be strong or weak, few or many; and what the land is that they dwell in, whether it be good or bad; and what cities they be that they dwell in, whether in tents, or in strong holds; and what the land is, whether it be fat or lean, whether there be wood therein, or not. And be ye of good courage, and bring of the fruit of the land. Now the time was the time of the first ripe grapes" (Num 13:17-20).

## The Opportunity Rejected

Why did faith need spies? "We walk by faith, not by sight" (2 Co 5:7). For forty days these men spied out the land. In their reconnaissance they had gone from one end of the land to the other. To all intents, they investigated in order to verify divine veracity. But real faith takes God at His word. Two years of experience had taught them that God was able and willing to provide for their every need and to meet every emergency. This period of time was filled with such evidence. The same God could meet whatever peril the land of Canaan contained.

"But with whom was he grieved forty years? Was it not with them that had sinned, whose carcases fell in the wilderness? And to whom sware he that they should not enter into his rest, but to them that believed not? So we see that they could not enter in because of unbelief" (Heb 3:17-19).

True faith is not governed by circumstances or by the often mysterious nature of divine providence but by reliance upon God Himself. Faith rests in a person. "Without faith it is impossible to please him: for he that cometh to God must believe that he is, and that he is a rewarder of them that diligently seek him" (11:6).

After forty days the twelve spies returned to make their report and to announce their findings. What they reported was not based upon what they saw but upon the interpretation given to the facts of their experience. Ten of the spies brought a majority report, which is called in Scripture an evil report.

"And they went and came to Moses, and to Aaron, and to all the congregation of the children of Israel, unto the wilderness of Paran, to Kadesh; and brought back word unto them, and unto all the congregation, and shewed them the fruit of the land. And they told him, and said, We came unto the land whither thou sentest us, and surely it floweth with milk and honey, and this is the fruit of it. Nevertheless the people be strong that dwell in the land, and the cities are walled, and very great: and moreover we saw the children of Anak there. The Amalekites dwell in the land of the south: and the Hittites, and the Jebusites, and the Amorites, dwell in the mountains: and the Canaanites dwell by the sea, and by the coast of Jordan" (Num 13:26-29).

They were willing to admit that the land was all that God had represented it to be, as proven by the grapes of Eshcol. They admitted that it was a "land flowing with milk and honey" (v. 27). But they introduced into their report a "nevertheless." They saw walled towns and giants. They saw themselves as grasshoppers and said, "And so were we in their sight" (v. 33). It is an obvious fact that in our day there are many "grasshopper Christians."

The ten spies interpreted God in the light of circumstances. Caleb and Joshua interpreted circumstances in the light of God. This is the difference between the majority and the minority reports. "And Caleb stilled the people before Moses, and said, Let us go up at once, and possess it; for we are well able to overcome it" (v. 30).

Joshua and Caleb saw the same difficulties as the others, but they viewed them through the eyes of faith. Two phrases stand out in this minority report: "at once" and "we are well able." Herein lies the difference between defeat and failure. The majority said, "they are stronger than we" (v. 31); Joshua and Caleb said, "we are well able" (v. 30). It was true then, and it is true today. "Ye are of God, little children, and have overcome them: because greater is he that is in you, than he that is in the world" (1 Jn 4:4).

There is another distinction between the "evil" and the "good" reports. One involves ownership with no hope of possession. The other involves ownership with the assurance of possession. The ten, by right of divine gift, owned the land but did not wish to possess it. Joshua and Caleb were in favor of turning ownership into possession. How few Christians that we know ever possess their possessions. "They could not enter in because of unbelief" (Heb 3:19). In order to possess our possessions we must move in and stake out our claims. The question may be asked, How extensive are our possessions? The answer: "All things are yours." All that He is, we are in Him. Here again, faith is the secret. Accept it as true and if it is in the Book and designated to Christians, it is yours. God said it, I believe it, and that settles it.

It was sad enough for the ten to be affected, but the real tragedy lay in the fact that they represented an unfavorable influence on others. "And they went and came to Moses, and to Aaron, and to all the congregation of the children of Israel, unto the wilderness of Paran, to Kadesh; and brought back word unto them, and unto all the congregation, and shewed them the fruit of the land" (Num 13:26). They influenced the course of a whole nation. "And all the congregation lifted up their voice, and cried; and the people wept that night" (14:1). Again we are reminded, "None of us liveth to himself, and no man dieth to himself" (Ro 14:7). Here we are confronted again with the very solemn thought of man's responsibility before God and man.

### The Opportunity Lost

Immediately after the evil report had been rendered, rebellion broke out. In order for Caleb to give his report, we are told that he "stilled the people before Moses" (Num 14:30). Afterward, bedlam reigned. Mob psychology took over.

"And all the children of Israel murmured against Moses and against Aaron: and the whole congregation said unto them, Would God that we had died in the land of Egypt! or would God we had died in this wilderness! And wherefore hath the Lord brought us unto this land, to fall by the sword, that our wives and our children should be a prey? were it not better for us to return into Egypt? And they said one to another, Let us make a captain, and let us return into Egypt" (Num 14:2-4).

In desperation Joshua and Caleb sought to restrain the people in this crucial hour (Num 14:5-9). Instead of listening to and heeding these men of faith, we find the sad answer recorded, "But all the congregation bade stone them with stones" (v. 10). God has never majored on majorities. Many churches have been divided and many pastors' hearts broken under similar conditions, where reason was dethroned and prejudice and passion ruled. Where the contest is between faith and human sentiments, truth rarely prevails.

Joshua and Caleb had to encounter in their day what all true witnesses have had to face in every succeeding generation. Being found in the minority, they had to listen to a multitude of voices that were raised against them. Joshua and Caleb were calm, while others were agitated. The unbelieving people were held to their choice.

## The Result of Israel's Mistake

First, all those over twenty years of age were doomed to die in the wilderness period. What a sad prospect—death in the wilderness. Where hope is dead, despair reigns. There are few things more dominant in the human heart when the final hour upon this earth becomes apparent. Then the longing,

"Let me go home to die," could not be so with this people. They could neither die in Egypt, the land they had known so well, nor in Canaan, the land they had so long anticipated.

Second, they were doomed to a life of wandering. They would have to travel thirty-eight more years, waiting to die. They were God's people; they had been redeemed by the blood of the paschal lamb. They were saved people, but they were condemned to a life and career of fruitlessness and misery. Here we behold Israel's lost opportunity. Here we see failure at Kadesh-barnea as the people stood on the border of their inheritance. We could wish that matters had been otherwise, but they were not.

Third, Canaan was lost—even though the people repented after they saw the results of their failure. It was too late. They were doomed to abide by their fateful decision. They missed so much. How sad it must have been for this generation that came so near and yet missed God's plan. To know what they missed, one must turn to the book of Joshua and read of the romance of possession and the thrill of victorious conflicts.

## Israel's Experience—Our Warning

"Now these things were our examples, to the intent we should not lust after evil things, as they also lusted" (1 Co 10:6).

In a true sense every individual stands one day at his or her Kadesh-barnea; he stands at the fork of the way that holds eternal potential for weal or woe. Decisions, after all, are the hinges upon which the doors of destiny turn. For the unsaved it can be the door of heaven or the door of hell, the door of faith or the door of despair.

As individual Christians, we are all in our own place of experience in a wilderness journey. In this journey, first and last, we come to the hour of decision.

Through many years, the writer has had related to him many sad experiences, some of them by people who turned back at their Kadesh-barnea. He has heard them say, "God called me to preach," or, "God called me to go as a missionary or to serve Him in a life of stewardship, but I was afraid of the walled towns and the giants; I was afraid of the difficulties. I turned back at my Kadesh-barnea, and I have meandered through these years in a spiritual wilderness." There are tens of thousands of people who know this regrettable experience.

It is true of individuals and it is true of churches. We have witnessed churches coming to their Kadesh-barnea. It could be the decision to enlarge the facilities, join in a missionary program, or embark on a program of soul winning, but all too often churches are willing to retain the status quo. In some instances we have seen churches standing at their Kadesh-barnea in the matter of relocating, where the need was imperative, but a majority saw only the walled towns and the giants.

When individuals or churches, for lack of vision and faith, repeat Israel's mistakes of long ago, a wilderness experience of some sort is the next step.

It will be well for us to keep in mind that God has in the past set aside one whole generation while another grew up. Sometimes God has to wait for one generation in a church to die before that church can move forward on the promises of God. It is sad for the church and doubly sad for the generation that has no vision.

# 20

# DANGERS IN THE DESERT

CRISES DO NOT PRODUCE HEROES, nor do emergencies make cowards; however, extraordinary circumstances often serve to reveal strengths or weaknesses that have long been dormant. The storm that felled the mighty oak only brought to light the hidden decay that had been eating at its heart for years. The outburst of a glaring weakness or evil tendency in an unguarded moment only serves to bring to attention that which is but the climax of a protracted course of thought and purpose. We are not what we are because of what we do; we do what we do because of what we are. The thief is a thief long before he pilfers. Character determines the deed. The deed only reveals the character.

During Israel's wilderness wanderings, three exalted characters, each called of God and each occupying a place of high privilege and dignity, failed one way or another in a time of crisis. The failure of these three persons, Moses, Miriam, and Korah, seems to exemplify the three cardinal sins that are often found among those who are closest to Jehovah.

Moses was one of the greatest characters of all history. In fairness to the record, we must note that his sin was a sin-of-the-moment, a failure under extreme provocation; but it was nonetheless serious, as is all sin. Moses' momentary weakness is more glaring when viewed against the background of one of the most noble characters depicted for us in the Scriptures. Moses' sin was *discouragement.* This provoked a rashness that in turn charged God with unfairness. Had God placed more responsibility on Moses than he could bear? Moses' defection was more surprising because of who he was and what he was before God. He was "faithful in all his house" (Heb 3:2). The sin of discouragement was followed by the sin of *impatience.*

Miriam, the sister of Moses and Aaron, allowed her *jealousy* toward her sister-in-law to bring her to the brink of ruin and misery, to say nothing of the disappointment she brought those closest to her.

Korah's sin of *rebellion* was the most despicable sin of all. The sin of Korah and his cohorts was that of treason against God and the divine order.

These sins appear before us on a descending scale of moral turpitude. But all are subtle and emanate from the master mind of a great adversary.

### The Danger of Discouragement

"And Moses said unto the Lord, Wherefore hast thou afflicted thy servant? . . . I am not able to bear all this people alone, because it is too heavy for me." (Num 11:11, 14).

Moses was provoked by the rash grumbling of the mixed multitude and by the resultant murmuring and crying of their Hebrew companions. He lost his patience and inquired of Jehovah, "Wherefore hast thou afflicted thy servant? . . . Have I conceived all this people? . . . Whence should I have flesh to give unto all this people?" (vv. 11-13). Moses was caught in one of the weak moments of his life, but surely this cannot be the Moses who spent forty days with God in the Mount! Momentarily, at least, Moses lost sight of God and became sorry for himself.

Self-pity, even if it is only spasmodic, works with destructive reaction that reflects itself in both a person's moral life and his spiritual life. There are few maladies more impairing than self-pity and which offer less success to those who would like to make friends and influence people.

Discouragement, certainly in this case, was aggravated by a protracted irritation resulting from the unending complaints and criticisms issuing from the lips of those for whom he had done the most. Discouragements are usually associated with men and women of action. The sluggard meets with little or no opposition because he undertakes little.

Another factor in Moses' complaint was the weariness that he permitted to exhaust his patience. The exhaustion of soul and body can render the best of God's servants vulnerable to Satan's attack. This truth is graphically set forth in two other Old Testament examples, namely, Elijah and Jonah.

The great Elijah sat under a juniper tree, praying that he might die. "But he himself went a day's journey into the wilderness, and came and sat down under a juniper tree: and he requested for himself that he might die; and said, It is enough; now, O LORD, take away my life; for I am not better than my fathers" (1 Ki 19:4). What was the background of such an irrational and unexpected display of weakness and discouragement? This was the man who, many years later, appeared with Moses on the mount of transfiguration. He had spent himself, 450 prophets of Baal, and 400 prophets of the grove on Mount Carmel in a test of fire. He had not only called down fire from heaven, he had won the battle and destroyed the prophets who opposed him. Still under the impact of divine power, and prodded by the excitement of victory and the sight of a little cloud the size of a man's hand, the prophet ran ahead of the chariots of King Ahab all the way from Carmel to Jezreel, some seventeen miles away (1 Ki 18:45-46). (The little cloud was an indication of the coming rain that was destined to break the three-and-one-half years famine.) Having arrived in Jezreel, Elijah was told that Jezebel was after him. Upon hearing such news, the prophet took off on another day's run for the wilderness. It was there under the juniper tree that the Lord found him pleading to die. But the Lord ministered to him: "And as he lay and slept under a juniper tree, behold, then an angel touched him, and said unto him, Arise and eat. And he looked, and, behold, there was a cake baken on the coals, and a cruse of water at his head. And he did eat and drink, and laid him down again" (19:5-6).

The second instance of total discouragement and childish complaint was displayed in the person of Jonah under the gourd vine, praying that he, too, might die. Piqued over a worm and a withering gourd vine, Jonah was ready to give up. Here again we see a condition similiar to that which prevailed with the prophet Elijah. Jonah had traversed the great city of Nineveh crying, "Yet forty days, and Nineveh shall be overthrown" (Jon 3:4). Then there was the letdown! As a matter of fact, Jonah had had quite an exhausting experience before he had begun this day's journey toward the city of Nineveh.

Three people seem to personify the major dangers that confront every child of God.

Moses was known in Scripture as the meekest among men. This means that he was in no sense self-assertive, vindictive, or quick to defend himself, even when he was severely provoked and unjustly criticized by those about him. This virtue manifests itself again and again as Moses faces the murmurings that often contained even threats upon his life. We hear him say at Kadesh-barnea, "But all the congregation bade stone them with stones. And the glory of the LORD appeared in the tabernacle of the congregation before all the children of Israel" (Num 14:10). Hitherto when such criticisms were uttered against Moses and Aaron, we read that Moses did one of two things; either he fell on his face before God and the people or he prayed earnestly for divine help and deliverance. In his meekness, he referred the matter of his own vindication to the Lord. In this he offers us an important example.

The loss of patience that resulted in criticism of the Lord on the part of Moses is found in Numbers 11. The people of Israel had arrived at Taberah in their journey through the wilderness. "And when the people complained, it displeased the LORD: and the LORD heard it; and his anger was kindled; and the fire of the LORD burnt among them, and consumed them that were in the uttermost parts of the camp. And the people cried unto Moses; and when Moses prayed unto the LORD, the fire was quenched. And he called the name of the place Taberah: because the fire of the LORD burnt among them" (vv. 1-3). Furthermore, Moses had to listen to the whining complaints of the mixed multitude as they made known their distaste for, and their disgust with, the heavenly manna (vv. 4-6). Moses, it seems, had reached the end of his patience, first with Israel and then with God. It is at this point that his soul seems to falter and all but sink beneath the weight of his responsibility. "Moses heard the people weeping, not over their sinful lusts and murmurings, but in their vexations with God. . . . But God's eye is upon everything, and He can bring many different things to light by the same set of circumstances. The evil state of the people became a crucible in which Moses was tested. A state of general unfaithfulness brings peculiar testing upon those who are faithful; they are not exempt from the searching of God, for the nearer one is to God, the greater becomes the demands for purity of motive" (C. A. Coates, *An Outline of the Book of Numbers*).

We have here another demonstration of the gracious dealings and the long-sufferings of God with His people. This exhibition of divine patience is brought out repeatedly as God deals with His servant Moses. Whenever the Lord places a man in a position of responsibility, He will both fit that man for the place and maintain him in that place. Moses said that his burden was too great. God answered by taking a portion of the spirit that was upon Moses and putting it upon the seventy. "And the LORD came down in a cloud, and spake unto him, and took of the spirit that was upon him, and gave it unto the seventy elders: and it came to pass, that, when the spirit rested upon them, they prophesied, and did not cease" (v. 25).

It was a pity that Moses, in this big moment, did not realize that his God was sufficient. In answer to his plea, there was no more power, just more machinery. The power that was given to the seventy was not increased but simply distributed. There were seventy men instead of one, but the multiplying of men brought no increase of spiritual power. While this transaction under the permissive will of God saved Moses from trouble and gave him seventy helpers, it also meant the loss of power and a dignity that hitherto had been his own. Moses lost something he never regained. We can well understand Moses' human weariness. The question should have been: Was it all too heavy for God? Was not the living God with him? Herein Moses, one of the greatest among men, displaying a prevailing human weakness, encourages us to have faith in God. This passage does not close without a blessed exhibition of Moses' former magnificence.

Joshua, the servant of Moses, became jealous for Moses' honor on discovering two men, Eldad and Medad, who had prophesied in the camp, but who had not come up to the tabernacle. The reaction of Moses was not only immediate but gracious. "And Joshua, the son of Nun, the servant of

Moses, one of his young men, answered and said, My lord Moses, forbid them. And Moses said unto him, Enviest thou for my sake? Would God that all the LORD's people were prophets, and that the LORD would put his spirit upon them!" (vv. 28-29).

There are few Christian virtues greater than the grace that enables one to rejoice in the success of others—even in the success of his competitors.

## THE DANGER OF JEALOUSY

In Numbers 12 there appears another danger in the desert —the jealousy of Miriam. None escape the searchings and discipline of the Lord, not even the most eminent or spiritual. Miriam and Aaron were placed in the divine crucible. Moses, Aaron, and Miriam were all children of the same parents. They formed one of the greatest families in Scripture. They were all mightily used of God. Herein lies the lesson for us.

This display of jealousy was precipitated by a changed situation in the life of Moses. "And Miriam and Aaron spake against Moses because of the Ethiopian woman whom he had married: for he had married an Ethiopian woman" (Num 12:1). Evidently Moses' brother and sister thought his new wife was beneath the family dignity. It could be that this jealousy grew out of the fact that Moses' wife held a place in the inner circle that was now denied to Miriam. Miriam had played the part of a worthy elder sister, who watched over the baby Moses as she kept vigil by the Nile River. Could this be the Miriam who sang the refrain to Moses' song when they celebrated the victorious passage through the Red Sea? It is most difficult now to think of Miriam as caustic and censorious.

It seems evident also that Miriam affected Aaron and brought him into the quarrel and the rebellion. Very often it is difficult in families for the older brothers and sisters to give proper attention to the younger.

The course of jealousy, as usual, took a hypocritical turn. Instead of complaining about Moses' wife, Aaron and Miriam struck their blow by challenging Moses' authority. "And they said, Hath the LORD indeed spoken only by Moses? Hath he not spoken also by us? And the LORD heard it" (v. 2). If believers would always remember that the Lord is listening, many gossiping tongues would be immobilized. Someone has said, "When we think we are judging another, God is often judging our own state." It is a trait of the flesh, when aroused to jealousy, to cut others down to its own pattern. The idea seems to prevail that a person can exhalt himself by deprecating others.

The sin of Miriam and of Aaron, the high priest, did not go by without notice. Moses did not defend himself. "Now the man Moses was very meek, above all the men which were upon the face of the earth" (v. 3). But God took up his cause. "And the LORD spake suddenly unto Moses, and unto Aaron, and unto Miriam, Come out ye three unto the tabernacle of the congregation. And they three came out" (v. 4). We are further told, "The anger of the LORD was kindled against them; and he departed. And the cloud departed from off the tabernacle; and, behold, Miriam became leprous, white as snow: and Aaron looked upon Miriam, and, behold, she was leprous" (vv. 9-10).

The seriousness of this sin was emphasized by several important factors. First was the sobering fact that God heard the complaint. Second, "The LORD spake suddenly" (v. 4). Third, "And the LORD came down in the pillar of the cloud" (v. 5). Fourth, Miriam was temporarily stricken with leprosy. Fifth, Aaron, the high priest, found favor and forgiveness by confession. Sixth, Miriam was healed after seven days through the intercessory prayer of Moses.

## THE DANGER OF REBELLION

In our consideration of dangers in the desert, we find ourselves on the descending scale. First, we witness the sin of discouragement that becomes the temptation of God's tried and tired servants. Second, we witness what jealousy can do to a person. Finally, we deal with the most serious of all sins found among God's people—rebellion.

We are struck with the serious nature of the sin of Korah and his associates. This was revealed in the fact that Moses fell on his face, leaving the rebels to face God. "Now Korah, the son of Izhar, the son of Kohath, the son of Levi, and Dathan and Abiram, the sons of Eliab, and On, the son of Peleth, sons of Reuben, took men: and they rose up before Moses, with certain of the children of Israel, two hundred and fifty princes of the assembly, famous in the congregation, men of renown" (Num 16:1-2).

Korah was a Levite to whom the services of the tabernacle were committed and entrusted. Associated with Korah were Dathan and Abiram and two-hundred and fifty princes. All these men were exhalted leaders in Israel. Evidently Korah was a man who by nature was shrewd, clever, and energetic; a man of dominant and striking personality. This was evidenced by the fact that he was able to persuade others to join him in this terrible sin of rebellion. It is this type of strong character that Satan picks to initiate and to promote his schemes. Such men know how to stir up the passions of the masses and capitalize on aroused emotions.

It is worthwhile to note the charges trumped up against Moses and Aaron by this band of rebels. Their movement was subtle. They pretended to champion the causes and rights of others. Korah moved upon the pretext that his group was for the preservation of the holy character and the democracy of the assembly. He publicly charged Moses and Aaron, telling them: "Ye take too much upon you, seeing all the congregation are holy, every one of them" (v. 3). Such a charge could appeal to the natural man. In addition to this the rebels could have sought to promote their cause upon the grounds that the national leadership was in the hands of one family. Were not Moses and Aaron brothers? Was not Miriam the leader among the women? This complaint could have carried with it a plausible legitimacy, had it not been for one important fact—these people were God's choice. They had been divinely appointed, and they were responsible to Him. There are few things more sobering in the midst of difficulties such as this than to remember the sovereignty of God. We hear Him say again, "Who art thou that judgest another man's servant?" (Ro 14:4).

It is evident from the Word that the majority of the children of Israel were deceived, since following the visitation of divine judgment upon Korah and his group we hear the people say, "But on the morrow all the congregation of the children of Israel murmured against Moses and against Aaron, saying, Ye have killed the people of the LORD" (Num 16:41).

Notice also the character of the sin of Korah. In the book of Jude it is called "the gainsaying of Core (Korah)" (v. 11). The awfulness of Korah's sin can be measured by the penalty inflicted. Our souls are struck with horror as we read, "The earth opened her mouth, and swallowed them up, and their houses, and all the men that appertained unto Korah, and all their goods. They, and all that appertained to them, went down alive into the pit, and the earth closed upon them: and they perished from among the congregation" (Num 16:32-33).

But the remedy was applied: "Speak unto Eleazar the son of Aaron the priest, that he take up the censers out of the burning, and scatter thou the fire yonder; for they are hallowed" (v. 37). There is something here that lies deeper than what appears to the natural eye. Without doubt, the seriousness of Korah's sin consisted in this: Korah was striking at the very heart of divine mediatorial work. If, as Korah claimed, all men are holy, then there is no need for a separate priesthood. This implies that all men can approach God without sacrifice and without an intermediary. We hear this today: "All men are the sons of God. God is the Father of all mankind." If this were true, then man was not ruined by the fall, and logically he needs no redemption. This nullifies the typical meaning of Aaron's high priestly functions and ministries. These, as we know, were but prototypes of our great High Priest, the Lord Jesus Christ, who was "called of God an high priest after the order of Melchisedec" (Heb 5:10). The seriousness of Korah's crime must be seen in the light of two things: the sin of rebellion and the sin of destroying one of God's important types—one that relates to His Son, the coming Messiah. At the very heart of the system of revealed redemption, foreshadowed in the Old Testament and fulfilled in Christ, is the doctrine of substitution. This life-for-life principle of blood redemption and mediatorial ministry was finally completed in Christ. Apart from such mediatorial work, Christianity degenerates and can be classified among the pagan religions of the earth. Only in the grace found in the Old Testament and in the work of Christ do we find the gospel of redemption, based upon substitutionary atonement.

Repeatedly in these studies we have been brought face to face with the seriousness of intruding into divine things, and attention has been called to the peril of breaking God's types. We have seen this in the sin of Nadab and Abihu, who offered strange fire on the altar of Jehovah and were visited with immediate fiery judgment of God that consumed them. At Meribah, Moses was commanded to speak to the rock with the rod of the high priest in his hand, but he chose to strike the rock twice, resulting in the judgment of exclusion from the promised land.

The proof that the sin of Korah and his followers struck at the vital truth of a divinely-appointed priesthood was to be found in the twelve rods laid up before the Lord according to divine command—only Aaron's rod blossomed and bore fruit (Num 17).

If the priesthood of Christ is discarded, Christianity is destroyed. But if it is an eternal ministry, and He is a royal Priest, without beginning or ending of days, then Christianity is of God and is all that it claims to be.

# 21

# THE ROCK OF MERIBAH

"And the LORD spake unto Moses, saying, Take the rod, and gather thou the assembly together, thou, and Aaron thy brother, and speak ye unto the rock before eyes; and it shall give forth his water, and thou shalt bring forth to them water out of the rock: so thou shalt give the congregation and their beasts drink. And Moses took the rod before the LORD as he commanded him. And Moses and Aaron gathered the congregation together before the rock, and he said unto them, Hear now, ye rebels; must we fetch you water out of this rock? And Moses lifted up his hand, and with his rod he smote the rock twice: and the water came out abundantly, and the congregation drank, and their beasts also.

"And the LORD spake unto Moses and Aaron, Because ye believed me not, to sanctify me in the eyes of the children of Israel, therefore ye shall not bring this congregation into the land which I have given them. This is the water of Meribah; because the children of Israel strove with the LORD, and he was sanctified in them" (Num 20:7-13).

In many respects, the account contained in this passage constitutes one of the most crucial moments in the life of Moses. It should hold for us a serious and solemn lesson. In one brief moment, by one impulsive act, the great man of God, who was doubtless the greatest character in the Old Testament, forfeited his opportunity to lead Israel into the promised land after having led them for nearly forty years.

The act described in this passage meant that Moses, instead of experiencing the incomparable thrill of leading the people across Jordan and into the land that flowed with milk and honey, had to die in the wilderness and be buried by the Lord on a lonely mountain within sight of the land.

Seen from the point of view of human reason, the divine penalty inflicted upon Moses and Aaron seemed to be completely out of proportion to the act that caused God's displeasure. The record tells us that Moses smote the rock that he was told to speak to. It is true that he lost his temper, but it was not without severe provocation, in view of the complaints of his own people, Israel. There was no water and people complained strongly to Moses, saying, "Would God that we had died when our brethren died before the LORD" (v. 3). This was a mere introduction to their complaints. They continued with most exasperating provocations and even insults (vv. 4-6). Moses and Aaron lost their patience indeed, and Moses smote the rock twice. This act of disobedience was followed by summary and severe divine judgment. There must have been a reason for chastisement on the part of Jehovah. Since God is always justified in all of His dealings, it behooves us to pause here and inquire reverently concerning the deeper seriousness of Moses' mistake. The results of such a search are both rewarding and startling.

## God Safeguards His Sacred Things

In all of God's dealings with man, He has two unfailing methods of communicating His will. The first is by the spoken or written word; the second is by types and institutions such as are found in the levitical system. The most authorative communication is transmitted through human language. The second is in the form of a picture. Both the Old and the New Testaments are filled with these.

In the Old Testament we have the word in types and institutions. In the New Testament we have parables. The ear and the eye must agree. One substantiates and corrects the other. Herein is found the importance of verbal inspiration of Scripture. Verbal inspiration is accompanied by certain sacred types. While these hold a place of secondary importance, they are nonetheless divinely safeguarded in the economy of revelation. This is particularly true concerning those types and institutions that foreshadow the person, the work, and the glory of the Son of God. It is of great importance that this truth be understood.

To further analyze this truth, as revealed in Scripture, we note God's sacred things and the safeguards that He has placed about them. In what may well be called the vestibule of revelation, certain types, like wax figures, are provided to warn those who enter. In the vestibule of the tabernacle worship, God struck dead the two sons of Aaron—Nadab and Abihu. Their sin was offering strange fire, typical of carnality, in worship.

Think for a moment who these two men were. They were the sons of Aaron. Nadab was to be the successor to his father in the high priestly office. Notice where they were—in the tabernacle. To offer "strange fire" does not seem so serious to man or so sinful as to call for sudden death, but in God's eyes, it was a heinous crime. In the vestibule of the kingdom age, God struck Uzzah dead for putting his hand forth to steady the ark as it was being moved on the new cart instead of being carried, as God had designed, on the shoulders of the Levites (2 Sa 6). The adoption of a Philistine expedient entailed the violation, touching the ark, that was followed immediately by death. This was a demonstration of carnality in service.

In the vestibule of the church age, God struck dead Ananias and Sapphira for lying to the Holy Spirit. They evidenced carnality in giving. God is jealous over the pictures and ordinances that depict the great truths of redemption associated with His beloved Son. The picture and the word must agree. Too much is involved to permit the marring of either. In the New Testament church, our Lord instituted two pictorial ordinances—baptism and the Lord's Supper. They should not be tampered with, altered, or ignored. Like the Old Testament types, and even more important, these two ordinances are guards to the cross and its message and are set to depict the heart of the gospel—the death, burial, and resurrection of Christ according to Scriptures.

There are those among us who claim that it doesn't make much difference if the form of these ordinances is altered. In this connection it is interesting to note the record in 1 Corinthians, where warning is given concerning observing the Lord's Supper without discernment. "Wherefore whosoever shall eat this bread, and drink this cup of the Lord, unworthily, shall be guilty of the body and blood of the Lord. But let a man examine himself, and so let him eat of that bread, and drink of that cup. For he that eateth and drinketh unworthily, eateth and drinketh damnation to himself, not discerning the Lord's body. For this cause many are weak and sickly among you, and many sleep" (11:27-30).

How solemn are the words, "For this cause many are weak and sickly among you, and many sleep" (v. 30). This can only mean that many *were* sick and many *were* dead. God must place much importance upon the ordinances, or the pictures, that He has provided to keep alive and true the story of redemption as wrought on Calvary's cross. "For as often as ye eat this bread, and drink this cup, ye do shew the Lord's death till he come" (v. 26).

## Truth Exemplified in Contrast

To gather the full meaning of Moses' mistake—a mistake

that resulted in the application of such a severe penalty—we must refer to the account of Moses obtaining water from the rock in Horeb. This was the rock that Moses *was* commanded to smite. Much is to be learned in the contrast between these two occasions. In the first instance, God told Moses to take the elders of Israel and stand before the rock of Horeb and smite it. In the case of the rock at Meribah, more than thirty years later, God told Moses to take the rod of Aaron and to speak to the rock.

Both of these rocks speak of Christ. "And did all drink the same spiritual drink: for they drank of that spiritual Rock that followed them: and that Rock was Christ" (1 Co 10:4). The fact that each rock speaks of Christ constitutes the major factor in both pictures, and this must determine all else. While both rocks speak of Christ, one speaks of Him on the cross, the Savior wounded for our transgressions and bruised for our iniquities (Is 53:5). The other speaks of Christ as the resurrected High Priest. The Hebrew words themselves indicate this. In Exodus 17 the word for rock in *tsur,* which means low rock. In Numbers 20 it is *sela,* cliff or high rock. Here we have Christ set forth in two aspects. First, we see Him in His redemptive work on the cross and second in His High Priestly work after His resurrection, ascension, and exaltation to the right hand of the Father. "For Christ is . . . entered . . . into heaven itself, now to appear in the presence of God for us" (Heb 9:24).

## The Two Rods

The rod at Horeb was the rod of judgment. "Take . . . thy rod, wherewith thou smotest the river, take in thine hand, and go" (Ex 17:5). "Yet it pleased the Lord to bruise him; he hath put him to grief: when thou shalt make his soul an offering for sin, he shall see his seed, he shall prolong his days, and the pleasure of the Lord shall prosper in his hand.

He shall see the travail of his soul, and shall be satisfied: by his knowledge shall my righteous servant justify many; for he shall bear their iniquities" (Is 53:10-11).

The rod of Meribah was the rod of Aaron the high priest, the rod that budded. In Numbers 17 we have the account of the contest among the twelve rods, a rod from each of the tribes of Israel, including the rod of Aaron. Aaron's rod that budded, blossomed, and yielded almonds spoke of divine acceptance in resurrection. This rod of Aaron was laid up before the Lord as a testimony. The rod was later left in the ark of th covenant (Heb 9:4), and here it speaks of resurrection. Christ was only a high priest after His resurrection, as set forth in Hebrews 9. While He was on earth, He could not be a high priest, but rather He is the High Priest after the order of Melchisedec. In this second instance, Moses did not take the rod of judgment, as he was told to do at Horeb, but the "rod from before the LORD" (Num 20:9).

## Two Commandments

In Horeb, Moses was told to stand alone in the presence of the elders of Israel and to smite the rock (Ex 17:6). In the second instance, years later, Moses was told to take Aaron, with the gathered assembly (no longer just the elders), and speak to the rock. Great significance is to be found in the reason for the two different commands.

Instead of obeying God and speaking to the rock, Moses smote the rock twice (Num 20:11). Here again the double striking is significant. The provocation of Moses came from two sources. First, it came from the people themselves, who gave so little evidence of being a redeemed people. Second, Moses acted in self-will. He said, "Hear now, ye rebels; must we fetch you water out of this rock?" (Num 20:10).

## Divine Grace Acts

The abundant waters tell of the presence of a refreshing supply, despite the errors of the leader of the people. Grace acts even where God is poorly represented. It is significant to note that the passage closes with these words: "This is the water of Meribah; because the children of Israel strove with the Lord, and he was sanctified in them" (Num 20:13). The flowing waters of Meribah speak of the sanctification of God's name. As someone has said, "God strikes many straight blows with crooked sticks."

There are several lessons to be learned from the contrast. First, Christ, our Rock, was to be smitten only once. To do otherwise is to imply that Calvary's work was ineffectual. "If they shall fall away, to renew them again unto repentance; seeing they crucify to themselves the Son of God afresh, and put him to an open shame" (Heb 6:6). Second, the sin that kept Moses out of the promised land was but an example of the present-day teaching that one coming under the benefits of Christ's death can lose such benefits and must be saved again and again. Third, the water, that in each case represents the Holy Spirit, was given once, this truth being based upon the smiting of the Rock. It is never to be repeated. Thereafter He is freely and continuously given to those who confess Jesus Christ as Saviour and Lord.

# 22

# THE BRAZEN SERPENT

IN HUMAN NATURE, certain characteristics are found that are so dominant and deep-rooted as to perpetuate themselves from generation to generation. To put it more strongly, the adamic nature never changes. "The carnal mind . . . is not subject to the law of God, neither indeed can be" (Ro 8:7). Nowhere is this fact so clearly evidenced as in the Scriptures themselves. In this account of the brazen serpent we behold a candid picture of human nature in the raw.

At this point in Israel's journey from Egypt to Canaan a new crisis has developed. Thirty-eight years have passed. These descendants of Abraham, Isaac, and Jacob have been consistent in one respect at least—they have sustained their chorus of murmuring and complaining. As they had been warned when they turned back at Kadesh-barnea thirty-eight years earlier, not one of those who left Egypt above twenty years old, except Joshua and Caleb, was to enter the land. This divine decree had been all but fulfilled. Aaron was dead; only Moses was left. A new generation was on the scene, but it had proved itself to be of the same stock as the previous group.

"They journeyed from Mount Hor by the way of the Red Sea" (Num 21:4). They were almost at the place where their ancestors had camped a generation earlier. When Edom denied them passage, they wheeled around and once more moved toward the south. "And the soul of the people was much discouraged because of the way" (v. 4). Nothing reveals the nature of the human heart as accurately as trials and discouragements.

## Sin Is Against God

Israel's sin and rebellion reached a new low in degradation. Formerly, the people complained to Moses and Aaron. Their complaints had been somewhat veiled and indirect, but now they broke out in open mutiny. "The people spake against God, and against Moses" (Num 21:5).

God loved Israel. His infinite patience and the meekness of His servant Moses had been graciously displayed, but a holy God had to deal with rebellion if His righteous government was to be maintained on the earth. In their complaint against God, the hidden, deep-rooted sin, long dormant, became open transgression akin to blasphemy. The people were tempting Jehovah. "Neither let us tempt Christ, as some of them also tempted, and were destroyed of serpents" (2 Co 10:9). The nature of Israel's sin is brought out repeatedly in Scripture. "They sinned yet more against him by provoking the most High in the wilderness. And they tempted God in their heart by asking meat for their lust. Yea, they spake against God; they said, Can God furnish a table in the wilderness?" (Ps 78:17-19).

All sin is measured by, and derives its heinousness from, the dignity of the person sinned against. How terrible sin appears in this light! David's eyes were washed by tears and his soul was oppressed by the enormity of his crime. He cried out, "Against thee, thee only, have I sinned, and done this evil in thy sight" (Ps 51:4). Every sin against man, in fact, strikes at the image of God in man (Gen 9:6).

## Sin, Judgment, and Death

A holy God must judge sin. Only mercy and grace can delay the hour of its execution, but it must come. It must come upon either the sinner or the sinner's substitute. In the Old Testament, temporary respite or covering was found in the blood of bulls and goats, but these could never take away sin. In the death of Christ, grace found a way to take away sin, to the praise and glory of His name.

Judgment in the case of the Israelites came in the form of physical death. This is but a visible demonstration of spiritual death which separates man from God. "And the Lord sent fiery serpents among the people" (Num 21:6). Note that *God* sent the serpents! While God is a God of love, His righteousness demands punishment. This age we live in is so characterized by the synthetic and the artificial—stimulated by pep pills, tranquilized by sedatives, calmed by opiates—that man under false impressions is ready to rule out the fact and the necessity of pain both here and hereafter. Pain is all but eradicated, hell is vetoed, and the law of retribution is derided by soft and easy sentimentality. But God is righteous, and He still reigns. God is not mocked, nor are His judgments suspended.

The fiery serpents, we are told, still infest the neighborhood of Elath, at the head of the Gulf of Akaba. God could have used natural means to perform His will, but He sent the fiery serpents. These venomous reptiles were either marked with fiery red spots, or they were called "fiery serpents" because of the inflamation produced by their bites. "God made the serpents," as Alexander MacLaren tells us, "though they were hatched by eggs laid by their mothers. God brought Israel to this place; He willed the poisonous stings" (*Expositions of Holy Scripture*). God uses the ordinary to accomplish the extraordinary and the natural to perform the supernatural.

The serpent is a type of Satan and evil. This is depicted in Genesis 3, as well as in Revelation 12:9: "The great dragon was cast out, that old serpent, called the Devil, and Satan, which deceiveth the whole world: he was cast out into the earth, and his angels were cast out with him." Sin, like the serpent, is subtle, sly, deceptive, and deadly. Its venom coagulates the blood, resulting in sure and painful death.

Death was wholesale in the camp that day. "And much people of Israel died" (Num 21:6). "The soul that sinneth, it shall die" (Eze 18:4). There is a universal reign of death, and what wreckage! The devastating, destroying, corrupting, corroding effects of sin are evidenced by history, in nature, and in conscience. No wonder it took the blood of the Son of God to stay its flow and to quench its fires in the souls of man. How wonderful is the love that wrought it and the grace that brought it down to man!

## Death Brings a Cry

"Therefore the people came to Moses, and said, We have sinned, for we have spoken against the Lord, and against thee; pray unto the Lord, that he take away the serpents from us" (Num 21:7). The stroke of judgement fell without warning, but no voice was needed to tell these wanderers where it came from or why. Their hearts knew; the request for Moses' intercession witnessed to the instinct of conscience requiring a mediator. The man they had hated was the man they now sought for intercession. The one they had loathed, they now wanted; the one they had criticized, they now besought for favor. This is always true. The serpent's bite brought the people of Israel to a sense of their need. It seems that little short of judgment will avail to bring man to repentance and confession. All too often men wait until their sins have caught up with them before they are willing or disposed to say, "I have sinned." This was true with Achan, Balaam, Saul, and Judas. The Lord has to catch most men on the bounce after they have bitten the dust. Few men seek the Lord, it seems, in times of prosperity.

The request with the confession was a natural one. The people asked that the serpents be removed. If their request had been granted, it would have spared the ones who were not bitten. That is man's way. But God's way is best. An antidote was given instead of the requested temporary expedient.

## A Cry Brings Mercy

Here God finds an occasion to display divine grace in meeting man's needs. Our God delights in mercy, but it must be mercy that is consistent with His holiness. The moment Israel could say, "I have sinned," all hindrances to the operation of abundant mercy were removed. Murmuring brought the sting of the serpents' venom; confession was answered by grace and forgiveness.

On this occasion the serpent was the instrument of their wretchedness; on the other, it was the instrument of their restoration and blessing.

Nowhere is human depravity and obstinate self-will better displayed than in man's reluctance to accept God's grace on God's sovereign terms. Some, it seems, would rather die and go to hell than confess themselves to be sinners. "And the Lord said unto Moses, Make thee a fiery serpent, and set it upon a pole: and it shall come to pass, that everyone that is bitten, when he looketh upon it, shall live" (Num 21:8). The very image of that which had done the mischief was set up to be the channel through which divine mercy might flow in rich abundance to poor wounded sinners. What a beautiful type this is of Christ on the cross!

Some striking observations are at once apparent when one considers the similarity and the dissimilarity existing between the enemy and the remedy. "Moses made a serpent of brass" (Num 21:9). Brass is typical of judgment. "For he hath made him to be sin for us, who knew no sin, that we might be made the righteousness of God in him" (2 Co 5:21). The command to make a fiery serpent and to set it in a conspicuous place is remarkable, not only as sanctioning the formation of an image but also as associating healing power with a material object: Two questions must be considered: What did the method of cure say to the people who turned trusting eyes on it? What does it mean to us, who see it in the light of our Lord's great words about it? (Jn 3:14). As to the former question, we need not take into account the Old Testament symbolism which makes the serpent the emblem of Satan or of sin. Serpents had bitten the wounded. Here was one like them, but without poison, hanging harmless on the pole.

The pole was raised in the midst of the camp, available to all. The pole must speak of two things as we turn to the Antitype, Christ, as He said, "As Moses lifted up the serpent in the wilderness, even so must the Son of man be lifted up: that whosoever believeth in him should not perish, but have eternal life" (Jn 3:14-15).

First, it speaks of the nature of His death—on a cross, suspended between heaven and earth. "Cursed is every one that hangeth on a tree" (Gal 3:13). "Now is the judgement of this world: now shall the prince of this world be cast out. And I, if I be lifted up from the earth, will draw all men unto me. This he said, signifying what death he should die" (Jn 12:31-33).

Second, the cross not only marked the depths of His humiliation but also the glory of His triumph over death, sin, the grave, and Satan.

## The Remedy Depicted

First, let us consider the remedy negatively. It is interesting to note what the people were not told to do or the things that would appeal to reason. The remedy was not to be accomplished by some homemade concoction or .ointment. It was not by helping others, by getting busy for the Lord, or by organizing a society for the extermination of serpents.

Second, let us consider the remedy positively. God said, "Make thee a fiery serpent, and set it upon a pole: and it shall come to pass, that every one that is bitten, when he looketh upon it, shall live" (Num 21:8).

## The Type Fulfilled

Here we rest upon solid ground in the interpretation of Old Testament types. As someone has said, "Our Lord gives us the deepest meaning of the brazen serpent. Taught by Him, we see in it a type of Himself, the significance of which could not be apprehended till Calvary had given the key." In speaking to Nicodemus (Jn 3), our Lord drew three parallels between Himself and the brazen serpent in the wilderness. First, He took the serpent as an emblem of Himself. Each was made like the venomous serpents of death, yet without their poison or sin. Second, the Lord Jesus laid stress on "lifting up" the serpent, since this "lifting up" speaks of His death on the cross. In a later chapter of John His words are recorded: "And I, if I be lifted up from the earth, will draw all men unto me" (Jn 12:32). Third, the conditions of healing are paralleled. "When he beheld the serpent of brass, he lived" (Num 21:9). "That whosoever believeth in him should not perish, but have eternal life" (Jn 3:15). There is life, eternal life, in the look of faith at the crucified one. But many do not choose to look. Their foolish hope is elsewhere, so death reigns. But for those who heed, "where sin abounded, grace did much more abound" (Ro 5:20).

# 23

# EGYPT, THE WILDERNESS, AND CANAAN

THERE ARE JUST THREE WINDOWS to the human soul. These three windows are called lusts. The lust of the flesh is the desire to enjoy something, the lust of the eyes is the desire to obtain something, and the pride of life is the desire to be something (1 Jn 2:15-17). There are three enemies of the human soul—the world, the flesh, and the devil. All three of these inward lusts find a counterpart in outward enticements. Egypt is typical of the world, the wilderness is typical of the flesh, and Canaan is typical of satanic warfare. In our present study it will greatly aid us to remember that, like Israel, believers are "in Egypt." In terms of experience, they are "in the wilderness," and in position they are "in Canaan."

## EGYPT—THE HOUSE OF BONDAGE

"Their dead bodies shall lie in the street of the great city, which spiritually is called Sodom and Egypt, where also our Lord was crucified" (Rev 11:8). Egypt represents this world-system. Like the world, Egypt epitomized wealth, power, prestige and pleasure. The evidences of her ancient grandeur are still with us. The rich Nile Delta made her the granary of the world. Her armies, all but invincible, were implemented with the finest of chariots, horses, and men. Her architecture is exemplified by her ancient ruins such as Luxor, Karnak, and Memphis. Her accomplishments in science, astronomy, and mathematics are renowned. The culture of the ancient world was centered in the city of Alexandria, which was renowned for its schools and libraries.

It is evident that Moses had all of these in mind when he forsook Egypt. "By faith Moses, when he was come to years, refused to be called the son of Pharaoh's daughter; choosing rather to suffer affliction with the people of God, than to enjoy the pleasures of sin for a season; esteeming the reproach of Christ greater riches than the treasures in Egypt: for he had respect unto the recompence of the reward. By faith he forsook Egypt, not fearing the wrath of the king: for he endured, as seeing him who is invisible" (Heb 11:24-27).

Egypt represents our world in its deceptive appeal, its enticing glamour, and its fascinating prospects. Those who are wise must readily admit that the world's display of wealth, honor, fame, and pleasure makes a strong appeal to the sons of Adam's race. To recognize this, and at the same time remember its tinsel nature and its temporary aspect, is to have the battle half won. Merely to downgrade or minimize the appeal of the world can be a questionable procedure. The Scriptures recognize that sin has its temporary pleasures. The Christian way is: "Esteeming the reproach of Christ greater riches than the treasurers in Egypt" (v. 26).

The typical aspect of Egypt presents her darker side. Egypt, for God's children, was a house of bondage and servitude. It is true that the land had its fleshpots and its cucumbers, melons, leeks, onions, and garlic. Beyond all this, while Israel was in Egypt, it was accustomed to the sound of the clank of chains and the crack of the taskmaster's lash.

Egypt was a land of darkness. George Henderson wrote,

"In helpless servitude, without a single ray of hope to lighten the gloom, they possessed neither wisdom to devise a way of escape nor the power to carry it out even if devised. That land in which Israel toiled for so many long years is a perfect picture of the world. There is no bondage so absolute as the bondage of sin and no slavery so abject as that which is the lot of those who are led captive by the devil at his will" (*Studies in the Book of Exodus*).

Egypt is like the world in another respect—it is a land of death. Pharaoh is clearly typical of Satan, called by the apostle Paul, "the god of this world" (2 Cor 4:3-4). Like Egypt, our world-system, or cosmos, is under the domination of the devil, or Satan. How important it is to recognize this fact which is often neglected by many Christians.

Egypt today is a land of death and spiritual darkness. One can hardly think of its ancient glory without recalling its architecture. This magnificence exhausted itself in the pyramids that encased the bodies of its dead rulers. The science of the land seemed to have reached its zenith in the art of embalming; Egyptian mummies are seen in the museums of the world. In spite of its boasted learning, wealth, accomplishments, and glory, our world is a land of death, both physical and spiritual. Egypt with its wealth, power, prestige, and culture was a land of plagues and death. Tragedy stalked every household from the king's palace to the mud house. Spiritual darkness and death encompassed the nation, while its gods were sacred bulls, scarabs, and the forces of nature. This death was far more serious than physical death.

While Egypt is a type of death and condemnation, grace intervened to bring life, deliverance, and hope.

## The Wilderness—the Place of Testing

The wilderness represents the flesh. It is taken up with food, drink, weariness, complaint, and carnal warfare with

Amalek, the kinsman in the flesh. But the wilderness speaks of a brighter side. All of God's children are redeemed by blood and by power. The power of the world has been broken, Egypt is behind them, the Red Sea has been crossed, Canaan is before them, and God is with them. God opened the Red Sea in front of them to let them out and closed it behind them to keep them out. Their entire resource was in God, who provided everything for them. The wilderness was and is God's school. It is here that His soldiers receive their preliminary training before the combat "against principalities, against powers, against the rulers of the darkness of this world, against the spiritual wickedness in high places" (Eph 6:12) that await them in Canaan.

It is in the wilderness experience that we discover our true nature as pilgrims and strangers. This world is not our home; we are going somewhere, and we are on the move. Therefore we must travel lightly, free from encumbrances, using, but not abusing, the things that are available.

### Canaan—the Sphere of Victory

Canaan has often been mistaken for a type of heaven. This error is especially prevalent in hymnology. Canaan is far from being typical of heaven, since it was inhabited by seven apostate nations and given over to warfare. Canaan is a promised possession, a rich and fertile land flowing with milk and honey, but a land that had to be conquered, appropriated, and possessed. In a true sense, the land belonged to Israel by divine gift, yet every inch had to be won. Israel's seasoned army was now under the command of Joshua. What is described historically in the book of Joshua is set forth doctrinally in the epistle to the Ephesians. The warfare in both is not merely against flesh and blood, "but against principalities, against powers, against the rulers of darkness of this world, against spiritual wickedness in high places"

(Eph 6:12). The same powerful monstrosities that brought on the judgment of the flood, the giants (nephilim, "fallen ones") were in possession of Canaan (Num 13:32-33). This fact alone seems to account for Joshua's war of extermination. The iniquity of the Amorites was at last full (Gen 15:16). The liberals and the so-called modernists have made much of this war of extermination. Faith sees it through different eyes.

Our Canaan is a place of spiritual warfare waged against the apostate forces unleashed by Satan. He who has not come into an awareness of this is still a babe and unable to bear arms. The epistle to the Ephesians should arouse us to battle. It is a call to arms, and the believer must put on the full armor of God (chap. 6).

As we view the children of Israel in Egypt, in the wilderness, and in Canaan, we do well to keep before us the words of the apostle: "Now all these things happened unto them for ensamples: and they are written for our admonition, upon whom the ends of the world are come" (1 Co 10:11).

# 24

# A GENTILE PROPHET—BALAAM, THE MAN

THE HEALING LOOK at the brazen serpent marked the end of one era and the beginning of another. The succession of murmurings reached a climax in the new generation, the one that had arisen to succeed the people who had fallen in the wilderness as a result of their failure at Kadesh-barnea. One generation had been set aside. Another generation, comprised of younger men and women, now assumed responsibility. Our first view of this second generation must convince us that they are truly the children of their fathers. Miriam is dead, Aaron is dead, and the march towards the promised land is resumed.

As with their fathers, so with the children. When the going became difficult, murmurings flowed from their lips in a steady stream. "And they journeyed from Mount Hor by the way of the Red sea, to compass the land of Edom: and the soul of the people was much discouraged because of the way. And the people spake against God, and against Moses, Wherefore have ye brought us up out of Egypt to die in the wilderness? for there is no bread, neither is there any water; and our soul loatheth this light bread" (Num 21:4-5). They charged God with their miseries and murmured against His providences.

The question naturally arises: What will God do with

these children of the people who left Egypt forty years ago? Will He be as patient and as long-suffering as formerly, or will He teach them a lesson so severe and conclusive as to turn them from their sins and prepare them for the destiny that was set before them?

God responded to their complaints by sending fiery serpents that inflicted suffering and death. The supreme manifestation of human depravity formed the background for a luminous display of divine grace. It was this Old Testament incident that our Lord used in talking to Nicodemus, applying it to Himself to show forth the nature of His redemptive death. This experience with the brazen serpent marked a great change in Israel. It was to Israel what the cross is to the Christian. It marked a great transition. After this time, we hear no more murmuring; we are made acquainted with the joy that accompanies salvation. They drank from the wells of Beer (pronounced "Beh-ere"). "Then Israel sang this song, Spring up, O well; sing ye unto it" (Num 21:17).

First, the brazen serpent is set forth as a type of redemption. Then follows the waters of Beer. Water is the symbol of the Holy Spirit bestowed (Jn 7:37-39). The joy that comes from the Spirit, symbolized by the refreshing waters, was followed by power. Immediately Israel had two great victories. The first was over Sihon, the king of the Ammorites, who refused to let Israel pass through the land. The other was over Og, the king of Bashan. As suggested by Dr. C. I. Scofield in the *Scofield Reference Bible,* "The spiritual order here is beautiful: (1) atonement (vs. 8, 9; John 3.14, 15); (2) water, symbol of the Spirit bestowed (v. 16; John 7.37-39); (3) joy (vs. 17, 18; Rom. 14.17); (4) power (vs. 21-24)."

## The Man

This last victory brings Israel to the border of the land of Moab, ruled over by Balak, the son of Zippor. Filled with fear as a result of Israel's recent and earlier victories, Balak sent for Balaam the son of Peor, a strange and contradictory person, a Gentile prophet and a soothsayer, with the hope that Balaam would come and place a curse or spell upon the people of Israel.

With this introduction to Balaam, we are brought face to face with two great facts: the strangeness of his character and the magnificence of his gifts. First let us consider Balaam, the man; later we will deal with Balaam, the prophet.

Of Balaam's origin we know practically nothing except that he was a native of Pethor, meaning "interpretation." A study of his character reveals the fact that he was a man with a split personality. He possessed a strange mixture of vice and virtue, of decision and indecision, and of lofty hopes and despicable practices. He could well be characterized as the man who would run with the hare and with the hounds, who would eat his cake and keep it too, and who would serve both God and man. He was a double-minded man who longed to die the death of the righteous, but who, in fact, died the death of a dog.

## His Character

Through Balaam was a Gentile, he had many rare privileges. He was brought into close contact with God. God spoke to him directly and answered his prayers. He had the Word of the Lord in his mouth (Num 23:29). His privileges were extraordinary. His eyes were opened to see the angel that stood in the way (Num 22:31-35). At times he was moved by the Holy Spirit (Num 24:2). He had a lofty concept of righteousness. He knew how to pray. As seen by his prophetic utterances, he was an exceedingly brilliant man. As an orator and poet he was unsurpassed.

Balaam's character was marked by many contradictions and weaknesses. First, he wanted so serve two masters. While recognizing divine authority, Balaam sought to change God to suit his own whims. He represents those who seek to follow the permissive, rather than the directive, will of God.

Second, he wanted two kinds of wages. Peter speaks of those who have forsaken the right way, and are gone astray, following the way of Balaam the son of Bosor, who loved the wages of unrighteousness" (2 Pe 2:15). Balaam was unwilling to do anything that would deprive him of either kind. Balaam was a man who bartered his soul for greed. He was as cautious and cunning as he was coveteous. He was a hireling prophet who let it be known that his pious services were available for the proper price with the guarantee that they were accompanied by divine sanction.

Many who follow in his train seek to capitalize on God by diluting the gospel from a bloodred to a pale pink, from a shout to a whisper, and from a conviction to an opinion.

Third, Balaam wanted to support diverging viewpoints at the same time. He tried, as it were, to ride two horses going in opposite directions. He wished both to bless and to curse. He wanted to obey the word of the Lord, and at the same time he desired to go to Balak to curse God's people. How similar this is to so many who want to serve God and yet find themselves unwilling to give up the world. Their yoke with the world is too binding for them to find easy release.

Fourth, Balaam wanted two kinds of friends. He willingly would have been friends with everybody. He was a timid soul, perhaps one who loved peace at any price, and a hail-fellow-well-met—a yes-man on all occasions. "Ye adulterers and adulteresses, know ye not that the friendship of the world is enmity with God? whosoever therefore will be a friend of the world is the enemy of God" (Ja 4:4).

Fifth, Balaam wanted two religions. He could adapt himself to any conditions, provided the wages were right and the new alignment promised favorable advancement and reasonable security. He had a flexible conscience that was capable of change to meet existing conditions.

Sixth, Balaam wanted two philosophies. He held to a doctrine that was unrelated to practice. He wanted to live like the devil and die like a saint. "Who can count the dust of Jacob, and the number of the fourth part of Israel? Let me die the death of the righteous, and let my last end be like his!" (Num 23:10). Following a lesson on the rich man and Lazarus (Lk 16:19-31), a Sunday school student was asked which of the two he would like to be. He replied, "I'd rather be the rich man while I live and Lazarus when I die."

## Balaam's Character as Depicted in the New Testament

Balaam is never named among the honored saints of the Bible. His name is not found on the roll call of faithful men in the New Testament. Three of the New Testament writers, Peter, Jude, and John, mention him, but all do so with a disparaging note of warning.

In 2 Peter we learn of the "way" of Balaam. "Which have forsaken the right way, and are gone astray, following the way of Balaam the son of Bosor, who loved the wages of unrighteousness" (2:15). Here Balaam is seen as the typical hireling prophet, representing those who refuse to speak out or stand up and be counted. As one preacher said to another, "Between what I would like to do and what I can do there is a great gulf fixed." In other words, "My job depends upon cooperation with, and conformity to, the powers that be."

Jude speaks of the "error" of Balaam. "Woe unto them! for they have gone in the way of Cain, and ran greedily after the error of Balaam for reward, and perished in the gainsaying of Core" (Jude 11). The notes of the *Scofield Reference Bible* comment: "The 'error' of Balaam was that, reasoning from natural morality, and seeing the evil in Israel, he supposed a righteous God *must* curse them. He was blind to the higher morality of the Cross, through which God maintains and enforces the authority and awful sanction of His law, so that He can be just and the justifier of a believing sinner."

The late Dr. John J. Van Gorder, in his book *The Alphabet of Christian Experience,* very aptly commented "It is at this very point that the proponents of the 'insecurity' of the believer fail." "But to him that worketh not, but believeth on him that justifieth the ungodly, his faith is counted for righteousness. Even as David also describeth the blessedness of the man, unto whom God imputeth righteousness without works. Saying, Blessed are they whose iniquities are forgiven, and whose sins are covered. Blessed is the man to whom the Lord will not impute sin" (Ro 4:5-8).

In the book of Revelation we have the "doctrine" of Balaam. "But I have a few things against thee, because thou has there them that hold the doctrine of Balaam, who taught Balac to cast a stumblingblock before the children of Israel, to eat things sacrificed unto idols, and to commit fornication" (Rev 2:14). Here the *Scofield Reference Bible* says: "The 'doctrine of Balaam' . . . was his teaching Balak to corrupt the people who could not be cursed . . ., by tempting them to marry women of Moab, defile their separation, and abandon their pilgrim character." This is emphasized in the message of the risen Christ to the church of Pergamos. This great change came to the historical church in the time of Constantine the Great in the fourth century A.D., when the church became the patron of the state.

# 25

# A GENTILE PROPHET—BALAAM'S MESSAGE

To Balaam, the only Gentile prophet whose words are recorded in Scripture, was given some of the most sublime words of prophecy ever uttered. These prophecies were in the form of parables. It must strike us with some degree of a shock to realize that God often employs ungodly men to carry out His will. As men, we are prone to assume that God only uses men because of their piety and their spiritual perception and consecration. We now learn that He often resorts, as in the case of Samson, to the employment of men in which are found many contradictions and inconsistencies.

It is one of the mysteries of the Bible that the gift of prophecy can be possessed apart from moral chacter. The unwilling prophet is forced to say what God puts in his mouth. Even Caiaphas the high priest, who was instrumental in bringing Christ to judgment and the cross, had this to say, "Ye know nothing at all, nor consider that it is expedient for us, that one man should die for the people, and that the whole nation perish not. And this spake he not of himself: but being high priest that year, he prophesied that Jesus should die for that nation" (Jn 11:49-51).

We must never forget that God is sovereign. The fact that God uses such men to proclaim His message is well established in the Scriptures. The mistaken concept that God can only use good men to deliver a divine message has apparently led many Bible expositors to assume that little importance should be attached to these four parables of Balaam. We are bold to assert that the contrary is true. As a matter of fact, the prophecies of Balaam, the Gentile prophet, give us a panoramic view of Israel's entire history, reaching even to the millennium. Similarly, the prophet Daniel in a Gentile court prophesied a panoramic view of the times of the Gentiles.

It is interesting to observe both the likeness and the contrast that exist between Daniel and Balaam. In character, in personality, and in disposition, the two men stand poles apart; yet their prophecies are equally important. The recognition of this fact is essential to the understanding of all biblical prophecy.

Balaam viewed from the wilderness an unpromising people, a nation of strangers and pilgrims who were outwordly despised, yet who were destined to be the key both to redemption and to the ultimate world order. In contrast, Daniel spoke his prophecy in the Babylonian court, surrounded with pomp, splendor, power, and magnificence. In the midst of the debauchery of this oriental court, the prophet was granted the privilege of looking down the corridors of time and viewing the whole panorama of the times of the Gentiles.

Daniel's prophecy was extended and in many instances given in minute detail. Balaam's prophecy, on the other hand, was brief and spoken in parables from the top of the rock. Daniel looked *down* the corridors of time to behold the far distant scenes of desolation and ruin that would most certainly be visited upon the Gentile nations. Balaam, in his turn, looked *up* the corridors of time to view the history of Israel as it involved the coming glory that God would bestow upon this ancient and holy nation.

The prophecies given to the two men were similar in that

they both dealth primarily with the end time—Daniel with the end time of the Gentiles and Balaam with the end time of Israel. The two prophecies taken together give us a picture of the whole of the world's history. "Prophecy is history prewritten," it has been said; or, "Prophecy is the mold of history." This fact alone should challenge us to give heed to Balaam's parables. A failure to observe this prophecy, or a misinterpretation of it, can cause much confusion and misunderstanding among Bible expositors.

Balaam uttered four prophecies concerning Israel, and much of what he said awaits fulfillment. Four words can express and characterize these four parables: *separation, justification, sanctification,* and *exaltation.*

## Separation

The first utterance of Balaam spoke of the general character of the chosen people of God. His first words formed the foundation and the keynote of all that he was about to say under divine inspiration. In truth, he was speaking to Balak, son of Zippor, the king of Moab, and the words of the Lord were put in his mouth. "And the LORD put a word in Balaam's mouth, and said, Return unto Balak, and thus thou shalt speak. And he returned unto him, and, lo, he stood by his burnt sacrifice, he, and all the princes of Moab. And he took up his parable, and said, Balak the king of Moab hath brought me from Aram, out of the mountains of the east, saying, Come, curse me Jacob, and come, defy Israel. How shall I curse, whom God hath not cursed? or how shall I defy, whom the LORD hath not defied? For from the top of the rocks I see him, and from the hills I behold him: lo, the people shall dwell alone, and shall not be reckoned among the nations. Who can count the dust of Jacob, and the number of the fourth part of Israel? Let me die the death of the righteous, and let my last end be like his!" (Num 23:5-10).

This call to separation, along with Israel's response to it in either obedience or failure, marks the whole history of Jehovah's ancient people. Since Israel, according to the Abrahamic covenant, was and is the key to world conditions for good or evil, the parables take on tremendous significance.

Keeping in mind this truth, that one has before him the key to the entire field of ethnology, every word seems to weigh a ton. Let us proceed with our examination.

First, we see the impossibility of man cursing what God has not cursed. If only the nations had recognized this truth down through the ages, there would have been no anti-Semitism (hatred of the Jewish people).

Second, God's people are to be a separate people. They are to dwell alone. This has always characterized the history of the Jews. There are two distinct divisions of people in the Old Testament—the Jews and the Gentiles.

Third, Israel's separateness or its failure to be separate has been a guiding factor in the pattern and course of the world order. This is historically evident today. A holy people out of a holy land means world chaos. A holy people in a holy land means a divine cosmos. History is replete with evidence that when Israel lost her separateness and mixed with other people, forgetful of her God, and engaged in idolatry, she experienced confusion, sin, and judgment. The same was true of other nations. The Abrahamic covenant is a criterion for the moral and spiritual order of this world. When Israel is in fellowship, the world is blessed. When it is out of fellowship with Jehovah, the world suffers. This is not only the key to the past but also to the present and to the future.

Fourth, Israel's separateness has made it a miracle people. All the nations of antiquity, such as the Egyptians, the Assyrians, the Babylonians, and even the ancient Greeks and Romans, have long since perished and moldered in the dust of a vanished civilization. But here are the Jews today—separate and distinct, a people of destiny.

Like the three Hebrew children in the fiery furnace, who were preserved from death by a divine miracle, the nation of Israel stands to this day as an indestructible people. In spite of the many attempts to erradicate the nation, including the Nazi slaughter of six million Jews in World War II, and in spite of her sufferings and scatterings and unparalleled persecution, Israel has increased. In the glory of the coming kingdom, when the Messiah, the one whom Israel pierced, will be recognized, Israel will be without number—a blessed and mighty people.

The fifth thing we notice here is Balaam's cry: "Let me die the death of the righteous, and let my last end be like his!" (Num 23:10). This indicates that Balaam was given a glimpse of Israel's ultimate glory.

## Justification

Just as the first parable was spoken from the high place of Baal, the second was spoken from the summit of Pisgah and the last two from the top of Peor. Each succeeding point was nearer the camp and afforded a better view. Doubtless Balak, by this gradual procedure, hoped to induce Balaam more effectively to curse Israel.

The first view is from the high place of Baal. Here only a partial view of the camp was presented. The last view was from Peor, and from here was brought into range the entire camp of some three million people. Imagine the astounding view that was presented to Balaam as he beheld in the valley an ordered camp with its many-colored tents and the glory cloud over the tabernacle, the place of the divine presence.

Balaam's second parable was spoken, as we have noticed, from the summit of Pisgah. Having spoken of Israel's separation, he began speaking of Israel's justification: "And he took up his parable, and said, Rise up, Balak, and hear; hearken unto me, thou son of Zippor: God is not a man, that he should lie; neither the son of man, that he should repent: hath he said, and shall he not do it? or hath he spoken, and shall he not make it good? Behold, I have received commandment to bless: and he hath blessed; and I cannot reverse it. He hath not beheld iniquity in Jacob, neither hath he seen perverseness in Israel: the LORD his God is with him, and the shout of a king is among them. God brought them out of Egypt; he hath as it were the strength of an unicorn. Surely there is no enchantment against Jacob, neither is there any divination against Israel: according to this time it shall be said of Jacob and of Israel, What hath God wrought! Behold, the people shall rise up as a great lion, and lift up himself as a young lion: he shall not lie down until he eat of the prey, and drink the blood of the slain" (Num 23:18-24). Here we see the standing of this people before God.

"And the LORD put a word in Balaam's mouth" (v. 5). Here we have full and complete inspiration. It is God who has chosen, separated, and blessed Israel. This, after all, is the unshakable foundation upon which Jehovah's eternal salvation rests, both for Israel and for the church. At no point are the thoughts of human reason and the facts of divine revelation so far apart. The great mystery of justification is a revelation and must be spiritually discerned. Neither iniquity in Jacob nor perverseness in Israel was visible to the divine eye, because that eye rested upon the perfections of Him in whom Israel was chosen.

"Who shall lay any thing to the charge of God's elect? It is God that justifieth" (Ro 8:33). On the basis of complete redemption, God declares righteousness and imputes righteousness to those who believe. What a blessed thought it is that by His grace He reckons us righteous as He beholds us in His Son. "And hope maketh not ashamed; because the love of God is shed abroad in our hearts by the Holy Ghost which is given unto us. For when we were yet without strength, in due time Christ died for the ungodly. For scarcely for a righteous man will one die: yet peradventure for a good man some would even dare to die. But God commendeth his love toward us, in that, while we were yet sinners, Christ died for us" (5:5-8).

There is little happiness in the heart of even the believer until he apprehends and appropriates this truth. We must receive by faith what God's Word has proclaimed to be. "There is therefore now no condemnation to them which are in Christ Jesus" (8:1).

Concerning this passage, the late Dr. Arno C. Gaebelein said, "It seems a very significant fact that in all of Balaam's parables, sin and guilt are not mentioned. However, it does not say here that Israel is without iniquity or evil travail, but the statement is that God has not beheld iniquity and not seen perverseness in Israel" (*The Annotated Bible*).

It is this truth, so clearly set forth in Balaam's second parable and supported by the entire body of Scriptures, that is so little understood by those who hate the Jews as well as by those Bible expositors who reckon God to be through with His ancient people. A lack of acceptance and understanding of this fact has caused much anti-Semitism. No system of eschatology can be understood that omits the people of Israel.

Along with this justification, Balaam's prophetic eye seems to pierce the clouds of glory to behold God's presence and the anticipation of a king yet unseen by the natural eye. "The LORD his God is with him, and the shout of a king is among them" (Num 23:21).

## Sanctification

The third parable tells of the final exaltation of Israel and the humiliation of its enemies. "And when Balaam saw that it pleased the Lord to bless Israel, he went not, as at other times, to seek for enchantments, but he set his face toward the wilderness. And Balaam lifted up his eyes, and he saw Israel abiding in his tents according to their tribes; and the spirit of God came upon him. And he took up his parable, and said, Balaam the son of Beor hath said, and the man whose eyes are open hath said: He hath said, which heard the words of God, which saw the vision of the Almighty, falling into a trance, but having his eyes open: How goodly are thy tents, O Jacob, and thy tabernacles, O Israel! As the valleys are they spread forth, as gardens by the river's side, as the trees of lign aloes which the Lord hath planted, and as cedar trees beside the waters. He shall pour the water out of his buckets, and his seed shall be in many waters, and his king shall be higher than Agag, and his kingdom shall be exalted. God brought him forth out of Egypt; he hath as it were the strength of an unicorn: he shall eat up the nations his enemies, and shall break their bones, and pierce them through with his arrows. He couched, he lay down as a lion, and as a great lion: who shall stir him up? Blessed is he that blesseth thee, and cursed is he that curseth thee" (Num. 24:1-9).

Bear in mind that Israel is still living in the wilderness and dwelling in the lowly habitation of tents as a journeying people. But the prophetic eye, with God, views the centuries to behold the time when Israel's unbelief will end and that nation, with her king, will be exalted in the earth. Here Agag, the king of the Amalekites, a people who were the natural enemies of Israel, could well represent the coming Antichrist. Here again we behold in miniature an outline and preview of things to come.

## Exaltation

In this fourth parable we behold the Messiah Himself as the Star and Scepter. "And he took up his parable, and said, Balaam the son of Beor hath said, and the man whose eyes are open hath said: he hath said, which heard the words of God, and knew the knowledge of the most High, which saw the vision of the Almighty, falling into a trance, but having his eyes open: I shall see him, but not now: I shall behold him, but not nigh: there shall come a Star out of Jacob, and a Scepter shall rise out of Israel, and shall smite the corners of Moab, and destroy all the children of Sheth" (Num 24:15-17).

In the first three parables we have viewed the nation, and now we are about to behold the person. Concerning this parable, Dr. Arno C. Gaebelein said, "It is a very pronounced Messianic prophecy relating to the time when the kingdom is to be restored to Israel. Many teachers of God's Word have made the mistake of applying this prophecy to the time of the first coming of the Lord Jesus Christ. The Jews recognize the prophecy as relating to the King Messiah"

In concluding our study of the messages of Balaam, let us again note the importance of the prophecy itself. Even though the utterances, inspired of God, fell from the unwilling lips of an unworthy prophet, we have herein a preview of the entire history of God's ancient people. To know Israel's past, present, and future is to know about the world in which we live as well as God's ultimate program for the ages to come. To fail in obtaining this knowledge is to fail miserably.

# 26

# ISRAEL'S WILDERNESS LESSONS

NEARLY FORTY YEARS had passed since the children of Israel left Egypt. A new generation had arisen to replace those who had disqualified themselves from entering the promised land through complaint born of unbelief. Their complaining ultimately reached its climax of rebellion at Kadesh-barnea, where the people failed to enter into their inheritance. Of this former generation, only Joshua, Caleb, and Moses remained. Moses was soon to be summoned to Pisgah's stormy heights. There he would be shown the land of promise before his undimmed eyes were closed in death and he was buried by his Lord in a lonely grave.

From the human side, the scene is most pathetic. Moses, too, had failed at Meribah. He had failed to sanctify God before the people when he struck the rock, to which he was commanded to speak. His tragic failure had cost him the coveted privilege of leading the children of Israel into the promised land. Though he had pleaded with the Lord to be granted this privilege, God refused his request.

"And I besought the LORD at that time, saying, O Lord GOD, thou hast begun to show thy servant thy greatness, and thy mighty hand: for what God is there in heaven or in earth, that can do according to thy works, and according to thy might? I pray thee, let me go over, and see the good land that is beyond Jordan, that goodly mountain, and Lebanon.

But the LORD was wroth with me for your sakes, and would not hear me: and the LORD said unto me, Let it suffice thee; speak no more unto me of this matter" (Deu 3:23-26).

The last work this great man of God was privileged to do was that of training this second generation preparatory to entering the land under the new leadership of Joshua. It is this preparation that forms the subject of our present study. Deuteronomy 8 seems to epitomize these great lessons born out of an unforgettable experience that came to a people dedicated to God. In this chapter there are four words that seem to jump at us. They are: *observe* (v. 1), *remember* (v. 2), *consider* (v. 5), *and beware* (v. 11).

## OBSERVE

The first lesson God would have His creatures learn is, "Observe to do" (Deu 8:1). Obedience is so basic and essential that nothing else will count with God until obedience is in evidence. It was disobedience that caused man's fall. Obedience through grace, begotten of faith, restores man to the orbit of the divine will. Only judgment remains for those who do not obey.

With obedience, Israel is promised three things: "All the commandments which I command thee this day shall ye observe to do, that ye may live, and multiply, and go in and possess the land which the LORD sware unto your fathers" (Deu 8:1). First, there was the promise of life. To Israel, it was a promise of the continuation of physical life, conditioned on their keeping of the law. For us, the promise of life is based upon grace, the gift of God through faith. Second, Israel was promised growth or prosperity in the physical realm. Our obedience brings spiritual blessings. Third, they were promised a land—earthly possessions. Our promise is that all things are ours, both here and hereafter.

The ownership of the land of Canaan was granted to Israel

by an oath through Abraham, Isaac, and Jacob. The time element of the possession of the land depended on obedience. The right of ownership has never been abrogated, but full possession has been delayed by disobedience. It is one thing to own land; it is another thing to move in and possess it.

### Remember

"And thou shalt remember all the way which the Lord thy God led thee these forty years in the wilderness, to humble thee, and to prove thee, to know what was in thine heart, whether thou wouldest keep his commandments, or no" (Deu 8:2).

There is no human attribute more essential to personality, more needful for the depths of living, and more pertinent to a degree of intelligent existence and personal safety than the function of memory. Apart from it there can be no growth, no profit by experience, no gratitude of recall, no continuity of personality, no sense of identity with the past, no fellowship with the infinite, and no hope for an intelligent future, either here or hereafter.

One cannot read the Scriptures with scrutiny without being impressed by the recurring divine exhortation, "Remember." So this important passage seems to epitomize the essentials of Israel's wilderness experience as it says, "Remember all the way."

First, it was a way of discipline. It was the way God had led them—through the sea, to the bitter waters of Marah, by the way of the wilderness, through dark valleys, and over barren and treacherous mountains. The way was not smooth. They found no path for their feet in a trackless wilderness—only a cloud that guided; they found no food for their hunger except the bread from heaven; they found no water except that obtained from the smitten rock; they found no diversion except the daily refreshing from God's overshadowing providence and manifest presence; they had no passion except that which was made real by the hand of faith that appropriated divine promises and made them present riches.

"Now faith is the substance of things hoped for, the evidence of things not seen" (Heb 11:1). It was the way of discipline. This is always true for those whom God would greatly use. He must first subject them to fiery trials and severe discipline. This was true with men like Abraham, Joseph, Moses, Daniel, and Paul. Bishop Hall wrote: "God has had but one Son without sin, but none without suffering." To apprehend God's way with His children is to go a long way on the road of joyous Christian living. The punishment that God permits is not always retributive but educative. However, let us make it plain that the people of Israel suffered much and were punished for their own sins.

Concerning the people of Israel, the psalmist wrote: "Our fathers understood not thy wonders in Egypt; they remembered not the multitude of thy mercies; but provoked him at the sea, even at the Red sea. Nevertheless he saved them for his name's sake, that he might make his mighty power to be known. He rebuked the Red sea also, and it was dried up: so he led them through the depths, as through the wilderness. And he saved them from the hand of him that hated them, and redeemed them from the hand of the enemy. And the waters covered their enemies: there was not one of them left. Then believed they his words; they sang his praise. They soon forgat his works; they waited not for his counsel: but lusted exceedingly in the wilderness, and tempted God in the desert. And he gave them their request; but sent leanness into their soul. They envied Moses also in the camp, and Aaron the saint of the LORD. The earth opened and swallowed up Dathan, and covered the company of Abiram. And a fire was kindled in their company; the flame burned up the wicked.

They made a calf in Horeb, and worshipped the molten image. Thus they changed their glory into the similitude of an ox that eateth grass. They forgot God their saviour, which had done great things in Egypt; wondrous works in the land of Ham, and terrible things by the Red sea. Therefore he said that he would destroy them, had not Moses his chosen stood before him in the breach, to turn away his wrath, lest he should destroy them. Yea, they despised the pleasant land, they believed not his word: but murmured in their tents, and hearkened not unto the voice of the LORD. Therefore he lifted up his hand against them, to overthrow them in the wilderness" (Ps 106:7-26).

"Neither hath this man sinned, nor his parents: but that the works of God should be made manifest in him" (Jn 9:3). This was our Lord's reply to the disciples who asked, "Master, who did sin, this man or his parents, that he was born blind?" (v. 2).

Second, it was a hazardous way. The path they were told to recall had been hazardous. Reluctant feet had traversed the howling waste of the wilderness. God Himself said it was a "great and terrible wilderness, wherein were fiery serpents, and scorpions, and drought" (Deu 8:15). Besides all this, their course was through enemy territory. There the foe, filled with envy and hatred, waited to oppose, to molest, and to destroy. Yet it was God who was leading them. Only faith can submit with resignation and hope to such an experience, where the flesh only finds cause for murmuring, complaint, and rebellion.

Third, it was a severe way. God allowed His people to suffer hunger. Psalm 107:5 says, "Hungry and thirsty, their soul fainted in them." It is logical to conclude that at times the people doubted God's love and even His presence and care.

Among the people of the Near East there are weavers of exquisite and expensive tapestries who weave from the reverse side. Uninitiated eyes, watching the work, see only a riot of colors and loose ends with little or no art. To comprehend, one must see the other side. In the same way, from our point of view it often appears that God's dealing has but little meaning, because we view only the movements of His hands as He combines and arranges the dark trials, hardships, disappointments, and sorrows with the bright threads of spiritual blessing. We must try to see the design on the other side, where faith displays His love and grace in a tapestry that is destined to hang in the King's gallery.

Fourth, it was a right way. "And thou shalt remember all the way which the LORD thy God led thee these forty years in the wilderness" (Deu 8:2). Many man bear with fortitude the severe trials of a torturous experience if it only lasts for a short time. It is when there seems to be no end in sight and no relief near, and when hopes are deferred, that the heart grows faint, the nerves grow frayed, and tempers grow short. In Psalm 107 where these wilderness experiences are recounted, we read in verse 7 and 8: "And he led them forth by the right way, that they might go to a city of habitation. Oh that men would praise the LORD for his goodness, and for his wonderful works to the children of men!" At the beginning of these forty years we read: "And it came to pass, when Pharaoh had let the people go, that God led them not through the way of the land of the Philistines, although that was near; for God said, Lest peradventure the people repent when they see war, and they return to Egypt" (Ex 13:17).

When we fret and complain at God's way, Satan is pleased. Sin most often comes in disguise and reveals its hand in impatience and rebellion against God's providential leadings.

### Consider

"Thou shalt also consider in thine heart, that, as a man chasteneth his son, so the Lord thy God chasteneth thee" (Deu 8:5).

There arises before us that unending question, Why? Why does God allow His children to suffer? Surely He who redeemed Israel has not forgotten them or ceased to love them. The answer must lie elsewhere, and this verse gives it to us. We are now at the end of the forty years. James wrote: "Behold, we count them happy which endure. Ye have heard of the patience of Job, and have seen the end of the Lord; that the Lord is very pitiful, and of tender mercy" (Ja 5:11). We see it, but Job did not see it at the time. This very fact constituted the severity of the trial. The verse of our text calls us to "consider," and there is a threefold purpose.

First, "to humble thee" says Deuteronomy 8:2. It is strikingly evident that God did not call the Israelites because they were docile. Like many of us, they were stiff-necked, stubborn people. Scripture proves that God can use men of multiplied weaknesses, but He can use no one who is proud, self-willed, and stubborn. This He must cure if He would use an individual. Nothing so humbles a man as the fiery trials of sufferings. We are taking the privilege of using a story from the late E. W. Black's book entitled *Living Messages from the Canaan Journey*:

"The following story about a shepherd and his sheep may help us to a better understanding of God's dealings with His people. It is said that a lady was spending the summer in Switzerland. One day she started out for a walk. Presently, as she climbed a mountainside, she came to a shepherd's fold. She walked to the door and looked in. There sat the shepherd. Around him lay his flock. Near at hand, on a pile of straw, lay a single sheep. It seemed to be suffering. Scanning it closely, the lady saw that its leg was broken. At once her sympathy went out to the suffering sheep. She looked up inquiringly to the shepherd.

" 'How did it happen?' she asked.

"To her amazement the shepherd answered: 'Madam, I broke that sheep's leg.'

"A look of pain swept over the visitor's face. Seeing it, the shepherd went on: 'Madam, of all the sheep in my flock, this one was the most wayward. It would not obey my voice. It would not follow in the pathway in which I was leading the flock. It wandered on the verge of many a perilous cliff and dizzy abyss. And not only was it disobedient itself, but it was leading the other sheep of my flock astray. I had had experience with sheep of this kind before, so I broke its leg. The first day I went to it with food, it tried to bite me. I let it lie alone for a couple of days. Then I went back to it. And now, it not only took the food, but licked my hand and showed every sign of submission and even affection.

" 'And, now, let me tell you something. When this sheep is well, as it soon will be, it will be the model sheep of my flock. No sheep will hear my voice so quickly. None will follow so closely at my side. Instead of leading its mates astray, it will now be an example and a guide for the wayward ones, leading them, with itself, in the path of obedience to my call. In short, a complete transformation will have come into the life of this wayward sheep. It has learned obedience through its sufferings.' "

In order to comprehend the full benefits of these forty years of hardship, we only have to compare the second generation, at the end of the forty years, with those who began the journey. The older generation murmured until they all died; the new generation, having passed through these years of trials, murmured but once, and God sent the brazen serpents. That cured them. The first generation failed at Kadesh-barnea and was condemed to die in the wilderness.

Here is the new generation: "And they answered Joshua, saying, All that thou commandest us we will do, and whithersoever thou sendest us, we will go" (Jo 1:16). Here we have an example of what we find written in Hebrews 11:9-11: "By faith he sojourned in the land of promise, as in a strange country, dwelling in tabernacles with Isaac and Jacob, the heirs with him of the same promise: for he looked for a city which hath foundations, whose builder and maker is God. Through faith also Sara herself received strength to conceive seed, and was delivered of a child when she was past age, because she judged him faithful who had promised."

There is a second purpose for God's testing of the Israelites. God chastised the people to prove them "and to prove thee" (Deu 8:2). We well understand that God needed no proof as to what was in man. It was Israel that needed this exhibition of its own depravity. This is one of the two great wilderness lessons referred to above. To know self and to know God have always remained the supreme lessons. God proved the people at Marah. "Then said the LORD unto Moses, Behold, I will rain bread from heaven for you; and the people shall go out and gather a certain rate every day, that I may prove them, whether they will walk in my law, or no" (Ex 16:4). When the law was given at Sinai, Moses said to the people, "God is come to prove you" (20:20). God tested Abraham in the offering of Isaac.

To understand God's testing, we must keep in mind three facts: Man must be revealed to himself for correction; man must be revealed to others for an example for good or bad; and, God operates in a moral universe of intelligent creations, heavenly and otherwise.

The third reason for testing was that God wanted Israel to have a proper evaluation of His word. "And he humbled thee, and suffered thee to hunger, and fed thee with manna, which thou knewest not, neither did thy fathers know; that he might make thee know that man doth not live by bread only, but by every word that proceedeth out of the mouth of the Lord doth man live" (Deu 8:3). These are the very words quoted by our Lord in another wilderness (Mt 4:4). It was this "sword of the Spirit" (Eph 6:17) that put to rout the tempter. To learn to trust God's word is the highest attainment of faith.

### Beware

"Beware that thou forget not the Lord thy God, in not keeping his commandments, and his judgments, and his statutes, which I command thee this day" (Deu 8:11).

There is a negative aspect, as well as a positive one, to this comand. "Beware" alerts men to the things they must guard against.

First, Israel was told, "Beware that thou forget not the Lord thy God" (v. 11). A new day was before them. "The Lord thy God bringeth thee into a good land, a land of brooks of water, of fountains and depths that spring out of valleys and hills; a land of wheat, and barley, and vines, and fig trees, and pomegranates; a land of oil olive, and honey; a land wherein thou shalt eat bread without scarceness, thou shalt not lack any thing in it; a land whose stones are iron, and out of whose hills thou mayest dig brass. When thou hast eaten and art full, then thou shalt bless the Lord thy God for the good land which he hath given thee" (vv. 7-10).

With this new day came new perils. The perils of prosperity are often more subtle and dangerous than the perils of adversity. How tragic it is for men to forget God! In Hosea we read: "According to their pasture, so were they filled; they were filled, and their heart was exalted; therefore have they forgotten me" (13:6). To be godless, and we are often warned against this, is simply a state of mind and heart in which we ignore God and act as though He did not exist. How many live like that? This is exactly the state of the rich farmer of Luke 12, who was called a fool. He was successful, but he retained no sense of God's presence or man's need.

The second thing God warned against was self-indulgence. "Lest when thou hast eaten and art full, and hast built goodly houses, and dwelt therein" (8:12). Prosperity leads to self-indulgence, and few sins are more destructive. Those who burn incense to ungodly lust will sacrifice the happiness of their families, their friends, and their own good name on the altar of their own lust. Countless husbands spend their wages for drink while their families suffer with hunger.

Mel Trotter once told how low he was brought by drink. He said when his baby girl died, some neighbors bought a pair of shoes and put them on the child's body. Her father came in, and while his wife was out of the room, he opened the casket, took off the shoes, and sold them to buy whiskey.

The warning in this passage is against pride of heart. "Then thine heart be lifted up" (8:14). No one, preacher or layman, is immune to such a danger. Jeremiah reminds us: "The heart is deceitful above all things, and desperately wicked: who can know it?" (Jer 17:9). Pride of heart is the corroding worship of self. Included here is pride of opinion, pride of fact, pride of race, pride of place, and pride of grace.

In meditating on this, it might be well for us to recall what happened to the boastful Simon Peter. He said, "Though all men shall be offended because of thee, yet will I never be offended" (Mt 26:33). He was soon to be disillusioned.

Think of what happened to Nebuchadnezzar because of his self-glorification. "The king spake, and said, Is not this great Babylon, that I have built for the house of the kingdom by the might of my power, and for the honour of my majesty?" (Dan 4:30). God sent him out to live as a demented man, to eat grass, and to associate with the wild beasts for seven years. But concerning his return we read: "And at the end of the days I Nebuchadnezzar lifted up mine eyes unto heaven, and mine understanding returned unto me, and I blessed the most High, and I praised and honoured him that liveth for ever, whose dominion is an everlasting dominion, and his kingdom is from generation to generation: and all the inhabitants of the earth are reputed as nothing: and he doeth according to his will in the army of heaven, and among the inhabitants of the earth: and none can stay his hand, or say unto him, What doest thou? At the same time my reason returned unto me; and for the glory of my kingdom, mine honour and brightness returned unto me; and my counsellors and my lords sought unto me; and I was established in my kingdom, and excellent majesty was added unto me. Now I Nebuchadnezzar praise and extol and honour the King of heaven, all whose works are truth, and his ways judgment: and those that walk in pride he is able to abase" (Dan 4:34-37).

Fourth, Israel was warned against self-sufficiency. "And thou say in thine heart, My power and the might of mine hand hath gotten me this wealth" (Deu 8:17). Solomon says, "He that trusteth in his own heart is a fool: but whoso walketh wisely, he shall be delivered" (Pr 28:26).

A group of Christian workers went to a rich man and asked for a donation, reminding him at the same time that it was God who had given him his wealth. The miser replied, "Maybe so, but I was there when it happened." Here again we are reminded of the danger of covetousness. "The love of money is the root of all evil: which while some coveted after, they have erred from the faith, and pierced themselves through with many sorrows" (1 Ti 6:10).

Fifth, Israel was facing the prospect of entrance into the land, and the nation was again warned against disobedience. This chapter opens and closes with the same warning. How serious this is for those living in our day, including ourselves!

# 27

# JOSHUA, THE KIND OF MAN GOD USES

MOSES WAS DEAD! "Now after the death of Moses the servant of the LORD it came to pass that the LORD spake unto Joshua the son of Nun, Moses' minister, saying, Moses my servant is dead" (Jos 1:1-2). Human leaders must die, but God's work moves on. Moses represented the Law. The Law could never lead Israel into the promised land, only to its portals. *Joshua* is the Hebrew word corresponding to the Greek word *Jesus*.

"But Christ as a son over his own house; whose house are we, if we hold fast the confidence and the rejoicing of the hope firm unto the end. Wherefore (as the Holy Ghost saith, To day if ye will hear his voice, harden not your hearts, as in the provocation, in the day of temptation in the wilderness: when your fathers tempted me, proved me, and saw my works forty years. Wherefore I was grieved with that generation, and said, They do alway err in their heart; and they have not known my ways. So I sware in my wrath, They shall not enter into my rest)" (Heb 3:6-11).

Joshua was a type of our blessed Lord. He led Israel into a place and time of rest. Rest, however, sounds like a paradox in view of the fact that the nation fought for more than a decade to capture the land and to drive out the enemy. This is the kind of rest that we read about in Hebrews—a rest from our own labors, and then complete rest in the finished work of Christ. Rest must precede labor. There is, however, the perfect rest that will be realized, both for the land and the people, in the coming millennial kingdom of our Lord. This rest is described in the fourth chapter of Hebrews.

"For he spake in a certain place of the seventh day on this wise, And God did rest the seventh day from all his works. And in this place again, If they shall enter into my rest. Seeing therefore it remaineth that some must enter therein, and they to whom it was first preached entered not in because of unbelief: again, he limiteth a certain day, saying in David, To day, after so long a time; as it is said, To day if ye will hear his voice, harden not your hearts. For if Jesus [Joshua] had given them rest, then would he not afterward have spoken of another day. There remaineth therefore a rest to the people of God. For he that is entered into his rest, he also hath ceased from his own works, as God did from his. Let us labour therefore to enter into that rest, lest any man fall after the same example of unbelief" (Heb 4:4-11).

Of this much we can be sure: Joshua represented grace while Moses represented the Law. Also, Joshua represents the type of man God can use. Four sources of strength are depicted in the first chapter of the book of Joshua.

## Joshua Was a Faithful Minister

"Now after the death of Moses the servant of the Lord it came to pass, that the Lord spake unto Joshua the son of Nun, Moses' minister" (Jos 1:1). He was born in Egypt in the midst of hardships and trials. As we read the Scriptures and the annals of human history, and as we contemplate the deeds of mankind, we discover that most people whose lives have been of significant value have been men and women who came up under hardships. Not many who were born with a silver spoon in their mouths were ever able to overcome that handicap. Abraham Lincoln was an example of a person capitalizing on hardship, and tens of thousands have had similar experiences. There are some fruits common to the South that are not palatable until they have been frostbitten. Even the persimmon that puckers the mouth when green becomes a delicious fruit after the fields are covered with hoary frost. Faith thrives best under trial.

Another thing we notice about this minister is that he was faithful in the service of Moses. He is referred to in Joshua 1:1 as Moses' minister. He was willing to play second fiddle, to take an inferior place, but having served well there, he became the kind of man that God could use.

The whole philosophy of Christianity is the reverse of natural philosophy. Human philosophy dictates, "God helps those who help themselves," while Christian philosophy tells us that God helps those who help others. Our blessed Lord said to His disciples, "Whosoever will be great among you, let him be your minister" (Mt 20:26). This has been one of the most difficult lessons for Christians to learn. It seems so natural to gain greatness by promoting oneself. The great Socrates had as a motto with which he challenged his pupils, "Know thyself." Several centuries later a Roman philosopher, Epictetus, added this, "Control thyself." It was Christ, the greatest of all, who said, "Lose thyself."

One of the characteristics of a great minister is the virtue of patience. As we read of the history of this man Joshua, we are made aware of his patience. He waited forty years, and finally he succeeded Moses. There was found in him no unholy ambition, grasping, or self-promotion. He waited, and presently his day arrived. In the midst of this service of ministering, he was found to be a man full of faith. When ten of the twelve spies brought back an evil report to Moses at Kadesh-barnea, Joshua and Caleb brought back a faithful report and recommended that the children of Israel go up at once and possess the land. In this respect he also manifested courage—a courage that led him to dare stand in the minority. Only persons of strong character can endure what he endured. Unfortunately there are some who would stand alone because of their determination to be different. This was not so with Joshua.

### Joshua Called of God

"There shall not any man be able to stand before thee all the days of thy life: as I was with Moses, so I will be with thee: I will not fail thee, nor forsake thee. Be strong and of a good courage: for unto this people shalt thou divide for an inheritance the land, which I sware unto their fathers to give them. . . . Have not I commanded thee? Be strong and of a good courage; be not afraid, neither be thou dismayed: for the Lord thy God is with thee whithersoever thou goest" (Jos 1:5-6, 9).

Of all the indispensable convictions, none is more essential to a successful Christian ministry than the conviction that one has received a divine call. Sad to say, there are many men who have entered into the gospel ministry by mere choice of profession. There is such a thing as success on the natural plane that may elicit the plaudits of men and flatter a fickle public opinion. But actually there are few things that are sadder than running without being sent or answering without being called. Conversely, there is no force that holds and reassures amid the hours of difficulty and discouragement like the towering consciousness that one is in the will of God and has been called of God to fulfill a destiny that is divinely appointed. Joshua was God's man in God's place.

Out of an experience of more than a half century of preaching and more than forty years as the pastor of one church, permit me to offer this advice to young servants of the Lord: If you are conscious that God has called you, don't run when the first shot is fired or the first opposition arises. This in no sense means that one never feels like resigning. Perhaps there are many Sunday evenings when a pastor feels it is time to quit. First of all, resign to your wife, but don't tell anybody else about it until you have full instructions from the Lord. Certainly never resign on the impulse of a moment.

Along this same line, I would give a word of warning to churches: If churches were conscious that they had God's man in God's place and that God had led them to the man of His choice, they would be more reluctant to change pastors or even to become restive under a ministry that was sometimes chafing. It is true, as in the case of Moses and Aaron, that when the people lost the sense of God's presence, they jumped on the human leadership. The Israelites derided Moses and Aaron for their leadership out of Egypt into the wilderness of trial and difficulty.

The man who is conscious of a divine call and who is living in fellowship with the Lord is a man who is invincible. He cannot be defeated, even by death. What would happen to our missionaries if they were not conscious that God had led them away from home into a distant land where they were unwanted and often mistreated? Was this not also true of their blessed Lord and Master? Are we better than He is? The Christian minister does not go because man calls him; neither does he run when man warns him. Stability, patience, and endurance are begotten with the living sense of a divine call.

## Joshua Indwelt by the Word of God

"This book of the law shall not depart out of thy mouth;

but thou shalt meditate therein day and night, that thou mayest observe to do according to all that is written therein: for then thou shalt make thy way prosperous, and then thou shalt have good success" (Jos 1:8).

The secret of power is to know the Word. This is the raw material of every Christian product. It is the Word that God blesses. It is the Word that sustains, directs, and keeps God's servants. Notice in particular that Joshua was to meditate upon the Law. He was to eat it, chew it, and digest it. It is said of the blessed man: "In his law doth he meditate day and night" (Ps 1:2). No wonder the next verse goes on to say, "And he shall be like a tree planted by the rivers of water."

Perhaps our best biblical illustration of meditation is found in the words of the prophet who tells us about the command to eat the book (Rev 10:8-11). He ate it, and it was sweet to the taste but bitter in the stomach. The Word and the communion that we receive from it are blessed and sweet, but often when we understand prophecy there is a deep bitterness associated with judgment.

The secret of knowledge is obedience. "That thou mayest observe to do according to all that is written therein" (Jos 1:8). God only gives us additional information as we make proper use of the knowledge we have. This is clearly set forth in John 7:17: "If any man will do his will, he shall know of the doctrine, whether it be of God, or whether I speak of myself." We cannot window-shop on God. It is vain for us to pray that God would show us what He wants us to do and then let us make up our minds. True faith is faith in a person. The greatest compliment that we can pay to any man is to believe in the man, not in his acts. The greatest compliment we can pay Almighty God is to believe in Him, even though we may not understand His providences. We must place implicit trust in Him. Too often we want

God to show us the distant scenes and then to allow us the right of choice. We must let Him choose, because He knows best, and He can be trusted.

### Joshua and the Divine Presence

"Have not I commanded thee? Be strong and of a good courage; be not afraid, neither be thou dismayed: for the Lord thy God is with thee whithersoever thou goest" (Jos 1:9).

Not only did Joshua have a conviction that God had called him, he lived with the consciousness that God was seeing him and that He was present. God had so promised. Think for a moment what would happen to you, to me, and to all men if we could realize that God is really present.

One of the most dynamic little books that I have read is *When Christ Came to Church* by the late Dr. A. J. Gordon. The theme of the book deals with a dream that Dr. Gordon had, a dream that a strange person came to church one morning as he was about to preach and watched him all the way through. According to this dream, after services were dismissed, Dr. Gordon asked one of the ushers who the man was. "Did you not know? That was the Lord Jesus Christ." Dr. Gordon then reveals the transforming effect that grows out of the realization of the actual presence of Christ.

# 28

# CROSSING THE JORDAN

As we consider the wonderful account of Israel's wilderness journey, we arrive at a point that is especially meaningful in terms of typical and historical richness. The importance of all of these events is best understood when we remember that it was designed and ordered by Jehovah. Nothing was left to chance or accident. On the occasion of the crossing of the river Jordan, we have another demonstration of a divine intervention. God undertakes in behalf of His people.

Before we begin to study the third chapter of the book of Joshua, it is well for us to notice something about the river Jordan itself. The word *Jordan* is derived from the Hebrew word *Hayyarden,* meaning "flowing downward" or "the descender." From a point where the Jordan flows out of the sea of Galilee to where it enters the Dead Sea is a distance by air of about 70 miles, but the river itself, because of its serpentine curves, is about 200 miles long. These two hundred miles are marked by some twenty-seven rapids and a descent of some 595 feet to the Dead Sea about 1290 feet below sea level. The river carries no traffic, it is bordered by no cities, and it is bound by a forbidding wilderness with a terminus in a sea of death. These factors led George Adams Smith, with his unusual brilliance, to write, "There may be something on the surface of some other planet to match the

Jordan Valley; there is nothing on this" (*The Historical Geography of the Holy Land*).

In our attempt to analyze and draw lessons from this historic crossing of the Jordan River by the hosts of Israel, let us divide the study into four sections.

## The Marvels of Divine Leadership

In all the annals of history there is nothing akin to the exodus of an entire nation out of another nation. Nor has any other people sustained itself in a wilderness for forty years. In this experience, God was further training His chosen people for a destiny. The end of the journey was at hand. Israel had finally reached the eastern bank of the Jordan River, and just beyond lay the promised land—a land "flowing with milk and honey." As the host of Israel encamped there, there must have come again and again the haunting memories of their fathers' failure at Kadesh-barnea some thirty-eight years earlier.

Israel failed to enter in at that time because of unbelief. Judgment had removed that generation by death. Their children must act upon a different principle. Ada R. Habershon regarding their situation, in her book *The Study of the Types,* wrote, "The Jordan River divided the people from the promised land. To be in the land, Jordan had to be crossed. Jordan overflowed all of its banks at this time (Jos 3:15) Its dark, forbidding waters rose between them and their God-given possessions. There were no bridges, no human means by which yonder side could be gained. Only the power of God was sufficient. 'Man's extremity is God's opportunity.' " Human extremity prepares one to look up. Rarely do men seek God until they have exhausted their own resources. Israel was face to face with a new crisis.

Jordan does not speak of one's experience in physical

death, but it does speak of and typify the death of Christ and the believer's position in Him. There are five types of death in Israel's journey from Egypt to Canaan. In the Passover we have noted in the death of the paschal lamb a type that speaks of our Lord Jesus Christ, who delivers from the penalty of sin. The second figure of death is found in the passage through the Red Sea. Here we behold a type of death to the world as the power of Egypt was broken. The Red Sea flowed between the people and their former servitude; Pharaoh's armies had been drowned. In the smitten rock we saw death that brings life—the refreshing waters from the cleft rock, Christ. The waters that flowed from that rock speak of the spiritual waters of Pentecost (Jn 7:37-38). The brazen serpent speaks of death to the flesh. The crossing of the Jordan is another figure of death and points to the work of the Lord Jesus Christ. This is the topic of our present study.

The marvels of God's leadership are found in the fact that the details were divinely arranged. "And it came to pass after three days, that the officers went through the host; and they commanded the people, saying, When ye see the ark of the covenant of the LORD your God, and the priests the Levites bearing it, then ye shall remove from your place, and go after it. Yet there shall be a space between you and it, about two thousand cubits by measure: come not near unto it, that ye may know the way by which ye must go: for ye have not passed this way heretofore" (Jos 3:2-4). It was an untried experience, and thus we find the officers going among the people for three days instructing them about what to do. The children of Israel were about to enter on the basis of faith, and faith operates in full only where man rests upon His promises and His power. And so the command is given and the march is on.

## The Miracle

Secular as well as divine history moves forward on a series of crises. The key idea in the book of Joshua is the victory of faith. As far as their vision was concerned, the people of Israel looked upon the turbulent waters of the overflowing Jordan River. The sight was not much different from that which faced their fathers a generation earlier when they stood on the banks of the Red Sea, pursued by the armies of Pharaoh. These people must have been fully aware of the nature of the enemy on the other side—the enemy that had baffled ten of the men who had spied out the land nearly four decades earlier. They certainly knew of the "walled towns" and the giants who lived in the land of their possession. Only faith can properly motivate obedience. Canaan was a place of conquest and conflict, but it was to be a new experience for this wilderness people.

## The Manifestation of a New Instrument

When Israel had crossed the Red Sea, it was the pillar of cloud that had led them. It was the pillar of cloud that had hindered the approach of Pharaoh's army. Throughout the forty years journey, the cloud had been their guide. As they prepare to cross the Jordan River, a new guide was introduced—the ark of the covenant. The pillar of the cloud had served well for a childish race, but now a new order had dawned. The new superseded the old.

Admittedly, the cloud that led Israel through their journeyings was far more spectacular than this acacia chest, being carried on the shoulders of the priests, that stayed the waters of the swollen Jordan. The time of multiplied miracles had to pass, and the Law and the redemption that was spoken of by the mercy seat and the sprinkling of the blood had to serve an adult nation. The sacred ark of the covenant symbolized the presence of God, who lived in the midst of His people, on the grounds of redemption. Israel did not consider the ark as a fetish but as a symbol of the presence of God. It is the consciousness of this presence in every age that transforms and makes radiant the living of individuals. The ark speaks of Christ our High Priest in the heavenlies.

We are reminded in Joshua 3, "Yet there shall be a space between you and it, about two thousand cubits by measure: come not near it, that ye may know the way which ye must go, for ye have not passed this way heretofore" (v. 4). The people were commanded to keep at a reverent distance, where the view of the ark could be better maintained. It had to be fully impressed upon the Israelites that it was the presence of the ark that produced the miracle of their entrance.

## Messages in Typology

There seems to be a prevailing misunderstanding concerning the typical meaning of the river Jordan and the land of Canaan. It is important for us to recognize the rich, typical meaning of the entire journey from Egypt to Canaan as set forth in 1 Corinthians 10:1-11. However, we must be careful in the interpretation of these types.

First of all, the crossing of Jordan does not represent physical death, and Canaan does not represent heaven. Certainly Canaan cannot represent heaven, since it was occupied by seven apostate nations that had to be conquered before Israel could possess the land. In addition, in years to follow, Israel was dispossessed of Canaan and was sent into captivity. All too often one's theology is affected by hymnology. It is generally conceded that we remember better the things we sing than those we recite. This psychological truth is illustrated by the fact that the book of Psalms was originally set to music. The psalms were sung in the temple and later in the synagogues. Today many TV and radio commercials are sung rather than recited. Many of our Protestant hymns, such as, "On Jordan's Stormy Banks I Stand," "Beulah Land," and others, assume that Jordan is death and Canaan is heaven.

Neither does the passage through Jordan, as some hold, represent an experience of sanctification that eradicates the flesh. The group of people who hold to such tenets most often are highly emotional, giving more preeminence to the third Person than to the second Person of the Trinity.

Next, the crossing of the Jordan does not illustrate the passing of a soul into eternity; rather it illustrates the passing of a Christian from one level of Christian life to another. It marks the end of the self-life and the beginning of the Christ-life, the end of a life lived on the principle of human effort and the beginning of a life lived on the principle of faith and obedience. Between these two rose the mighty Jordan—the river of impossibility.

The passage through Jordan does represent a crisis and the beginning of a new experience of adulthood. While we are called upon to put on the whole armor of God and be equipped for the battle "against principalities, against powers, against the rulers of the darkness of this world, against spiritual wickedness in high places" (Eph 6:12), this journey represents a sort of transition from children in the wilderness to adult warriors in the promised land. The salvation that delivered the Israelites from Egypt also took them into the promised land. Unbelief condemned them in the wilderness. A similar situation marked the early church. The epistle to the Romans teaches salvation from Egypt; Ephesians teaches salvation in Canaan. But unbelief hindered an immediate passage from the message of Romans to the message of Ephesians. Therefore coming between these two we have Corinthians and Galatians. Corinthians deals with moral failure, and Galatians deals with doctrinal error.

The land of Canaan, then, represents the truth as we find it in the book of Ephesians. It is both a land of rest and a land of warfare. We rest in the finished work of Christ.

# 29

# WHAT MEAN THESE STONES?

THERE ARE SERMONS IN STONE and messages in memorials. There are many kinds of stones—milestones, millstones, tombstones, and so on. "What mean ye by these stones?" (Jos 4:6) could well be written over the archway of every cemetery. Since the history of man began, he has tried to perpetuate his story in stones, in obelisks, and in monuments. Stones were used before books were written. Even today, most of our knowledge of ancient civilizations other than that which is found written in the Bible is gained from the field of archeology. This science is dependent largely upon the knowledge gained from the inscriptions on stones. The pyramids of Egypt, the silent sentinels of the centuries, have long borne their unforgettable message of an ancient grandeur—a culture of power, riches, and achievement as well as failure, disappointment, and death.

There stand the stones. God has also seen fit to erect many "Ebenezers" in the pathway of faith. We read concerning Jacob during his flight from the wrath of Esau his brother: "And Jacob rose up early in the morning, and took the stone that he had put for his pillows, and set it up for a pillar, and poured oil upon the top of it. And he called the name of that place Bethel. . . . And this stone, which I have set up for a pillar, shall be God's house: and of all that thou shalt give me, I will surely give the tenth unto thee," (Gen 28:18-19,22). Joshua, in his final charge to Israel at historic Shechem, closed with these words, "And Joshua said unto the people, Ye are witnesses against yourselves that ye have chosen you the LORD, to serve him. And they said, We are witnesses. . . . So Joshua made a covenant with the people that day, and set them a statute and an ordinance in Shechem. And Joshua wrote these words in the book of the law of God, and took a great stone, and set it there under an oak, that was by the sanctuary of the Lord" (Jos 24:22,25-26).

These stones that were divinely ordained as a memorial are described in the following passage: "And the people came up out of Jordan on the tenth day of the first month, and encamped in Gilgal, in the east border of Jericho. And those twelve stones, which they took out of Jordan, did Joshua pitch in Gilgal. And he spake unto the children of Israel, saying, When your children shall ask their fathers in time to come, saying, What mean these stones? Then ye shall let your children know, saying, Israel came over this Jordan on dry land. For the LORD your God dried up the waters of Jordan from before you, until ye were passed over, as the LORD your God did to the Red sea, which he dried up from before us, until we were gone over: that all the people of the earth might know the hand of the LORD, that it is mighty: that ye might fear the LORD your God for ever" (Jos 4:19-24).

We have here one of the great miracles of God—one that became His memorial. "All of God's memorials, like His miracles, are designed to advertise to the world and to the people therein the fact of God's presence in the world" (J. C. Massee). Therefore His miracles and His memorials are of such a nature as to proclaim God's faithfulness, to portray God's power, to provoke man's attention, to promote perpetual inquiry, and to provide a lasting testimony.

## To Proclaim God's Faithfulness

Two cairns or monumental piles are mentioned in Joshua 4. One was on the bank of the river, at Gilgal (v. 3), and the other was in the riverbed itself (v. 9). Each of these consisted of twelve stones, which represented the twelve tribes of Israel. The first speaks of divine faithfulness; the second speaks of divine power—faithfulness to fulfill, and power to stay the flood waters while the host of Israel passed over on dry land.

As we seek to answer the question, "What mean these stones," it is appropriate that we keep in mind the fact that, first and foremost, the design of these memorials was to set forth the faithfulness of God in fulfilling the promises made to His people. More than four-hundred and fifty years earlier, God had made a covenant with Abraham, and in these words He had promised to Abraham and his seed the land whereon he stood: "In the same day the Lord made a covenant with Abram, saying, Unto thy seed have I given this land, from the river of Egypt unto the great river, the river Euphrates" (Gen 15:18). Centuries later He renewed this promise to the children of Israel while they were still in Egypt: "And I have said, I will bring you up out of the affliction of Egypt unto the land of the Canaanites, and the Hittites, and the Amorites, and the Perizzites, and the Hivites, and the Jebusites, unto a land flowing with milk and honey" (Ex 3:17).

We know "the gifts and calling of God are without repentance" (Ro 11:29). Men may delay but never defeat the purposes of God. Man is accustomed to dealing with minutes, while God deals with millennia; man deals with time, but God deals with eternity. It is worthy of notice that God took in His own hands the prescription of the method by which these great events should be commemorated. Great mercies call for special recognition and observance.

God remembers and keeps His covenants, and in making a path through the river, God again demonstrated both His concern for His ancient people and His ability to fulfill that which He had promised. While many other things were involved with the erection of these stone memorials, the primary object and purpose was to keep man's mind centered on God's sovereign grace. No consideration should take precedent over the attempt to keep God constantly before the conscience of the believer.

### To Portray God's Power

"That all the people of the earth might know the hand of the Lord, that it is mighty: that ye might fear the Lord your God for ever" (Jos 4:24). "These stones were to be memorials of the Lord's power in cutting off the waters of Jordan and in bringing His people into the land. They were to be witnesses to the generations yet to come of the power of the Lord's right hand. These memorial stones, raised up from the place of death, and borne by a power outside of themselves to a new position, in which they were to bear witness for God, remind us of the present place of those who are risen and seated with Christ. Once, like these stones, they lay in death, under judgment, but now, by the grace and power of God, they have been raised up and seated together in reavenly places in Christ" (J. C. Massee, *Conflict and Conquest in Holiness*). What mean these stones? At Gilgal, Israel's last obstacle was rolled away, and the power of God was again manifested to all people.

Miracles such as the rolling back of the Jordan served as a necessary means of demonstrating the invincible power of God. All through the Old Testament we have the repeated demonstration of God's intervention in human affairs. He stopped the natural order of things without violating the laws of nature. Instead, the God of nature intervened, and with a superior force He overcame that which was natural with that which was supernatural.

In a true sense, miracles are just as essential in the day in which we live as they were in days of old. They were needed then, and they are needed now, to demonstrate the power of God and to exhibit His mightiness. While the days of material and physical miracles apparently passed with the completion of the New Testament, one notable miracle has continued. The miracle that is absolutely essential to the Christian testimony in this our day is the miracle of a new birth and a changed life. This is the exhibition of divine power for which the world and society wait. We can magnify our forms, we can garnish our rituals, we can make ornate our ceremonies, we can enlarge our programs, and we can intensify our campaigns. But unless we are able to demonstrate that power of God which transforms individuals and homes and produces a society of the redeemed, the world will despise the Christian's Christ, the Christian's God, and the Christian's church. Where transforming power is absent, testimony is silent.

Just as the presence of the ark upon the shoulders of the priests held back the devastating and death-dealing floods, so the cross of Christ has impounded the wrath of God for the human race. We may be tempted to inquire why it is that God waits so long before striking back in fearful judgment. Here we must remember, "The Lord is not slack concerning his promise, as some men count slackness; but is longsuffering to us-ward, not willing that any should perish, but that all should come to repentance" (2 Pe 3:9). For nineteen centuries this lake of divine wrath has been filling. It is the cross that stands between God's wrath and man's destruction, but one day this wrath will manifest its destructive power. Just as the flood waters returned to their place after the ark of the covenant was lifted from the river, one day God will say "enough," and His long-suffering will come to an end. The

Lamb will become the Lion of the tribe of Judah. What a great force awaits a guilty world! Only God's mercy, grace, and long-suffering delay His wrath. It is the work of the cross that has made this the longest of all dispensations.

## To Provoke Man's Attention

Another meaning of the stones in the river and those erected at Gilgal is found in the arresting power of their exhibition. "One great necessity of God with men is to get their attention; to arouse them from the habit of neglecting, disbelieving, ignoring or taking for granted His presence and His interest in the world" (J. C. Massee). The same writer has said, "One is not sure whether God is more neglected in His world or taken for granted with a kind of impersonal fanatical faith." To be convinced of this danger of forgetting God, all one has to do is to turn to a Bible concordance and look up the word *remember*. Many times God called upon His people to remember.

We have a striking example in Matthew 2 that is most pertinent to our day. Mary and Joseph, when they were returning to Jerusalem after observing the feast of the Passover, left Jesus behind and went a day's journey, supposing that He was in their midst. Is it not true that most of us take for granted that God is in our midst and in our programs and that He is accommodating Himself to our means and our ways? It cost Mary and Joseph three days of painful and pungent sorrow. How much is lost as a result of our failure to give attention with alert minds, ready wills, and warm hearts!

Picture the Lord Jesus Christ standing at the door of the church of the Laodiceans. This church was rich and increased in goods, having need of nothing, according to its self-analysis (Rev 3:14-22), but the Lord of the church is on the outside.

There He stands, charging them with such indifference that they were pronounced neither cold nor hot but lukewarm. As far as we recall, there is no other place in the Scriptures where it is stated that God is made sick or nauseated. What did it? It was an indifferent, dull, lethargic, phlegmatic people who rarely or never sensed the presence of God in His own world. Men and women are too much taken up with themselves, their own interests, their own pleasures, and their own substances. Stephen said concerning God's chosen people, "Ye do always resist the Holy Ghost" (Ac 7:51). Many professed Christians live as if God did not exist.

America was startled by the announcement that three prominent theologians were in search of, or had founded, a new theology based upon the theory, "God is dead." True, that is horrifying. But, we dare to ask, are they much worse than those who profess with their lips that God lives and act as though God were dead? There is only a slight difference between a professed atheist and a practical atheist. One denies God with his mouth, the other denies Him by his life. What is the difference? In the simplest terms, such an attitude is designated in Scripture as "godlessness." It means to live without God.

Someone has suggested that if the attention of men can once be riveted upon the fact of His presence in the world, they will inevitably begin to practice the presence of God and to exercise a daily consciousness of this presence that will vitally alter their lives. Men and women live as they do because they are not conscious of God's presence. All of us are aware of the restraint which is ours when we are conscious that we are in the presence of one person or a thousand persons.

Here we have the answer as to why God builds His miracles into memorials. One generation has the miracles and another generation has the memorials.

One striking feature about these memorials set on land and in the river was that they were God's trumpet to His people to awake. The memorials were not ornate or large, nor were they burnished or touched by human carving tools. They were simple memorials, but they were all that was needed. They were not like the proud temples or the glorious pyramids of Egypt, reared to the glory of man. They were plain and magnificent in their simplicity. The world has erected many gaudy and expensive monuments, chipped and hewn by the tools of men, lettered and embellished. Men want to be remembered after they are gone. God wants to be remembered while we are here.

All of God's memorials have a spiritual connotation. Following the flood, God set a rainbow in the sky so that men might remember the covenant that He made with Noah—a token of His promise that He would never again destroy the earth with water. The ceremonies and the feasts of Israel were designed to serve this same purpose. God does not expect us to worship the memorials. This accounts for their ruggedness. The world is prone to do this very thing: to worship the crucifix instead of the Christ and to magnify the place rather than the person. This is nothing short of idolatry. There are men in our day who worship programs and systems and institutions. To fall before a rough pile of stones at Gilgal and to adore it would have constituted an act of idolatry. However, to gaze upon these is to think of God and of His interest, His power, and His love.

May we hear again the words, "Behold, I stand at the door, and knock: if any man hear my voice, and open the door, I will come in to him, and will sup with him, and he with me" (Rev 3:20). Can this not well be His challenge to His church in this hour? He stands outside the door of many churches pleading in love for them to open and let Him in. He warns of impending judgments with the words, "I will spew thee out of my mouth" (v. 16). To gain our attention, many times God has to knock at the door of our hearts with some tragedy, some devastating experience, some loss, or some great sorrow. God has to catch most of us on the second bounce. He has to let us hit so hard that we bounce up. Not many people receive Him without such an experience. We are too busy otherwise to give Him any heed. These stones at Gilgal were erected to arrest attention. They were to serve as roadblocks on the highway of life, over which unborn generations would have to travel.

## To Promote Inquiry

"And he spake unto the children of Israel, saying, When your children shall ask their fathers in time to come, saying, What mean these stones?" (Jos 4:21). God sets His memorial by the course of history, not only to arrest man's attention but to challenge his inquiry. Moses, on the back side of the desert, as he attended the flocks of Jethro, looked upon a strange phenomenon—a burning bush, the uniqueness of which was the fact that it burned and yet was not consumed. Moses demonstrated his curiosity by turning aside to examine it, and then he heard the divine voice say, "Put off thy shoes from off thy feet, for the place whereon thou standest is holy ground" (Ex 3:5).

Somehow God meets upon holy ground those who have an investigative mind. It is promised to those who hunger and thirst after righteousness that they shall be filled. In the New Testament, we notice the challenges and invitations are always to those who need something: those who are thirsty, those who are hungry, or those who are weary. God passes by satisfied individuals and searches for those who have needs. Neither God nor man can do much for people who have no sense of want, no romance of inquiry, no stimulating curiosity. God challenges His people to search, to seek, to ask, to call, to remember, to study, and to explore the Word.

## To Provide a Testimony

These stones had a story to tell; they bore a message. The memorials were not an end within themselves; their significance was found in the association of ideas. God taught His ancient people in two ways. He taught them first pictorially. These pictures are found in types and shadows, in ceremonies, in burning altars, in bleeding lambs, in ministering priests, in holy days, in the lives of individuals, and in the drama of history. He also taught them through the written Word. God's pictures and God's words must always agree. It is through a failure to understand or the neglect of this fact that many of God's memorials have been altered and much of God's truth has been lost.

These stones should remind us of the divine memorials that God has set for us. Let us notice, in the first place, some of God's memorials to Israel. There was the Sabbath day. In the Sabbath observance, God reminded His people that one-seventh of their time was to be holy. The observance of the seventh sanctified the whole of time. How much was wrapped up in this reminder that God owned the world and that God owned individuals! In the Old Testament, under the law, man was to work six days and then rest, and was to earn his rest. But we have our memorial in the Lord's Day. Christ has earned our rest for us. He is the rest of the children of God. In grace we rest; we enter this rest and then work. The ordinance of the Sabbath was designed to keep before God's ancient people the fact that He was the Lord of the Sabbath and that they were His possession.

Another memorial is found in the tithe. "The tenth shall be holy unto the Lord" (Lev 27:32). God not only claims man's time, He claims man's wealth. "The world is mine, and the fulness thereof" (Ps 50:12). Men are prone to forget this. God does not need the tithe—the cattle upon a thousand hills are His—but man needs what the tithe teaches. It is here that so many fail. God doesn't want "ours," He wants us. The only reason He is asking for "ours" is that He might gain us.

Marriage, the foundation of the home, is the first divinely ordained institution, the foundation of the social order, and the bulwark of every civilization. The Christian home stands as a memorial and a mighty sentinel and witness to the basic plan of God for human good. As goes the home, so goes the nation.

The offerings in the levitical system set forth the holiness of God, the sinfulness of man, and the way that the two might come together through appropriate sacrifice. "Without shedding of blood is no remission" (Heb 9:22).

The Jewish feast days, seven in number, look back and also look forward. Each of them bore its own message.

In the New Testament we have two ordinances. Baptism is the initial ordinance, setting forth death, burial, and resurrection. In 1 Corinthians 15 we have a definition of the saving gospel: "Christ died for our sins according to the scriptures; . . . he was buried, and . . . he rose again the third day according to the scriptures" (vv. 3-4).

Baptism is a drama that looks in three directions. In regard to the past, it points to Christ and the believer's identification with Him on the cross, in the grave, and in resurrection. Baptism by the scriptural mode looks back to the cross of Christ who died, was buried, and rose the third day. Baptism tells this important story when the ordinance is properly observed.

In regard to the present, baptism tells the story of the individual and the great revolution that has transpired in his experience—the posture of death in the watery grave, the burial, and then the resurrection. Just as marriage symbolizes a new and a different life—the death to the world socially of the bride and the bridegroom as they enter into a new and living experience with each other—so baptism tells of the death, burial, and resurrection of the believer. "Verily, verily, I say unto you, He that heareth my word, and believeth on him that sent me, hath everlasting life, and shall not come into condemnation; but is passed from death unto life" (Jn 5:24). Baptism, then, is God's memorial and the picture that represents the gospel, the irreducible minimum of what one must do to be saved. We believe this same story is told by the two cairns: The twelve stones in the bed of the river, which experienced the flood tide, tell of the death of Christ; and the twelve stones on the bank tell forth His resurrection and the hope that we have in Him.

The other ordinance is the Lord's Supper. We are born once but we must eat often. The Lord's Supper is a memorial designed and commanded by our Lord. He took simple bread and the simple fruit of the vine and said "this is my body, which is broken for you: this do in remembrance of me. After the same manner also he took the cup, when he had supped, saying, This cup is the new testament in my blood: this do ye, as oft as ye drink it, in remembrance of me" (1 Co 11:24-25). This ordinance, like baptism, looks back to the death of Christ, up to His High Priestly work and our fellowship and participation with Him, and forward to His second coming. "For as often as ye eat this bread, and drink this cup, ye do shew the Lord's death till he come" (v. 26).

# 30

# BEYOND JORDAN AT GILGAL

GILGAL MARKED the first bridgehead in the land of Canaan. After a wait of more than four hundred years, Jehovah's promise to Abraham was at last being fulfilled. Jordan was behind them, the land was before them, and the Lord was with them. It was at Gilgal that the children of Israel encamped during the campaign led by Joshua in the conquering and dividing of the land among the twelve tribes of Israel. Gilgal, as we can well imagine, became a very sacred spot to subsequent generations. It was thought of in much the same way as Americans think of Plymouth Rock. More than that, it was a blessed and sacred remembrance, rich in lore and laden with radiant experiences. God ordained that Gilgal should hold a prominent place in the hearts and the minds of His people.

Allan Redpath, in his book *Victorious Christian Living* calls attention to six lessons learned at Gilgal. To these six we shall add a seventh, following somewhat the same general classification.

## PLACE OF REMEMBRANCE

"What mean these stones?" One's personality, to a large degree, is determined by one's ability to recall or to remember. We are what we are because of what we remembr, so personality is the sum total of our recollections in the light of a living presence and a hopeful future. We are what we are because of the storehouse of memory which must serve us, come what may. In this particular instance the memorial was to apply to future generations. The monument of stones taken from the bed of Jordan and erected at Gilgal was to serve the purpose of arresting the attention of the unborn generations.

The children of Israel found Gilgal a place of remembrance. "That this may be a sign among you, that when your children ask their fathers in time to come, saying, What mean ye by these stones? Then ye shall answer them, That the waters of Jordan were cut off before the ark of the covenant of the LORD; when it passed over Jordan, the waters of Jordan were cut off: and these stones shall be for a memorial unto the children of Israel for ever" (Jos 4:6-7). The antitype of Gilgal is Golgotha. Just as the children of Israel reflected upon their mighty deliverance by God in response to their venture of faith, so we as Christians look back to our Golgotha and the cross of Christ. It was here that the sin question was forever settled. As someone has said, "When He died, I died." To this bedrock truth of Jordan's passing we must return again and again. It is the touchstone of all our hopes, the rock of all our salvation, and the guiding star of enduring faith.

## Place of Resurection

"And the people came up out of Jordan on the tenth day of the first month, and encamped in Gilgal, in the east border of Jericho. And those twelve stones, which they took out of Jordan, did Joshua pitch in Gilgal" (Jos 4:19-20). The time of this encampment is mentioned—the tenth day of the first month. This was the fortieth anniversary to the day, of the taking of the Paschal lamb, a remembrance which was to be kept for forty days. "Gilgal" means the "reproach taken away." During all the preceding years Israel had been only a people with a promise. The divinely ordained memorial of twelve stones taken from the bottom of the river, where they had been buffeted and worn by the unending flow, now stood as a monument to a gracious redemption.

As we find ourselves on resurrection ground, the reproach of sin is gone, and uncleanness and death have been taken away. In Him we are justified. "There is therefore now no condemnation to them which are in Christ Jesus, who walk not after the flesh, but after the Spirit" (Ro 8:1). We are made righteous in Him. Israel's wilderness experience of forty years was dominated by the flesh, but now all of that was past. A new life, a new liberty, and a new hope were theirs. The defeat so common to the old wilderness life that was accompanied by weariness and defeat, murmuring and complaint, had at last been superseded by a new order and a new day. Similarly, the children of God have been "quickened . . . together with Christ . . . and [seated] together in heavenly places in Christ Jesus" (Eph 2:5-6). What else can we ask? God has given us all. To believe it is to receive it. To practice it is to experience it. To know it is to show it and to exemplify it in a consistent walk before others.

## The Place of Restraint

"And it came to pass, when all the kings of the Amorites, which were on the side of Jordan westward, and all the kings of the Canaanites, which were by the sea, heard that the Lord had dried up the waters of Jordan from before the children of Israel, until we were passed over, that their heart melted, neither was there spirit in them any more, because of the children of Israel" (Jos 5:1). In reading the account of Israel's passing over Jordan, especially following the wholesale circumcision that had taken place, who has not been made to wonder why the kings in the land of Canaan did not strike? The answer is here: "Their heart melted, neither was there spirit in them any more, because of the children of Israel."

There is a parallel truth in the book of Acts. Just as Israel was invincible before her enemies under Joshua's leadership, the church was remarkably invincible. The Christians lacked influence; they did not even have enough influence to keep themselves out of jail. They were often found there. But they had enough power with God to open the doors of their imprisonment. When God is in the midst of His people, they are like an army with banners. It was so under Joshua, it was true in apostolic times, it is especially true today. The gospel, preached and lived, is more potent than nuclear fission and more powerful than the hydrogen bomb.

It was said of the early church, "And great fear came upon all the church, and upon as many as heard these things. And by the hands of the apostles were many signs and wonders wrought among the people; (and they were all with one accord in Solomon's porch. And of the rest durst no man join himself to them: but the people magnified them)" (Ac 5:11-13). It is a compromising Christianity that knows no power. The Great Commission still stands for all who have the audacity and the boldness to believe and to accept by faith what God has promised. All power in heaven and in earth is still ours for the appropriation.

The history of Israel is a witness to the fact that as long as God's people obeyed, they knew nothing of defeat, and this very fact brought consternation and fear to the hearts of their enemies. In the years that followed, Israel lost its separateness and loyalty to Jehovah. That in itself resulted in the nation's becoming despised among other nations, even to this day.

The price of victory does not fluctuate. "The LORD is my light and my salvation; whom shall I fear? The LORD is the strength of my life; of whom shall I be afraid? When the wicked, even mine enemies and my foes, came upon me to eat up my flesh, they stumbled and fell. Though an host should encamp against me, my heart shall not fear: though war should rise against me, in this will I be confident" (Ps 27:1-3).

## A Place of Renunciation

"And this is the cause why Joshua did circumcise: All the people that came out of Egypt, that were males, even all the men of war, died in the wilderness by the way, after they came out of Egypt. Now all the people that came out were circumcised: but all the people that were born in the wilderness by the way as they came forth out of Egypt, them they had not circumcised" (Jos 5:4-5). Since there had been no practice of circumcision in the wilderness, only a few of the generation who passed into Canaan under Joshua had even been circumcised. All over the age of twenty, except Joshua and Caleb, had died as a result of their rebellion at Kadesh-barnea some thirty-eight years earlier.

It seemed entirely appropriate, now that Israel was in the land, that the institution that initiated their exodus from Egypt should be set up as it had been commanded as a memorial. The children of Israel were beginning a new life. They were in the land of promise. The sign of the Abrahamic covenant was circumcision. The time and place of this wholesale ceremony had great significance. To human reason it would appear strange that the armies of Israel should be circumcised when they were on the verge of a campaign for possession of the land and a warfare of extermination. This brings to mind the sad treachery of two of the sons of Jacob,

Simeon and Levi, who circumcised the citizens of Shalem after Shechem, the son of Hamor, had defiled their sister Dinah (Gen 33:18—34:31). In deceit they bargained with Hamor and his son Shechem, promising to exchange sons and daughters in marriage if the male inhabitants of Shalem would submit to circumcision. They submitted to the ritual, and we read of their fate: "And it came to pass on the third day, when they were sore, that two of the sons of Jacob, Simeon and Levi, Dinah's brethren, took each man his sword, and came upon the city boldly, and slew all the males. And they slew Hamor and Shechem his son with the edge of the sword, and took Dinah out of Shechem's house, and went out" (Gen 34:25-26).

The circumcising of the children of Israel at this point in their history was a sign of the fact that the land was to be taken in weakness. God was to receive the glory. Israel's battles were to be won, not through human ingenuity, but by divine power and wisdom.

Circumcision is a type of that "cutting off" of the impulse of sin, even the very root of our experience. Paul says, "In [God] also ye are circumcised with the circumcision made without hands, in putting off the body of the sins of the flesh by the circumcision of Christ" (Col 2:11). This is the surrender of our whole life unto death, as the basis of our vital and practical fellowship with Christ, the one who was crucified, who died, and who rose again.

This new life in Canaan was a prototype of the Christian's life as set forth in the book of Ephesians. This experience calls for the most painful of all pains—the renunciation of the flesh. There can be no halfway grounds. The flesh and all that pertains to the old man must go. This painful cutting off of the flesh is a spiritual task that must be wrought through submission and obedience.

## A Place of Restoration

The observance of circumcision makes way for the observance of the Passover. No uncircumcised person could partake of the Passover. We have occasion here to note two dates. The first is found in Joshua 4:19, where it is stated that the Israelites had camped in Gilgal on the tenth of the first month. Then in Joshua 5:10 we read: "And the children of Israel encamped in Gilgal, and kept the passover on the fourteenth day of the month at even in the plains of Jericho." The first date marks the time that the Passover lamb was taken up for observation. Four days later, on the fourteenth day of the first month, was the time of the celebration of the Passover. This was exactly forty years after the Passover in Egypt. God led them out in order to lead them in.

The great truth of the Passover was that the firstborn were spared only by the sacrifice of a substitute. A lamb took their place. This is a type of redemption from the penalty of sin. A new experience brought a new participation. What a glorious experience this first Passover in the land must have been! For most of the generation then present, this celebration was their first and only observance. We can well imagine the thrilling spectacle of such an event as it was celebrated on the plains of Jericho. When it was celebrated in Egypt (Ex 12), the children of Israel were in enemy territory; for the second celebration, they were in the wilderness (Num 9); for the third, they were in their own land, a land that was to be theirs by possession, by dedication, and by warfare. The Passover speaks of Christ in His initial work for us. "Christ our passover is sacrificed for us" (1 Co 5:7).

## A Place of Realization

"And they did eat of the old corn of the land on the morrow after the passover, unleavened cakes, and parched corn in the selfsame day" (Jos 5:11). Along with their new position in Canaan, the children of Israel had a change of diet. They no longer received manna. Manna speaks of Christ in humiliation, "after the flesh," giving His flesh for the believer's life. "The old corn of the land," on the other hand, speaks of Christ apprehended, as arisen, glorified, and seated in the heavenlies. Paul tells us this in 2 Corinthians 5:16: "Wherefore henceforth know we no man after the flesh: yea, though we have known Christ after the flesh, yet now henceforth know we him no more."

The food of the wilderness was heavenly, given by a miracle, fresh each morning. It was light and sweet and entailed no burden of transportation. It was available each day. It was like milk or like baby food. But now the army of Joshua must fight. Soldiers need more substantial victuals. Israel's food was commensurate with its needs; so is ours. A pilgrim people were becoming possessors.

Though the believer is in the world, he is not of it. It is important that we apprehend the great truth in Ephesians 1, that we are seated with Christ in the heavenlies and that we are there in God's sight already seated in Christ. We must appropriate our position by faith. As the Israelites were in Canaan, so are we, according to Ephesians, soldiers ready for battle. It is wonderful to partake of the "old corn in the land"—to see ourselves "chosen . . . in him before the foundation of the world, . . . predestinated . . . unto the adoption of children by Jesus Christ . . . . In whom we have redemption through his blood, the forgiveness of sins, according to the riches of his grace" (Eph 1:4-5,7).

It is probable that some who tasted the old corn for the first time still longed for the manna, even as their fathers had longed for the fleshpots of Egypt. Manna, as we know, was more spectacular and more easily appropriated. It was thrilling to eat "angels' food." There are still those among us who insist on feeding on a wilderness diet. Like children, they glory in the spectacular, they magnify sensations and emphasize feelings, and they long for the days of miracles and tongues. They live in an atmosphere of emotion. They must get it fresh every morning; a new sensation must appeal to their feelings and bring them spiritual gooseflesh.

Israel could have moved into Canaan thirty-eight years earlier, when the nation stood on the border of the land at Kadesh-barnea. If they had moved in, as it was God's purpose at that time when He permitted their representatives to spy out the land, there would have been no need of crossing Jordan, and there would have been no need of thirty-eight years of wandering. At that time they could have pushed forward and possessed the land, as recommended by Joshua and Caleb. Here we see something of the drama of Christianity preenacted.

In apostolic Christianity we have, first of all, the book of Romans, the great doctrinal book that speaks of deliverance from the penalty and power of sin. But between Romans and the books of Ephesians, Philippians, and Colossians there are two epistles to the Corinthians, which speak of carnal practices and childish divisions, and the book of Galatians, which speaks of false doctrines. This order need not exist outside of the formal arrangement of these books in the New Testament. It is possible for the Christian to experience the transition from Romans into the book of Ephesians, from Egypt into Canaan. This seems to have been the purpose of God in leading the children of Israel out of Egypt—to lead them into Canaan. It was the weakness of human flesh that dictated the sad course of the thirty-eight years which intervened. Some people reach the position outlined in Ephesians by experiencing the trials of Corinthians and Galatians, if they enter in at all. Others, at the time of salvation, experience the blessedness of Ephesians' heavenliness.

### A Place of Revelation

"And it came to pass, when Joshua was by Jericho, that he lifted up his eyes and looked, and, behold, there stood a man over against him with his sword drawn in his hand: and Joshua went unto him, and said unto him, Art thou for us, or for our adversaries? And he said, Nay; but as captain of the host of the LORD am I now come. And Joshua fell on his face to the earth, and did worship, and said unto him, What saith my Lord unto his servant? And the captain of the LORD's host said unto Joshua, Loose thy shoe from off thy foot; for the place whereon thou standest is holy. And Joshua did so" (Jos 5:13-15).

A revelation came in an hour of extremity. Israel was now in the land and open to enemy attack. The army itself was not up to its usual strength, since the men had just been circumcised. In the rear, the river Jordan barred their retreat. In front of them were the walled towns that forbade their advance. Their new leader was untried. Most of the Israelites had never seen a walled city. These sons of Jacob were human and naturally given to fear and misgivings. It was in this hour of crisis that a new and important vision was given. "Man's extremity is God's opportunity."

Without doubt Joshua was heavily burdened. Apparently he went somewhere alone to meditate on what his next step should be. Alexander MacLaren wrote: "Absorbed in thought, he lifted up his eyes mechanically, as brooding men will, not expecting to see anything, and is startled by the silent figure of 'a man with a sword drawn' in his hand, close beside him. There is nothing supernatural in his appearance; and the immediate thought of the leader is, 'Is this one of the enemy that has stolen upon my solitude?' So, promptly and boldly, he strides up to him with a quick challenge: 'Whose side are you on? Are you one of us, or from the enemy's camp?' And then the silent lips opened. 'Upon neither the one nor the other. I am not on your side, you are on mine. For as captain of the Lord's host, I am come up.' And then Joshua fell on his face, recognizes his commander-in-chief, owns himself a subordinate, and asks for orders. 'What saith my Lord unto his servant?'

"Certainly we have here what is called a Christophany or the appearance of Christ before His incarnation. This Captain of the Lord's host it seems was none other than a preliminary manifestation of the Eternal Word of God, who in the fulness of time became flesh and dwelt among us."

All through the Old Testament we find appearances of "the angel of the Lord." When the Captain of the Lord's host appeared to Joshua, He gave him the same command that Moses had obeyed as he stood before the burning bush some forty years before: "Loose thy shoe from off thy foot, for the place whereon thou standest is holy" (Jos 5:15). It seems fair to assume that the angelic being would have us identify the persons in the two great theophanies. In proof of this, as the conversation continues, divine attributes in the form of the sacred name are applied: "And the LORD said unto Joshua, See, I have given into thine hand Jericho and the king thereof, and the mighty men of valour" (Jos 6:2).

Humanly speaking, it was a vision of one who only appeared as a man, but who was in truth the Commander of all battles for the right. This vision, coupled with the statement found in Joshua 3:11, "Behold, the ark of the covenant of the Lord of all the earth passeth over before you into Jordan," brings Joshua and those who follow a broad horizon and a vision of God as the God of all the earth. The Lord of all the universe is none other than the Lord Jesus Christ, to whom this rule was given.

This man with his drawn sword bespeaks warfare. Here again we are reminded of the fact that our God is at war with all evil. This truth is further enforced in Ephesians 6. To be consecrated, dedicated, surrendered, and resting is not enough. The Christian's life is a life of warfare. We err grievously if we fail to apprehend the nature and the character of this spiritual warfare, a warfare that pits the invincible power of the Spirit against principalities, against powers, and against the rulers of the darkness of this world. It is a great day in the life of the believer when he realizes that his chief enemies are not to be found in the flesh or even in visible things but rather in the heavenlies, the spiritual hosts of wickedness.

One final word remains in dealing with this particular thought: We dare not make Joshua's mistake. We must not be satisfied to have God on our side; rather, we must be on God's side! The whole social gospel is predicated on the conclusion that God must be on man's side since man is striving to be beneficent. There is much zeal without knowledge and a vain attempt to commandeer God onto our side.

# 31

# CONQUEST THROUGH CONFLICT

As we near the close of Israel's journey from Egypt to Canaan, even the casual observer must be impressed with two salient facts—facts that are dominant both in the Old Testament and in the New Testament. These two facts have to do with the doctrine of divine sovereignty and human responsibility. These facts constitute what God has done and is doing and what man does in fulfilling the divine purpose. Both of these truths are prominent in the book of Joshua, the book of conquest.

First, we saw God acting alone. This was divine sovereignty. He opened the path through the river Jordan. Then He revealed to Joshua the unseen Captain of the Lord of hosts. Finally, He demonstrated in the fall of Jericho that victory is with the Lord.

The next cardinal truth, one which is but a corollary of the first, is human responsibility. This involves the conquest of the land, the defeat of the enemies, and the driving out of the seven apostate nations, a conquest through difficulty.

These same great truths are vividly set forth in Ephesians. In the first three chapters we have the believer's position in grace. "Even when we were dead in sins, [God] hath quickened us together with Christ, (by grace ye are saved;) and hath raised us up together, and made us sit together in heavenly places in Christ Jesus" (Eph 2:5-6). In Ephesians

4-6 we behold the believer's walk and farfare. It is this warfare that we wish to consider in particular.

Many professed Christians live under, and conform to, the false philosophy that "God is in His heaven and all is right with the world." God is in the heavens, but things are not right with the world. In fact, everything is wrong with the world. The earth is in rebellion, the ground is cursed, man is depraved, and the cosmos or world-system is under condemnation awaiting judgment. As a result of this philosophy, the process of amalgamation, admixture, and conformity have captured the overwhelming majority of church members.

These is little separation from the world, there is a sparse acceptance of human depravity, and there is alienation and deep-seated enmity against God. Out of all of this grows the state of the Laodicean church—"neither cold nor hot" (Rev. 3:15). This state is where two streams meet and merge. It is a state like that of Samson when he lay asleep on the lap of his seducer. It is a state of being self-satisfied, standing in need of nothing, with Christ left outside the door.

The church has lost her militant, uncompromising aggressiveness. There is little fight left in a self-satisfied, professing, worldly church which is not feared by the world, the flesh, or the devil.

This leads us into the final phase—warfare! In Ephesians, as in the book of Joshua, we find the dominant, martial note of warfare. Joshua's warfare was one of extermination. There was to be no mercy or agreed armistice; The iniquity of the Amorites was full. The bloodstream was corrupted, as it had been in the case of the antedeluvians. The Nephilim were in the land. Joshua's order of execution was from heaven. The liberals have made much of the ruthlessness of Joshua and his armies in conquering and destroying the inhabitants of the land. One has been so brazen as to refer to the God of the Old Testament as a "dirty bully." A sovereign God is full of love and mercy, but we do well to remember that He is also a God of justice. He loves righteousness, but He hates sin. A person's character, ranging from godliness to satanic wickedness, is determined by what one loves and what one hates. God loves the sinner, but He hates sin.

The lesson from the book of Joshua proves the costliness of compromise. Where the enemies were left, they became a thorn in the flesh of Israel throughout her history.

A holy and righteous God demands judgment where mercy is long spurned. Christ is first depicted as the Lamb and finally as the Lion. In this day of growing latitude, men need to remember that there are two sides to the shield.

The book of Ephesians, after viewing the heavenlies where Christ is seated and the believers seated with Him, finally comes to the question of our spiritual warfare. "Finally, my brethren, be strong in the Lord, and in the power of his might. Put on the whole armour of God, that ye may be able to stand against the wiles of the devil. For we wrestle not against flesh and blood, but against principalities, against powers, against the rulers of the darkness of this world, against spiritual wickedness in high places. Wherefore take unto you the whole armour of God, that ye may be able to withstand in the evil day, and having done all, to stand" (Eph 6:10-13). Oh, that Christians could see the enormity, the resourcefulness, and the power of this satanic foe that challenges the position of the child of God. Our warfare is not carnal.

The weakness of this hour and every hour is the failure to comprehend this conflict. The believer is here called upon to stand. "Wherefore take unto you the whole armour of God, that ye may be able to withstand in the evil day, and having done all, to stand. Stand therefore, having your loins girt about with truth, and having on the breastplate of righteousness" (vv. 13-14). To stand means to hold that which has already been taken for us by the Captain of our salvation. One cannot read the New Testament, especially the epistles, without being made aware of the intensity and absoluteness of this struggle.

Christianity in its New Testament purity gives no mercy and offers no peace; instead, it calls for absolute surrender on terms set forth in the councils of the Godhead. Christianity in the spiritual sphere, like Communism in the material, challenges ultimate world domination. There is no note in the New Testament that will justify complicity or compatability with this alienated world-system. The divine peace terms are absolute, unconditional, and worldwide. This ultimate victory must await the coming of Christ.

New Testament Christianity is aggressive, evangelical, and exclusive, claiming all for Christ until He comes to rule. The sad note that is becoming more dominant with every passing day is the cry for passivity, amalgamation, ecumenicity, and worldly ambitions. The days described for us in Revelation 17 seem to be near. "And there came one of the seven angels which had the seven vials, and talked with me, saying unto me, Come hither; I will shew unto thee the judgment of the great whore that sitteth upon many waters" (v. 1).

In the meantime our task is to rescue the perishing and care for the dying as we are energized by the Spirit and inspired by the hope of His return.

# BIBLIOGRAPHY

BLACK, Ernest W. *Living Messages from the Canaan Journey.* Kannapolis, N.C.: 1948.

CHADWICK, G. A. "The Book of Exodus." In The Expositor's Bible. Vol. 1. New York: Armstrong, 1905.

COATES, C. A. *An Outline of the Book of Exodus.* London: Stow Hill, n.d.

———. *An Outline of the Book of Numbers.* London: Stow Hill, n.d.

GAEBLEIN, Arno C. *The Annotated Bible.* Vol. 1. Chicago: Moody/Loizeaux, 1970.

HABERSHON, Ada R. *The Study of the Types.* London: Morgan & Scott, 1907.

HENDERSON, George. *Studies in the Book of Exodus.* Covington, Ky.: Calvary Book, 1956.

MACKINTOSH, Charles H. *Notes on the Book of Exodus.* New York: Revell, 1951.

MACLAREN, Alexander. *Expositions of Holy Scripture.* Vol. 1. Grand Rapids: Eerdmans, 1944.

MASSEE, J. C. *Conflict and Conquest in Holiness.* New York: Revell, 1924.

MOYER, Robert L. *The Saviour in the Shadows.* St. Paul: Northland, 1940.

PINK, Arthur W. *Gleanings in Exodus.* Chicago: Moody, n.d.

———. *Gleanings in Genesis.* Chicago: Moody, 1922.

———. *Gleanings in Joshua.* Chicago: Moody, 1969.

REDPATH, Allan. *Victorious Christian Living.* Westwood, N.J.: Revell, 1955.

RITCHIE, John. *From Egypt to Canaan.* Kilmarnock, Scotland: Young Watchman, n.d.

SEISS, Joseph A. *Holy Types; or, The Gospel in Leviticus*. Philadelphia: Smith, English, 1866.

SMITH, George Adams. *The Historical Geography of the Holy Land*. New York: Armstrong, 1907.

TODD, J. H. *Prophetic Pictures of Christ*. Chicago: Bible Inst. Col., 1928.

VAN GORDER, John J. *The Alphabet of Christian Experience*. Findlay, Ohio: Fundamental Truth, n.d.

EGYPT
The Passover
Judgment
Death of
Firstborn
Pillar of Cloud
Descends
Succoth
Rameses
Migdol
Kingdom of Pharaoh
Israel in Bondage
From Egypt to Canaan
THE EXODUS AND JOURNEYINGS OF
THE CHILDREN OF ISRAEL